A Practical Guide
for Advanced Writers
in English
as a Second Language

A Practical Guide for Advanced Writers in English as a Second Language

PAUL MUNSELL

Michigan State University

MARTHA CLOUGH

University of Houston

Maxwell Macmillan
International Publishing Group
New York   Oxford   Singapore   Sydney

Collier Macmillan Canada
Toronto

Maxwell Macmillan International Publishing Group
ESL/EFL Department
866 Third Avenue
New York, NY 10022

Library of Congress Cataloging in Publication Data

Munsell, Paul.
   A practical guide for advanced writers in English as
   a second language.

   Bibliography: p.
   1. English language—Text-books for foreign speakers.
2. English language—Rhetoric. I. Clough, Martha.
II. Title.
PE1128.M76   1984   808'.042   83-11307
ISBN 0-02-384910-X

Printing: 6 7 8   Year: 0 1 2

❧ PREFACE ☙

AUDIENCE

A Practical Guide for Advanced Writers is designed for students who are learning English as a second language at the university or graduate level, who are in an upper intermediate or advanced preacademic English course (above 65 on the Michigan or above 470 on TOEFL), or who can write as good a composition as the sample labeled 65 in Appendix II.

PURPOSE

A Practical Guide sets four major goals for students:

1. To write more accurately in English.
2. To select and organize ideas effectively and to present them in the most common and effective formats.
3. To gain confidence and experience in approaching academic writing requirements.
4. To make progress in reading, listening, and speaking skills as a byproduct of the readings and discussions.

METHOD

The principal method used is the writing of short compositions on topics of interest and importance. Each unit is designed to be completed in less than one class period, so a writing assignment can be given at each meeting if desired.

To complement this basic method four other fundamental means are also used. First, each unit contains extensive prewriting activities to help clarify and specify the topic. Second, the materials emphasize editing in three ways: before writing by means of the editing exercise, during writing by self-editing and use of the checklist, and after receiving the composition that has been marked by the teacher by correcting mistakes. Third, each unit provides special guidelines to make the writing form of that unit completely explicit. Fourth, five units give practice in one of the most important, and sometimes neglected, skills of good writing: rewriting a paper written earlier.

MAIN DIVISIONS

The textbook is divided into three parts:

Part I. This part introduces basic forms of writing, such as chronological order, description, and argumentation, using personal topics for which all students have ample information. The units cover fundamental concepts such as selection of a theme, paragraph development, use of support, and appropriate sentence length.

Part II.   This part treats the forms of writing in greater depth through the use of topics that are familiar but require extending personal knowledge and understanding to topics of high interest in our modern world. The exercises deal in detail with matters of topic development; organizational patterns; style; effect on the reader; and specific methods of support through use of examples, explanations, analogies, and facts.

Part III.   This part emphasizes topics that require research or the study of supplementary sources. The units assume competency in the basic principles introduced in Parts I and II and provide more practice of these principles, using such topics as the biographies of famous leaders, energy, the environment, technology, and economics. Units 50 through 58 cover the writing of formal research papers, from use of the library to the compilation of the bibliography.

SUGGESTIONS FOR USE

A Practical Guide is designed to give the teacher maximum flexibility, as indicated in the Instructor's Manual (available at no charge from the publisher) and in the introductions to each unit. As examples of this flexibility, there are more units than can be covered in a typical term, so some parts of units or even entire units can selectively be omitted or given as homework. There are choices of topics in each unit to appeal to a wide range of interests. Particularly in Part I, there are paired units that can be treated together by more advanced groups. Units can be covered in class without a writing assignment, or the writing assignment may be carried over several units to give opportunities for the writing of longer and more complex papers. The course can emphasize spoken skills by having well-planned class discussions, can provide for the writing of personal journals, and can encourgae peer correction. These and many more options are readily available to suit the needs of the class.

The teacher is strongly encouraged to keep a folder for each student and to put papers that the student has recorrected in it. This not only helps students to keep all their work in one place, but also provides the teacher with a ready reference for how many papers students are writing and reediting. The students should have access to these folders for all revising units (Units 11, 19, 32, 39, 50). In courses in which students will be graded, the folder is a convenient way for the teacher to have a large amount of material available with which to measure progress, effort, amount of work completed, and consistency. Students should be notified from the beginning of the purposes and responsibilities regarding the folders.

The students should also be encouraged to keep a notebook or folder in which to record common mistakes, grammatical notes, important words, and questions they intend to ask.

Finally, the students should be required to have at least one good dictionary and reference grammar. Since availability and teachers' preferences vary so widely, each teacher should announce at the beginning of the term which reference books are required.

❧ CONTENTS ❧

CONTENTS

A Practical Guide for Advanced Writers in English as a Second Language

❦ PART ❦

I

Introduction

Part I introduces basic organizational forms of writing: chronological order, spatial order, description, classification, process, comparison/ contrast, and argumentation. Within each of these forms the emphasis is on the choice of a theme, overall arrangement of the composition, paragraph development, and selection of content.

Through the editing exercises, the sample compositions and many of the warmup exercises, Part I also offers directed practice in correct use of structure, vocabulary, spelling, and mechanics. Two of the units are addressed to the conditional forms of verbs, a grammatical structure that represents a specific problem even for advanced writers.

Each unit is built around personal content that is not only interesting but that also offers the writer large quantities of useful information. If a topic such as "My Home" seems easy or removed from academic writing on the surface, experience with advanced writers suggests exactly the opposite. Not only is the topic ideally suited for eliciting a rich storehouse of information, providing the basis for a vivid example of descriptive writing, and making the concepts of theme and paragraph development convincingly clear, but the subject matter almost invariably allows writers to experience a warm memory that motivates rather than simply directs the writing.

However, for advanced writers who are experiencing little difficulty with the forms, organization, or language of Part I, these units should be done as quickly as possible. Personal writing, if extended too long, can become self-conscious or even embarrassing. One way to use the units efficiently and quickly is to view them as pairs, as in the following listing.

Units 2 and 3 (descriptions of a trip).
Units 5 and 6 (descriptions of a place).
Units 7 and 8 (classification of activities or influences).
Units 9 and 10 (how to do or make something).

1

Units 13 and 14 (comparison/contrast and
   advantages/disadvantages).
Units 15 and 16 (use of conditional verb forms).
Units 17 and 18 (argumentation and explanation).

Each of these pairs can be treated as a single unit and only one
writing assignment given. Only those exercises in each unit that
appear necessary for the class need be used.

Each unit is designed to be used in one fifty- to sixty-minute class
session. In fact, most of the units can effectively be completed in less
than thirty minutes, allowing students to begin or even finish
writing within the class period. Both writing under pressure in class
and writing at leisure outside of class should be encouraged.

The materials as designed are intended to be complete and
self-contained. However, each class should provide any additional
activities that will promote learning and satisfaction with the
course. Interesting class discussion, writing of personal journals, and
peer interaction are highly recommended.

Unit 1 contains the information necessary to prepare students to
use all of the following units. Even if no writing assignment is
given, the remainder of the unit should be completed. Similarly,
Units 11, 12, 19, and 20 are essential to the overall development of
a mature writer and should be covered. In the rest of Part I the
teacher's and students' needs should determine the selection and
speed of the units and the exercises.

❧ Unit 1 ❧

First Impressions

Writing forms: Description; chronology
Writing skills: An overview of the writing process; characteristics of a good composition

INTRODUCTION

Many students who are using this textbook have recently moved to a new place or have experienced a dramatic change in environment. But even if you have not traveled recently, you certainly must remember finding yourself at some time in your life in new and unusual circumstances. The first impressions of a trip, change of residence, or new environment are the topic of this unit.

TIP

Before you sit down to write, be sure you have the materials you need: the right type and size of paper, pen or pencil and eraser, proper lighting, a dictionary, and your writing assignment.

WARMUP EXERCISE I: AN OVERVIEW OF THE WRITING PROCESS

In this unit you will prepare for writing, and you will develop an overview of the goals and principles of this textbook by carefully examining a composition that has been written, edited, and revised by a proficient speaker of English. When you write your first draft of a composition, it will probably not be so long, clear, neat, or well organized. Nonetheless, there are many features that you should attempt to imitate, features that will be discussed and illustrated in the following exercise.

Before we look at the specific features of a good composition written in English, however, reviewing the general stages that a good writer uses in approaching the writing task will provide a broad, useful orientation. You should assume, since you are probably well educated in your native language, that indeed you are already highly proficient as a writer, and many of these concepts will serve largely as review.

3

INSTRUCTIONS:
Read the following stages of good writing. Reflect on your own experience and understanding and be prepared to comment, in a class discussion, on the overall process of writing.

1. *Think of ideas, facts, or events.* You obviously have to have something to write *about,* and an indispensable step is collecting your material. You may have the material clearly in mind or you may have to read extensively, conduct interviews, and complete a research project in order to collect your data. Frequently, even when you have the information stored somewhere in your mind, it is necessary to go through a stage of "brainstorming," review, or discussion to recall and clarify the information.

2. *Organize your content around a purpose or theme.* The content you have collected in step 1 might be only loosely organized, uneven in importance, and not directed toward a specific goal. You must group your ideas, discard weak or irrelevant details, and put them into order so that they produce an overall effect or theme.

3. *Rendering your content into language.* Steps 1 and 2 are to some degree independent of any particular language, but in step 3 you find ways of turning your ideas into words. This stage is especially hard in a second language, but even in one's native language it represents a real struggle, requires a high degree of skill and experience, and is always subject to revision.

4. *Evaluate what you have written and revise it.* No matter how carefully you have proceeded through steps 1 through 3, after you have written something, you will invariably find weaknesses or omissions, especially if you read it a long time after writing it. If you want to write something with which you are really satisifed, you must reexamine it carefully *after* you write it, repeating the steps outlined previously: thinking of things you ought to include; looking for better ways of organizing your thoughts; and working on better ways of turning your ideas into clear and interesting English.

WARMUP II: CHARACTERISTICS OF A GOOD COMPOSITION

The steps outlined previously will be practiced systematically throughout the units of this textbook. In this first unit, it will be useful to examine a composition that was written following these guidelines. The questions that follow will direct you to those significant aspects that should be present in your compositions.

INSTRUCTIONS:
1. Read the sample composition on pages 6–7 at least once, carefully noting the ideas, the organization, and the format. 2. Answer each of the questions. (For your convenience, if you are working independently of the teacher, the answers to the warmup exercises, where relevant, are provided in the answers section between Units 20 and 21. Never consult the answers until you have completely finished the exercise.)

1. What size and what color should the paper be for a composition?

2. How wide should the margins be at the top, at the bottom, on the left, on the right?

3. How many lines should there be on the page, and how close together?

4. Should the title, date, and author's name be on the composition? Where?

5. How many paragraphs are there?

6. In your own words, what is the main idea of each of the paragraphs?

7. For each of the main ideas of the paragraphs, list several details that support that idea. (For example, the bad impression of the hotel is emphasized by the facts that the paint was peeling from the walls and the windows didn't close.)

8. Quickly examine the length of the sentences. Find three that are short and three that are long. Are all the short or all the long sentences in the same part of the composition?

9. What in your opinion is the overall purpose or theme of the composition? There is one sentence that perhaps best expresses this idea. Try to find it.

EDITING

In most units you will read a paragraph or two in which there are typical mistakes. In all of the first twenty units, the mistakes are marked with the correction symbols listed on the inside back cover. Determine what the mistake is and correct it. Your teacher will either use the same symbols or provide you with an explanation of the correction method you will use. In Part I the editing exercise is taken from the sample composition, so you can check your work. Never consult the sample composition until you have completed the editing exercise.

At the rainy night I arrive, I must to walk through several block of dark

streets until I have come to "The Grand Hotel," an ugly building just beside

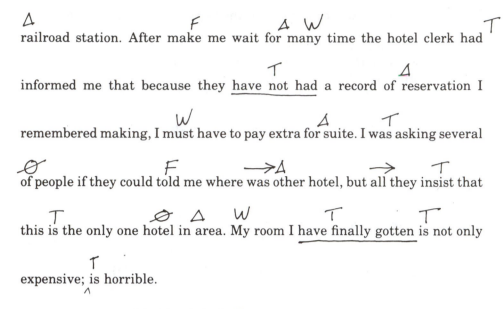

railroad station. After make me wait for many time the hotel clerk had

informed me that because they have not had a record of reservation I

remembered making, I must have to pay extra for suite. I was asking several

of people if they could told me where was other hotel, but all they insist that

this is the only one hotel in area. My room I have finally gotten is not only

expensive; is horrible.

PLANNING AND WRITING

Select one of the following topics:

1. My first impressions of the city where I am living now.
2. My first impressions of someone I know well now.
3. My first impressions of a school or program.

Following the first three steps just explained, think of details to include in your composition; organize them into groups so that there is an overall purpose and theme; use structures and vocabulary as accurately as you can to convey your idea in a clear, direct style; and reread your composition before you turn it in to see if you can identify and correct any mistakes.

The following organization was used in the sample composition and would be appropriate for your composition as well:

1. The first paragraph (the introduction) names the place you are going to describe and presents the impression that you *expected* to have.
2. The second paragraph describes (by means of a chronological description) a specific first impression.
3. The third paragraph describes a second major first impression.
4. The last paragraph describes the final or more permanent impression and offers an explanation for the other impressions. The last sentence is a type of summary and conclusion.

My First Impressions of a City

At first I supposed that the small city where I was headed several years ago for the purposes of attending a university would be a charming intellectual center where I would feel right at home. Several of my teachers had attended school there and told me what a good choice I was making. The university brochures certainly made the location seem attractive. Even some personal friends who had grown up there were warm in their praise. As the beginning of the school year approached I could hardly wait to get there.

The rainy night I arrived, I had to walk through several blocks of dark streets until I came to "The Grand Hotel," an ugly building right beside the railroad station. After making me wait for a long time the hotel clerk informed me that because they did not have a record of the reservation I remembered making, I would have to pay extra for a suite. I asked several people if they could tell me where another hotel was, but they all insisted that this was the only one in the area. The room I finally got was not only expensive, it was horrible. The paint was peeling off the walls, and the windows wouldn't close. I lay awake all night listening to the trains rumbling by and to the people who were having a party in the next room. Just after I finally fell asleep I was awakened by the noisy workers who came to remove the trash in the hallway.

The next day when the rain let up a little I decided to go for a walk. The sidewalks, where they existed, were muddy and slippery, and as the cars went past I had to jump to keep from getting splattered. Most of the buildings I saw were not just old but old fashioned and distasteful looking, many of them appearing to need extensive repairs. The air was heavy with a smell that I later learned came from the soap factory in the middle of the town. For some reason, the breeze never seemed to blow except from that direction. The sun didn't shine that day, nor for many days thereafter, and even then the sky was hazy.

Later on, after waiting an hour for a public bus which never came, I found out about the convenient university bus system. Once on campus I quickly discovered that the school I would attend was much nicer than the city itself and eventually, because I was having such a valuable experience, I came to love the university and its facilities. I was so pleased, in fact, that later on when someone asked me how I liked my new city I almost told them how wonderful it was. I then realized how I and most of my original sources of information really felt: the city was forgettable. But both its positive features, of which there were few, and its negative features, of which there were many, seemed quickly to fade from our memories as we became involved in the more interesting life on campus.

❧ Unit 2 ❧

Preparing for a Trip

Writing forms: Chronology; classification
**Writing skills: Developing a theme; eliminating unrelated ideas; short-
ening rambling sentences**

INTRODUCTION

A trip, especially one that will take a long time or that is important to us,
requires a lot of planning and preparation. For example, if we are going abroad,
we have to obtain the necessary legal documents and authorizations. We have to
choose the best means of travel and secure the necessary tickets. We have to find
people who can manage our affairs while we are away. Sometimes these
arrangements require almost as much time as the trip itself, but they are
unavoidable. What did you have to do to get ready for a trip you have taken?

TIP

Find a quiet and comfortable place where you can go whenever you want to
write.

WARMUP I: IDENTIFYING A THEME

You write something because you have a purpose. For example, you write a
letter to a friend when you are feeling lonely, or when you have some exciting
news, or when you need some information. Similarly, when you write a composition you should begin with some clear purpose in mind of what you are trying to
accomplish. Do you want the reader to laugh? To sympathize? To get useful
information?

In the following exercise there are many details that a writer could possibly
use in a composition about preparing for a trip; but if they were all included, the
composition would have no theme, no purpose. It would simply be a collection of
unorganized ideas.

INSTRUCTIONS:
1. Read all the numbered items in the following list, noting in general the content and
ideas included. 2. Then read through the list again, this time trying to determine

8

which of three themes (listed immediately following) the item would support and write the key word in the blank. If it supports none of the three themes, write NONE.

Possible Themes

Expensive (Planning for the trip was very expensive.)
Busy (I had many exhausting things to do in planning the trip.)
Sad (Planning for the trip made me feel sad or nostalgic.)

If the detail fits none of the above possible themes, write NONE.

Example

EXPENSIVE   I had to sell my car to pay for the airplane tickets.

1. _____ I had to leave just before my sister's wedding.

2. _____ I had to borrow money for the expensive hotels I would stay in.

3. _____ I was only able to get about five hours' sleep a night.

4. _____ I had to go back and forth to the travel agent many times.

5. _____ My parents cried and told me how much they would miss me.

6. _____ I had to buy a lot of new clothes to prepare for the trip.

7. _____ The houses along my street are pretty.

8. _____ I had to go to several hospitals for vaccinations, examinations, and health forms.

9. _____ I had to buy an extra suitcase and prepare to pay for excess baggage.

10. _____ There are two brothers and three sisters in my family.

11. _____ I could not find my passport and had to order a new one.

12. _____ My fiancée and I spent every spare minute together, wondering how we would endure the separation during my trip.

13. _____ I watched a good movie that I later saw on my trip.

14. _____ I had to ask three of my friends to spend a day doing last-minute errands to help me finish all the preparations.

WARMUP II: ELIMINATING UNRELATED IDEAS

A very important decision in writing a good composition is deciding what *not* to say. Things that you should omit include the following:

1. Details that weaken or contradict your theme.
2. Details that are uninteresting or trivial.
3. Details that are repetitious or that support an idea that is already clear or well supported.

4. Details that do not naturally fit into the theme or that are placed in a paragraph in which they seem out of place.

INSTRUCTIONS:
1. Read through the following imperfect paragraph to try to determine what the writer intended as the theme (main idea) of the paragraph. Either state the main idea in your own words or find and underline a sentence that expresses it. 2. Find four complete sentences that do *not* fit and cross them out. Be prepared to explain your decision.

My personal affairs made the planning hard. My younger sister, who is very close to me, was planning to get married about the time I was leaving and desperately wanted me to delay the trip for three weeks. The day of the wedding there was a terrible rainstorm and the electricity went off and her wedding pictures turned out very dark. Also, my mother and father wanted me to stay and help them in the family business because one of their partners had gotten sick. He was a friendly fellow and had been like an uncle to me over the years. In my own job my company had offered me a promotion and new responsibilities if I would stay, and I was seriously tempted to cancel the whole trip. The company is a leader in high technology and the company president will probably travel to Japan and other countries in the next year. Finally, my younger brother had a minor accident while driving me around doing the last-minute shopping, and while neither of us was seriously hurt, it did make both of us rather nervous. I have had only one other accident like that, and that mishap made me feel nervous and upset too.

WARMUP III: SHORTENING RAMBLING SENTENCES

Writers have two related tendencies that make their writing harder to understand or less interesting. The first, having overly long (rambling) sentences, will be discussed in this unit, and the second, having overly short (choppy) sentences, will be covered in Unit 3. Both will be reviewed in several other units.

A rambling sentence may have any of the following characteristics:

1. It is so complex and has so many interdependent, subordinated parts that it is either difficult to understand or confusing.

2. It is a long string of short, simple sentences connected by a word such as *and* into an unsophisticated and often monotonous sentence.

INSTRUCTIONS:
1. Read the following paragraph and note that it is just one long rambling sentence. Identify which of the two previous descriptions best describes it. 2. Correct the sentences in your own way. One possible correct form is included in the sample composition, which you should check only after you complete your own revision.

My personal affairs also made the planning hard because my younger sister, who is very close to me, was planning to get married about the time I was leaving and desperately wanted me to delay the trip for about three weeks, and also my mother and father wanted me to stay and help them in the family business because one of their partners had gotten sick, and in my own job my company had offered me a promotion and new responsibilities if I would stay, and I was seriously tempted to cancel the whole trip, and because finally my younger brother had a minor accident while driving me around doing the last-minute shopping, and although neither of us was seriously hurt, it did make both of us rather nervous.

EDITING

Leave home was one of most hard things I have ever have to do. At the first place, were the numerous details that have had to be taken care. I must get a passaport, and becuase mine apparently got misplaced so I must to make especial trip to the main passport office and to talk with head of department.

My visa not take many days for get but I must go to embassy a morning at the six o'clock and to stand in the line during about four hours. After, the airline told to me that I will no able to book passage during week I need to trip, but last after a dozen or more of phone call and special request they eventually have written me ticket. <u>At last</u>, my bank did not get clearance for convert my saving into the foreign currency until two weeks before I scheduled to leaving.

PLANNING AND WRITING

Choose one of the following four topics:

1. Preparing for a trip.
2. Preparing for a test or examination.
3. Preparing for a wedding.
4. Preparing to begin a new job or begin at a new school.

In writing on these topics, you will largely be telling about things in the order in which they happened. Begin by thinking of everything that happened, and then carefully select only those details that fit your theme and that are interesting.

The following outline would be appropriate for your composition:

I. First paragraph: A *short* introduction, telling what you were preparing for and at least hinting at your theme, as well as describing the first major phase of your preparation for your trip.

II. Second paragraph: The second major idea or phase of your preparation.

III. Third paragraph (if you have enough time and material): The third major idea or phase of your preparation.

IV. Last paragraph: A restatement or clarification of your theme, illustrated with examples that interestingly, humorously, or graphically capture and summarize your own feelings about the topic.

Be sure your composition has your name, the date of writing, a title, adequate margins, and space between the lines. Be sure, too, that it is on the type of paper your teacher asked you to use.

Preparing to Go Abroad to Study

Leaving home was one of the hardest things I have ever had to do. In the first place, there were the numerous details that I had to take care of. I had to get a passport, and because mine apparently got misplaced, I had to make a special trip to the main passport office and talk with the head of the department. My visa did not take many days to get, but I had to go to the embassy one morning at six o'clock and stand in line for about four hours. Then the airline told me that I would not be able to book passage during the week I needed to travel, but after a dozen or more phone calls and special requests, they eventually wrote me a ticket. Finally, my bank did not get clearance to convert my savings into foreign currency until two weeks before I was scheduled to leave, and by then the exchange rate was fluctuating widely, and I was worried that I was going to lose a lot of money.

My personal affairs also made the planning hard. My younger sister, who is very close to me, was planning to get married about the time I was leaving, and she desperately wanted me to delay the trip for three weeks. Also my mother and father wanted me to stay and help them in the family business because one of their partners had gotten sick. In my own job, my company had offered me a promotion and new responsibilities if I would stay, and I was seriously tempted to cancel the whole trip. Finally, my younger brother had a minor accident while driving me around doing the last-minute shopping, and although neither of us was seriously hurt, it did make us both rather nervous.

Fortunately, not everything was unpleasant. I had many wonderful parties with my friends. My family was very supportive of my reasons for leaving, and I felt exhilarated about the changes and opportunities I was facing. On the whole, however, it was an exhausting experience, and I was relieved, although somewhat sad, when I finally stepped on the airplane to begin a new phase of my life.

❧ Unit 3 ❧

An Exciting Trip

Writing form: Chronology
Writing skills: Selecting details to fit your theme; combining choppy
sentences

INTRODUCTION

A trip can be an adventure; a turning point; a new beginning leading to new experiences, responsibilities, and opportunities. Trips can be exciting or dull, dangerous or boring, expensive or cheap, wonderful or disappointing, tiring or exhilarating. Have you ever taken a memorable trip? What was it like?

TIP

There is an inexpensive tool that will greatly help you in writing: a dictionary. Have it with you and consult it while you write. Ask your teacher for advice in choosing a good dictionary for this course.

WARMUP I: CHOOSING DETAILS TO SUPPORT A THEME

Writing with a purpose requires that you select your material to suit that purpose. However, as you prepare to write, you often find that you do not have enough specific and interesting details to support your theme. The following two exercises will assist you both in planning the composition for this unit and in developing skills in building up ideas.

INSTRUCTIONS:
For each of the following ten possible details related to a trip, select additional words, phrases, or concepts to develop the detail. Work as a class or in smaller groups. Using your imagination freely, develop the detail separately for each of these three themes, as illustrated in the example:

Exciting
Tiring
Dangerous

14

Example: *Going to the Beach*

Exciting: big waves, beautiful coastline, riding a surfboard
Tiring: walking in the soft sand for miles, swimming all day long, playing volleyball
Dangerous: sharks in the water, deep water, an undertow, a storm

1. The taxi ride to the airport.

2. The airport and the boarding of the airplane.

3. The airplane ride itself.

4. Finding the hotel.

5. The hotel (lobby, elevators, room).

6. Walking along the streets of the city.

7. Shopping.

8. Visiting a famous location.

9. An excursion.

10. An evening event.

WARMUP II: CHOOSING DETAILS TO SUPPORT GENERAL STATEMENTS

INSTRUCTIONS:
In each of the following overly general sentences, add specific details that would support the theme or idea. You may either list possible key words or write one or two complete sentences.

> Example: *The airplane ride made me nervous.* Leaving the ground, strange bumps and noises, the wings of the airplane bending, memories of airplane crashes, feeling like the plane was falling, looking out the window at the ground far below.

1. The airport was depressing.

2. The customs officials were threatening.

3. The hotel was expensive.

4. The restaurant was wonderful.

5. The room was uncomfortable.

6. The roads were bad.

7. The scenery was beautiful.

WARMUP III: COMBINING CHOPPY SENTENCES

Too many short sentences make a paragraph seem choppy, tedious, and immature. A good writer is sensitive to the effect on the reader of various sentence lengths and maintains a proper balance. In the following exercise most of the sentences are either too short or incomplete.

INSTRUCTIONS:
1. Read through the following paragraph and find the three incomplete sentences.
2. Complete them, either by adding words or by combining them with another sentence. 3. Combine the other sentences, using a variety of connecting words and structures, so that there is a balance of short and long sentences without any run-on sentences. There are no "perfect" answers, but the sample composition provides a useful example. Consult it only after you complete your own work.

I finally arrived at my destination. I had no idea how to get to my hotel. I was afraid to ask. Because the people never seemed to understand me. They just talked louder and louder. They moved their hands dramatically. They made me frustrated and embarrassed. To make matters worse. Not all of my bags arrived at the terminal with me. When the airline agent asked me where I was staying. I did not understand why he was asking. The next morning I got a strange call on the phone. By then I was beginning to understand. I went down to get my suitcase. It had just been sent from the airport. I opened it hurriedly. I immediately took out what soon became my most valuable possession: my dictionary.

EDITING

After I got out of the plane and I walked to the custom, I had gotten in line that said "Citizens Only" because I don't understand what do they say and then must to go all way back through other line. When they pointed at my suitcase and say somethings I was thinking they was asking to me to showing

to them what was in the bottom, and I messed up my suitcase so bad that I had

to spending five minutes get it closed during the person behind me was acting

so impatient. After, I saw man in the uniform that looked like a porter,

although when I was asking him carry my bags, but he just was smiling,

saying something that I last recognized as the "policeman." In attempt to

carry all of suitcases up the escalator, I almost got caught in the mechanism

because I was tried to read the little signs telling me how should I use it.

PLANNING AND WRITING

Choose one of the following topics:

1. A business trip or a trip to a new place to live.
2. A pleasure trip.
3. An adventure (yours or someone else's).

Think about all the things that happened to you. Determine a purpose (theme or point of view) on which you can build a composition. Eliminate the weaker details (as you did in Unit 2) and also elaborate and make specific your central ideas (as you did in this unit) so that there is adequate support to make your theme clear, persuasive, and interesting. You may wish to read the sample composition for Unit 3 before beginning. The following outline would be appropriate:

  I. First paragraph: Give a short introduction in the first sentence or two, telling where and when the trip was and at least hinting at the theme. Finish the paragraph with support for the first major point or the first main activity.
 II. Second paragraph: Develop the second major point or activity.
III. Third paragraph: Develop the third major point or activity.
 IV. Final paragraph (if desired): Provide an overview or short summary and a conclusion.

My First Trip Abroad

My first trip abroad presented me with a large number of sensations and impressions, but one that stands out most vividly was the tremendous confusion surrounding almost everything I did the first few days. It started at the airport when I was told not only that there was a mistake on my ticket, but also that my original flight had been canceled, and I would have to wait two hours and pay a "late" fee for having made arrangements at the last minute. After finally getting the details straightened out, I was then unsure what to do with the friends who had come to see me off, who were getting a little bored just sitting around trying to be cheerful until I left. When I finally got on the plane and got seated, the attendant explained to me that only those who had paid extra for the movie could sit in that section, but I couldn't understand the instructions on how to make the payment, so I had to move to another seat. I was asked to pay $2.00 for the soft drink I ordered and then found out I had been served an alcoholic drink, which I did not want.

After I got off the plane and walked to customs, I got in the line that said "Citizens Only" because I did not understand what they said, and then had to go all the way back through the other line. When they pointed at my suitcase and said something, I thought they were asking me to show them what was at the bottom, and I messed up my suitcase so badly that I had to spend five minutes getting it closed while the person behind me was acting impatient. Afterwards, I saw a man in a uniform who looked like a porter, although when I asked him to carry my bags he just smiled, saying something that I finally recognized as "policeman." In attempting to carry all my suitcases up the escalator, I almost got caught in the mechanism because I was trying to read the little signs telling me how to use it.

Upon arrival at my final destination, I had no idea how to get to my hotel. I was afraid to ask because people never seemed to understand me and just talked louder and louder and moved their hands dramatically, making me feel frustrated and embarrassed. To make matters worse, not all of my bags arrived at the terminal with me. When the airline agent asked me where I was staying, I did not know why he was asking. The next morning I got a strange call on the phone, but by then I was beginning to understand. I went down to get my suitcase, which had just been sent from the airport. I opened it hurriedly and immediately took out what soon became my most valuable possession: my dictionary.

❧ Unit 4 ❧

My Autobiography

Writing forms: Chronology; description
Writing skills: Awareness of audience; appropriate level of specificity

INTRODUCTION

No one will ever be you, and you will never be anyone else. You are literally the center of your universe. You are, therefore, the most important person in the world. Not only do you matter to yourself, but without you the rest of the world would be different, would not have the same potential.

Who are you? Where are you from? What are your plans? What kinds of things do you like to do? Why are you here? These and other similar issues are the topic for this unit. Hopefully your classmates will be able to read what you say about yourself, and you will have an opportunity to read about them.

TIP

Always ask yourself before you write, "Who is going to read this, and what effects do I want to have on them?"

WARMUP I: BEING AWARE OF YOUR AUDIENCE

How you write is largely determined by the effect you want to have on your readers. For example, if you are writing an autobiography for the purpose of completing an application form for a university or a job, you will select information about yourself that will create an impression of stability, intelligence, expertise, and motivation. You will not include information that makes you appear playful, unpredictable, or strange. The following exercises are designed to help you select the appropriate type of information for the type of person who is reading your composition.

INSTRUCTIONS:
There are many facts listed in the following exercise that might be appropriate or inappropriate in an autobiography. Read each item and determine for which type of

reader the information would be most appropriate. Place the corresponding letter in the blank. If you feel the information would be appropriate for more than one of the types of readers, list more than one letter.

Type of Reader:

    A. An official in a university or company.
    B. Classmates in a writing course.
    C. A close personal friend.
    D. None of these readers. The information is irrelevant.

Example: __C__ My husband/wife and I are very romantic when we are alone.

1. _____ The exact date of my birth.

2. _____ Where I was born.

3. _____ My nationality.

4. _____ My occupation.

5. _____ When or how my mother and father met.

6. _____ The difference in age between my mother and father.

7. _____ The street address of my elementary school.

8. _____ The number of brothers and sisters I have.

9. _____ The mental health of the members of my family.

10. _____ The way our family practices its religion on a daily basis.

11. _____ The name of the president of my country.

12. _____ The grades that I made during high school or at the university.

13. _____ My salary when I worked.

14. _____ The things I like most about my husband/wife or mother.

15. _____ The reasons why I want to continue my studies.

16. _____ My hobbies related to my field, major, or profession.

17. _____ The kinds of parties I like to attend.

18. _____ How well I like this writing class.

19. _____ The type of house in which I grew up.

WARMUP II: CHOOSING THE RIGHT LEVEL OF SPECIFICITY

INSTRUCTIONS:
Some of the following sentences are too general and do not give the reader a clear idea of what you mean. Some are too specific, giving information that seems neither necessary nor interesting in a short, general autobiography. Some are just right.

Label each of the sentences as follows:

G   (Too general)
S   (Too specific)
OK   (About right)

1. _____ I was born at the beginning of my life.

2. _____ When I was born, my father was a banker in the second largest branch office of the Central Bank.

3. _____ We lived together in a house in a city in my country.

4. _____ I went to school when I was a child.

5. _____ I always liked school, especially mathematics.

6. _____ I went into the fifth grade on February 5, 1972.

7. _____ I come from a family of two brothers and two sisters.

8. _____ I came home from the university on holidays, on my father's birthdays, and to attend my sister's wedding.

9. _____ I felt lonely my first year in college.

10. _____ There were many organizations in my university, and I joined the tennis and chess teams.

11. _____ School was easy for some of my friends, difficult for others.

12. _____ I worked after I graduated.

13. _____ I was named the assistant coordinator of systems design and management in the division of general engineering and had three assistants.

14. _____ I came here to study for one year.

15. _____ My favorite type of entertainment is listening to live music in a good club or restaurant.

EDITING

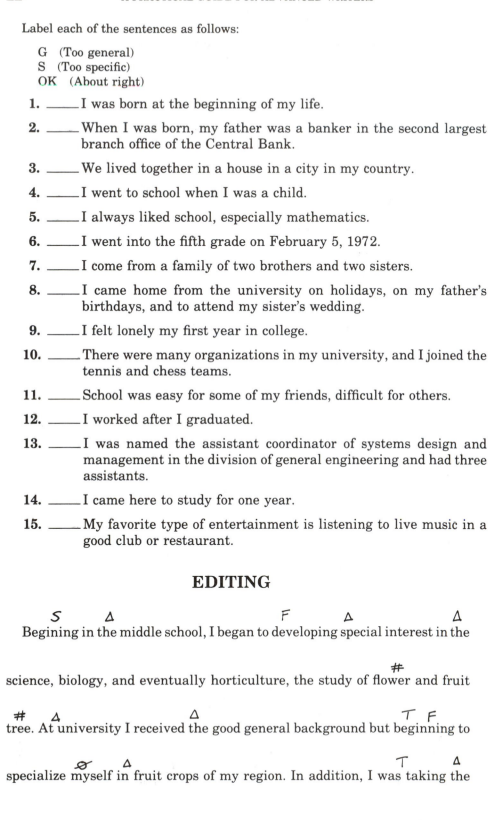

Begining in the middle school, I began to developing special interest in the

science, biology, and eventually horticulture, the study of flower and fruit

tree. At university I received the good general background but beginning to

specialize myself in fruit crops of my region. In addition, I was taking the courses in chemistry, maths and economics, along with laboratory course in

which we made experiments with the plants and trees and had concerned

ourselfs with the practical aspects of the irrigation, insect control, and

harvesting technique. In university as well, I had the lead guitarist in the

musical group. We have played contemporary music for student activity and

in a local clubs, and I was tempting at one time take on the music as the

career.

PLANNING AND WRITING

Write a short, concise autobiography that you feel would be of interest to the other members of your writing class. The following suggestions will help you to choose what to say. Read the sample composition for an example of a complete autobiography. The following items are *not* necessarily listed in the order in which they would be included in your composition, but are intended to help you develop ideas. To a large extent, your composition should be in chronological order. That is, it will start with the beginning of your life and continue up to the present.

1. Choose a level of intimacy with which you feel comfortable. That is, tell only what you really want the other students to know about, but feel free to give insights into your personality if it doesn't embarrass you.

2. Give details from the phases of your life that you consider important. For example, if you are just ready to begin at a university, your high school years are probably important. If you are a post-doctoral student, your elementary education is probably relatively unimportant and might warrant no more than a sentence. Include the basic facts of your place of birth, nationality and, if it does not make you uncomfortable, your age.

3. Mention important aspects of your family life. You could include a brief description of your parents and of your brothers and sisters, tell whether you are married and have children, and so on.

4. Explain what you are doing at the present, what you are studying, why you are in this class, and so on.

5. Briefly review your plans for the future.

6. Briefly describe yourself and discuss your favorite activities, hobbies, or pastimes.

7. Mention other aspects of yourself, such as your religious, political, or intellectual points of view, that would be of interest to others.

A Short Autobiography

I was born twenty-six years ago in a major commercial center in my country. I was the second child, and my sister was two years older than me. In the next three years another sister and brother came along, but the year after that, my father's death after a prolonged sickness forced the whole family to move to the capital city, where my grandparents lived. My mother's training as an accountant made it possible for her to get a good job with the ministry of finance, so we had an adequate, if somewhat difficult existence. After I completed my elementary education in a public school near my house and attended a good middle school, thanks to a scholarship and the encouragement of my teachers, I was able to go to a private preparatory school and to one of the best universities in the country.

Beginning in middle school, I began to develop a special interest in science, biology, and eventually horticulture, the study of flowers and fruit trees. At the university I received a good general background but began to specialize in the fruit crops of our region. In addition, I took courses in chemistry, math, and economics, along with laboratory courses in which we did experiments with plants and trees and concerned ourselves with the practical aspects of irrigation, insect control, and harvesting techniques. In the university as well, I was the lead guitarist in a musical group. We played contemporary music for student activities and in the local clubs, and I was tempted at one time to take up music as a career.

After graduating from the university, I went to work for a large agricultural concern to assist in the management of fruit production. I was given major responsibility for planning, designing, and overseeing the planting of a new orchard using the latest strains of plants and methods of irrigation. In a competition for a scholarship, I was fortunate to win one of three positions, but since my English was not quite adequate, I decided to enroll in this English course before beginning the program. When I finish my Master's degree, I will go back to work for the same company in a higher position than before.

I have several other interests in addition to horticulture. I still love to play the guitar and to meet people socially. I enjoy traveling very much and hope to visit many parts of the world as part of my work. I am a fan of adventure movies and do my best to go to a theater to see one at least once each month. I am not married yet, but I hope to be before too long. I am looking forward eagerly to the year that I will spend here and hope that I will learn a lot about my field, meet a lot of interesting people, travel, improve my English, and still have time to play my guitar occasionally.

❧ Unit 5 ❧

My Home

Writing form: Description
Writing skills: Arranging sentences into paragraphs; organizing ideas into paragraphs

INTRODUCTION

For most people, a home is a place with deep and happy memories, a place that we never forget and often dream of going back to.

How would you describe the appearance of your home, the way it is used, or its atmosphere? How can you share what it means to you? These are the issues for this unit. Don't make the mistake of assuming that this is an easy topic or one that is only for beginning writers. The principles you will practice and the challenge of providing a truly vivid description are of the highest order.

TIP

Reread each of your compositions within two or three days after the teacher has marked and returned them; promptly correct your mistakes and put your composition in your folder. To overcome your weaknesses, you must take an *active* role.

WARMUP I: IDENTIFYING MAIN IDEAS AND SEQUENCING SENTENCES

As you have learned, paragraphs are groups of sentences that have a purpose and a unifying idea or theme. In the following exercise, you will identify the theme of a group of sentences, find sentences that do not fit that theme, and put the sentences into the most logical order.

INSTRUCTIONS:
1. Read the following sentences, which have been taken in random order from a paragraph describing a particular aspect of a house. Determine precisely what the central purpose or theme of the paragraph is, and then find three sentences that do *not*

25

fit that purpose; cross them out. 2. Arrange the remaining sentences into a logical order of development by labeling each sentence with a number (1, 2, 3, and so on). After you finish, you can check your responses by looking at the sample composition.

1. _____ In front there are many tall bushes that have bright flowers on them most of the year.

2. _____ Upstairs there are the four bedrooms, one of which I had all to myself most of last year.

3. _____ Under the tree there are tables and chairs where we can sit in the late afternoon and have a cold drink and talk with our friends.

4. _____ There is a small yard in front and a large, more private yard in back.

5. _____ One of the neighbors owns a sports car, which I love to drive.

6. _____ The whole lot is surrounded by a low wall with a fancy iron fence on top of it.

7. _____ In back there is a huge tree that has brilliant red flowers from April through June, and there are numerous flower beds as well, with all types of tropical flowers and shrubs.

8. _____ On the outside the house looks like most of the others in the area and has two floors.

9. _____ Like the others, it has a high ceiling, large windows that let air in on hot nights, and a good view of both the outside and the inner courtyard.

WARMUP II: ORGANIZING IDEAS INTO PARAGRAPHS

There are two parts in this exercise that together illustrate two concepts. First, ideas come into your head in a rather disorganized manner; and second, it is possible to take these disorganized ideas and use them in a systematic way.

INSTRUCTIONS:
1. For five to ten minutes, write down, using notes and abbreviations, everything that you can think of about your house. Do not try to organize, criticize, or inhibit any ideas. Just work as fast as you can. 2. Looking at the list you just made, note the extent to which ideas are partially grouped together in meaningful clusters, but also the extent to which they are disorganized and are of different levels of interest and usefulness. 3. Now take these ideas and continue to add to them, but keep your notes grouped separately under the following categories:

- General neighborhood and setting.
- Outside appearance.
- The general organization of the house.
- The part that a visitor would see first.
- The kitchen and eating areas of the house.
- The types of activities that go on in the house.
- The sleeping areas.
- Your favorite part of the house.

In the short composition you will write for this unit, you will probably not be able to include all the information you generated in this exercise. Certainly you will not want to have eight paragraphs, each with one of these topics as the central idea. However, by organizing your ideas into groups first, you see more easily the type of information you have. Then you are able to organize it more effectively.

EDITING

My home is the old but comfortable building near to the downtown in my country's capital city. Is centrally locating near to my school, the bus lines, several of parks and museum. The people in the neighbor is friendly and cooperate. Is so little crime, polution, or dangerous in there, and childrens are found often playing on the less-traveling streets. Are small market and shop within walking distance and more large department store and shopping center less then ten blocks far away.

PLANNING AND WRITING

Referring to the warmup exercises, particularly the second half of Warmup II, select two, three, or four aspects about your home that you wish to describe. Select the details that give the most vivid, interesting, and unified description. A possible outline (used in the sample) looks like this:

I. The general neighborhood and setting.
II. The outside appearance of the house.
III. The inside of the house, arranged by the order in which people would see it if they came in and walked around.

My Home

My home is an old but comfortable building near the downtown area in the capital of my country. It is centrally located near my school, the bus lines, several parks, and a museum. The people in the neighborhood are friendly and cooperative. There is very little crime, pollution, or danger there, and children are often found playing on the less-traveled streets. There are small markets and shops within walking distance and larger department stores and a shopping center less than ten blocks away.

On the outside, the house looks like most in the area and has two floors. There is a small yard in front and a large, more private yard in back. The whole lot is surrounded by a low wall with a fancy iron fence on top of it. In front there are many tall bushes that have bright flowers on them most of the year and that branch out over the fence and are visible from the sidewalk and street. In back there is a huge tree that has brilliant red flowers from April through June, and there are numerous flower beds as well, with all types of tropical flowers and shrubs. Under the tree there are tables and chairs where we can sit in the late afternoon and have a cold drink or tea and talk with our friends.

Inside the house, in the very middle, there is an open courtyard with tropical plants and flowers and even a wild parrot that can say a few words and whistle. All around the courtyard is a kind of open corridor or porch with pillars and a railing. Plants hang from the edge of the roof, and there are comfortable chairs here and there around the porch. The rooms all open to this porch and courtyard. In the front is a large sitting room with fancy furniture. Here guests are greeted and entertained. In the back there is a large kitchen, on one side there is a formal dining area, and on the opposite side there is a comfortable study room where we keep all our books and family mementos. Upstairs are the four bedrooms, one of which I had all to myself most of last year. Like the others, it has a high ceiling, large windows that let the air in on hot nights, and a good view of both the outside and the inner courtyard. I had my room painted a rich blue with white trim, with curtains and bedspread to match, and my bed and desk and chairs were all made of a rare tropical wood that has a beautiful texture.

There are other houses in our neighborhood that are more expensive, bigger, or even prettier. But I have many fond memories of that home and all the things that I have done in it, and I often feel very homesick and eager to go back to it.

❦ Unit 6 ❦

My Favorite Place

Writing forms: Description; explanation
Writing skills: Choosing titles; writing introductions and conclusions

INTRODUCTION

If you could go anywhere in the world right now, where would you go? There are doubtless several places where you might feel extremely contented, comfortable, stimulated, or free. How would you describe one of them?

TIP

Keep a notebook or several extra pages handy on which to keep notes. Use this space to record words and structures that you are actively learning, mistakes that you make frequently, or questions that you want to ask.

WARMUP I: CHOOSING A TITLE

A title on a composition is like the name of a book, the label on a product, or the address of a friend. It will help you and the reader to identify it quickly, easily, and accurately. Here are some suggestions for choosing a title:

1. Keep it short.
2. Be sure it is an honest indicator of the topic.
3. Make it as interesting as possible.
4. Avoid an overly common, "cute," or silly phrase.

INSTRUCTIONS:
On the basis of the preceding rules, evaluate each of the following titles, deciding whether they are acceptable or unacceptable and stating why. They represent possible titles for the topics of the first five units.

1. _____ Like a Stranger in a Strange and Mysterious Land (Unit 1)

2. _____ Planning My Trip Abroad (Unit 2)

3. _____ The Greatest Adventure (Unit 3)

4. _____ Telling About Myself, Although It Is Hard for Me (Unit 4)

5. _____ My Wonderful Home Sweet Home! (Unit 5)

WARMUP II: WRITING INTRODUCTIONS

Writing an introduction, even a very short one, can sometimes be the hardest part of writing a composition. In fact, many good writers write the introduction last, after they have had additional time to think about it.

Include an introduction (as well as your name, the date, and the title) on each of your compositions. In short compositions or on examinations, the introduction should be no more than two sentences long, preferably contained within the first paragraph. You will study introductions in greater detail in Unit 25, but in the meantime here are several useful suggestions:

1. In your very first sentence, introduce the reader directly to your specific topic.
2. Keep the general introductory part as short as possible, two or three sentences at the very most.
3. Try to make the introduction interesting enough so that the reader will want to keep on reading. If possible, build in a little suspense or excitement to make the reader curious.
4. Even if you are trying to make your reader curious, however, avoid abstract, confusing, or vague statements.
5. Avoid making sweeping generalizations unless they are directly related to your topic.
6. Avoid offering irrelevant information, no matter how interesting it may seem.
7. Don't apologize to the reader for what you are going to say.

INSTRUCTIONS:
Each of the following introductions is very weak because it violates at *least* one of the preceding suggestions. Improve them, using the suggestions. You may wish to compare your corrections with the introductions used in the sample compositions.

1. (Unit 2) Have you ever taken a trip? Most people have, and usually find them exciting and useful. Of course, if the trip is a major one, you will have to do a lot of careful planning. If you do not, you will have a lot of problems. Sometimes the planning is easy, though sometimes it is difficult. In fact, for me, leaving home was one of the hardest things I have ever had to do. It was so hard that I almost decided to stay home.

2. (Unit 3) I will choose topic 1. Let me begin by specifying my topic. I will write about a trip that I took abroad. I had never gone abroad before this trip, so it was my first time. Traveling abroad presents many situations that are unique and sometimes difficult, especially because the language and customs are apt to be different.

3. (Unit 5) Since the beginning of time, humans have huddled together in the warmth of the family unit, first in caves, then in crude shacks, and finally in modern homes of all varieties. Some of the modern homes are luxurious, others painfully simple, but all have one aspect in common: the bond of love and affection that we know as "home." I will tell you about my home, where it is located, what it looks like, and how the interior space is used.

WARMUP II: WRITING CONCLUSIONS

Writing a conclusion, like writing an introduction, normally requires more care than writing the rest of the composition. It is the last thing the reader reads, so it determines the overall impression you create. (As you will study later, in the writing of newspaper stories and, to a large extent, in writing examination answers, the last part is the least important part and may not require a formal conclusion.) Here are some suggestions for writing effective conclusions:

1. Try to leave the reader with an idea that stands out or is unique, attractive, concise, or humorous.
2. Avoid merely summarizing what you have said. In a short composition, the reader can easily remember the main ideas; repeating them is both unnecessary and boring.
3. Draw conclusions or inferences that follow from your composition; avoid making sweeping generalizations that you have not supported.
4. Do not use the conclusion to introduce new, basic information that should have been introduced in the body of your composition.
5. Make sure the conclusion enhances, rather than weakens, the theme.
6. Keep the conclusion as short as possible. In a short composition, the conclusion should be two or three sentences at most. Because the conclusion is often quite different in purpose from the last main paragraph, it may be best to have it as a separate, short paragraph.
7. Don't apologize to the reader for what you have said or how you have said it.

INSTRUCTIONS:
Each of the following conclusions violates at *least* one of the guidelines just given. Each needs extensive revision. Improve them by following the preceding suggestions. After you have completed the exercise, consult the conclusions used in the sample compositions.

1. (Unit 2) In conclusion, my trip was difficult because I had many details to take care of, like getting a passport and visa, arranging to get the necessary tickets, and converting my money at the bank. I also had personal decisions that were difficult, like leaving my sister just before her wedding, abandoning my parents' business when they needed me, and walking out on a great professional opportunity. Also, I forgot to mention that I was asked to run for an important political office that I think I might easily have obtained.

2. (Unit 3) All these confusing experiences prove an important point that people should remember before traveling. Foreigners are simply not welcome in most places, and if you want to travel, you will have to put up with deliberate insults and inconveniences. Actually, I would rather have talked about a different topic because this one has been unpleasant for me.

3. (Unit 5) And that is what I have to say about my house. I hope you liked it, even though I have not been able to give a very clear explanation of my house, which is much nicer than I have said. For example, it won a small award once for the "most beautiful house on the block." Also my English is so poor. But I will try my best.

EDITING

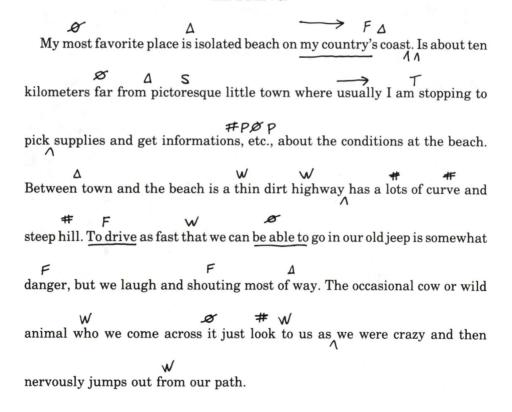

My most favorite place is isolated beach on my country's coast. Is about ten kilometers far from pictoresque little town where usually I am stopping to pick supplies and get informations, etc., about the conditions at the beach. Between town and the beach is a thin dirt highway has a lots of curve and steep hill. To drive as fast that we can be able to go in our old jeep is somewhat danger, but we laugh and shouting most of way. The occasional cow or wild animal who we come across it just look to us as we were crazy and then nervously jumps out from our path.

PLANNING AND WRITING

Choose one of the following topics:

1. My favorite place (other than home).
2. A place I would like to visit.
3. A place that is terrible (or lonely, or exciting, or expensive).

Using the suggestions you have followed in the previous units, think of and select ideas for your composition and organize them into paragraphs. Be sure you include your name and the date, a title, and a short introduction and conclusion. You will follow largely a spatial order in your description, describing your subject as if you were looking at it. However, you may also wish to include chronological events or other descriptions and explanations, as is done in the sample composition for this unit.

My Favorite Place

My favorite place is an isolated beach on the coast of my country. It is about ten kilometers from a picturesque little town where I usually stop to pick up supplies and get information about the conditions at the beach. Between the town and the beach is a narrow dirt road that has a lot of curves and steep hills. Driving as fast as we can go in our old jeep is somewhat dangerous, but we laugh and shout most of the way. The occasional cow or wild animal that we come across just looks at us as if we were crazy and then nervously jumps out of our path.

When we arrive at the beach, we park the jeep on the sand, set up a tent, and unload our equipment. The beach is in a kind of pocket, with the sea in front and a circle of wooded hills all around in back and on the sides. The sand is soft and silky and makes a kind of squeaking sound as we walk through it. It practically invites us to lie down on it and relax. The sun beats down gently but brightly; the sky is a pure blue with only a few scattered clouds. We can hear the wind whistling softly through the trees, the sea gulls calling, and the waves lapping.

For me the water itself is the most exciting part of the scene, at least once we get into it. It is warm and, except in early spring, is crystal clear. With the help of our skin-diving equipment, we enter the exquisite underwater environment, full of adventure and intrigue. Just a few meters from shore, there are all types of coral formations, unusual forms of plant life, and exotic and even dangerous fish and eels. There are also caves, boulders, and the ruins of broken ships. Who knows: maybe this cove was once the hiding place of bloodthirsty pirates, and maybe someday, in addition to all the natural treasures, we will find a buried chest full of gold, silver, and diamonds.

❦ Unit 7 ❦

My Favorite Activities

Writing forms: Listing; classification
**Writing skills: Identifying topic sentences; writing outlines with topic
sentences**

INTRODUCTION

What do you *like* to do? For most of us, life is a mosaic of activities, some
invigorating and some disappointing, some fulfilling and some tedious. In this
unit you will have a chance to list and describe your favorite activities: those
things that you find satisfying and that indirectly define who you are.

TIP

Don't apologize for what you say or how you say it. If you think that your English
is imperfect or that you have not eloquently said what you wanted to say, you
only intensify the weakness by mentioning it to the reader.

WARMUP I: IDENTIFYING TOPIC SENTENCES

Each of the preceding units has stressed the importance of writing with a
purpose. Not only the entire composition but each of the paragraphs as well
should have an identifiable theme. Frequently a paragraph will have one
sentence, often at the beginning, that clearly and concisely expresses that
purpose.

The type of composition you will write in this and the next unit requires clear
topic sentences; each paragraph will be a list, so you will need a sentence telling
the reader what type of list it is.

INSTRUCTIONS:
1. Read each of the paragraphs from previous units, as the directions state. Identify
the one sentence that best captures the main idea of the whole paragraph. 2. Express
in your own words the main idea and explain how the topic sentence serves its role.

34

3. Note whether the sentence is at the beginning, middle, or end of the paragraph and attempt to explain why.

Find the paragraphs in the sample composition in the units listed and identify the topic sentences.

   1. Unit 2, "Preparing to Go Abroad to Study," first paragraph.
   2. Unit 2, "Preparing to Go Abroad to Study," second paragraph.
   3. Unit 4, "A Short Autobiography," last paragraph.
   4. Unit 6, "My Favorite Place," last paragraph.
   5. Unit 7, "My Favorite Activities," first paragraph.
   6. Unit 7, "My Favorite Activities," second paragraph.

Note that many paragraphs that have a chronological order of development do *not* have topic sentences. The events contained in such paragraphs are all so clearly related to each other that no single sentence is needed to explain the central meaning.

WARMUP II: WRITING AN OUTLINE WITH TOPIC SENTENCES

In this unit you will do the planning and writing exercise as the warmup, and when you finish this exercise, you will be ready to begin writing.

INSTRUCTIONS:
1. Read the sample composition, noting the clear and direct way in which the activities are grouped and listed. 2. Choose one of the following topics for your composition:

   1. My favorite activities.
   2. The different activities I do during a typical week.
   3. The different types of friends I have.
   4. The different types of tools I use.

3. Make a list of about ten or more items or details concerning the topic. 4. Group these ten or more items into two or three groups, such as outdoor activities, social activities, artistic activities. 5. If within any of the groups you have too many activities to write about, eliminate some of the less interesting ones. If in another group you have too few, either try to think of more to include, or combine the items in that group with another group. 6. Write a sentence that summarizes or characterizes each of the groups that you have, and under this sentence list the specific activities that you intend to include. For maximum effect, put your most interesting ideas either first or last in the composition or paragraph, the least important or interesting in the middle. Use this outline form:

   I. The first type of activity I like to do (write a topic sentence).
      A. First example.
      B. Second example.
      C. Third example.
   II. The second type of activity (write a topic sentence).
      A. Example.
      B. Example.
   III. The third type of activity (write a topic sentence).
      A.
      B.

Example: In the sample composition the sentences are these:

  I. I love to be outdoors, to participate in sports, and to do daring things.
     A. Taking a trip down a wild river.
     B. Playing on the volleyball team.
  II. I also like to be around my friends, and I get bored if I have to sit at home with nothing to do for more than a few hours.
     A. Going to parties.
     B. Eating out with friends.
 III. In contrast, there are also many quiet, private things that I enjoy doing.
     A. Reading books.
     B. Watching movies.

EDITING

^F [#] [#] [#] ^F
In contrasting, there is also much quiet, private thing that I enjoy <u>to do</u>

^ø ^ø ^F [#] ^F ^Δ ^P ^F
them. I have been spending whole day <u>to read</u> book and I sometimes staying

^F ^Δ ^Δ ^F ^W ^Δ
up lately at the night with good novel. When I am tiring from the physical

^Δ
activities, I may find good movie or a light TV program very entertaining.

^F [#] ^Δ
Sometimes, too, I like spend a relaxed evening talk with friend about a
     [∧]

^W ^{WΔ} ^Δ ^Δ [#] ^W
serious materials by glass of a light wine. In another word, I want to do many

[#] ^Δ ^F ^W ^Δ
different kind of the things, depend of the mood I am in and the kind of the

people I am around.

PLANNING AND WRITING

Refer to Warmup II for the preliminary instructions on planning your composition. After you have stated the main ideas of each of your three paragraphs and listed the examples you are going to include, start with a first sentence that introduces the whole composition and then begin writing.

As you write, you may find a better way to state your main idea, you may remember other activities that you wish to include, or you may decide to rearrange your examples. Writing is a creative, not a mechanical activity, and you should not be alarmed if your outline, even if carefully planned, needs to be modified as you write.

My Favorite Activities

I like a wide variety of activities, from active and wild ones like camping, sports, and parties to quiet ones like watching TV and reading. I love to be outdoors, to participate in sports, and to do somewhat daring things. For example, several friends and I once took a trip down a wild river in a rubber raft. We spent over a week navigating rapids and dangerous currents, watching out for wild animals, camping on the banks of the river at night, fixing our own meals, and having a lot of fun talking and telling jokes. I am a member of a volleyball team, and for six months of the year we practice almost every day and compete with other teams. Two years ago we were one of the best city teams in the country and played a championship game on national television. I also like to do things that are risky, like skydiving, motorcycling, and swimming in the ocean at night, but quite honestly, I don't do them very often and am very careful.

I also like to be around my friends, and I get bored if I have to sit at home with nothing to do for more than a few hours. I usually get invited to at least one party a week. If I don't, then I arrange a party, even if it is very informal. I love to eat out, and my friends and I are experts on which restaurants serve the best food and which have the best atmosphere. I'm a good, if not excellent dancer, and whenever I have a chance, I go to a place where the lights are low and the music is loud and dance with someone who can teach me a few new moves.

In contrast, there are also many quiet, private things that I enjoy doing. I have spent whole days reading a book, and I sometimes stay up late at night with a good novel. When I am tired of physical activities, I may find a good movie or a light TV program very entertaining. Sometimes, too, I like to spend a relaxed evening talking with friends about serious matters over a glass of light wine. In other words, I like to do many different kinds of things, depending on the mood I am in and the kind of people I am around.

❧ Unit 8 ❧

The Three Major Influences on My Life

Writing forms: Classification; analysis
Writing skills: Planning the overall organization; supporting general statements

INTRODUCTION

Once there was a young prince who lived a life of fabulous luxury, sheltered by his family from all unpleasantness. But one day when he was riding in the royal park he encountered four things he had never seen before: an old man, a sick man, a dead body, and a religious teacher. From that instant his life was changed. He left his beloved family and all his wealth and dedicated himself to solving the riddle of human misery. In the process, he founded Buddhism, one of the world's great religions.

Each of us bears the indelible mark of physical, social, or intellectual influences. Which ones have most significantly shaped your life?

TIP

You will achieve your goal of becoming a mature and independent writer much more quickly if you correct as many of your own mistakes as you can *before* turning in your paper.

WARMUP I: PLANNING THE OVERALL ORGANIZATION

In many of the compositions you have written so far, the ordering has been quite simple. You simply put first what occurred first (as in describing a trip) or what you saw first (as in the description of a house). The following list includes these basic orders as well as those you will need for the next several units. Other types will be introduced throughout the book. Notice that these sequences can apply to individual paragraphs as well as to the whole composition.

1. **Chronological order.** The events are presented in the order in which they occurred, first things first and so on.
2. **Spatial order.** The ideas are presented in an order that follows spatial dimensions: front to back, left to right, top to bottom, and so on.
3. **Order of importance.** The ideas are arranged to produce a desired effect. There are two basic orders. In the order of *saliency*, the idea that the writer wants the reader most to notice comes *first*. In the order of *recency*, the idea the writer wants the reader to remember most (since it is the last thing the reader sees) comes at the *end*.

INSTRUCTIONS:
Reread the sample composition (or the compositions you have written) from the units listed here. Which of the preceding orders do you find? There may be more than one of these types in each composition.

1. Unit 4 (page 24)
2. Unit 5 (pages 27–28)
3. Unit 6 (page 33)
4. Unit 7 (page 37)

WARMUP II: SUPPORTING GENERAL STATEMENTS

To be effective, your writing must include more than merely general statements or opinions. You need to support your ideas with enough details so that the reader gets a clear and convincing idea of what you mean. In this unit, for example, you will be doing more than simply listing influences on your life. You will also be providing enough supporting information so that the reader will clearly see why you think these influences are significant.

INSTRUCTIONS:
1. Read the following sentences and decide whether they are generalizations (G) that need to be supported or whether they represent specific support (S). 2. For each of the sentences you have labeled G, write another sentence that would make it more specific.

Example: __G__ My older brother helped me get to college.

Support (step 2): He stayed up with me every night for weeks helping me prepare for the entrance examination.

1. _____ My childhood and early life were quite unusual.

2. _____ My parents spent hours with me, showing me how to work with my hands, pointing out the details of music, and discussing people's behavior.

3. _____ I had a lot of freedom.

4. _____ The most positive influence on my life was my friends.

5. _____ We developed honest friendships and were frank when we disagreed with others.

6. _____ In my country people were very conservative.

7. _____ My hobby has had a big influence on my life.

EDITING

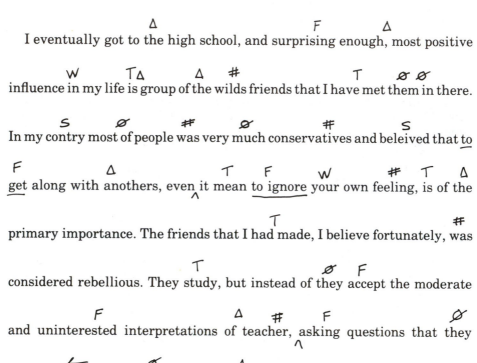

I eventually got to the high school, and surprising enough, most positive

influence in my life is group of the wilds friends that I have met them in there.

In my contry most of people was very much conservatives and beleived that to

get along with anothers, even it mean to ignore your own feeling, is of the

primary importance. The friends that I had made, I believe fortunately, was

considered rebellious. They study, but instead of they accept the moderate

and uninterested interpretations of teacher, asking questions that they

irritated often those who in charge of school.

PLANNING AND WRITING

The topic for your composition is "The Three Major Influences on My Life." You may use pimarily the order of saliency, giving the most important influence first. On the other hand, you may wish to list it last (recency), where it will leave a final strong impression in the reader's mind. To a certain extent, your order may also reflect a chronological sequence and resemble somewhat your autobiography.

After you have finished writing, but before you turn in your paper, count the number of sentences you have of each of the following types:

1. Sentences used as introduction.
2. Sentences used as conclusion.
3. Sentences that contain primarily generalizations.
4. Sentences that contain primarily support or explanations.

The introduction and conclusion (1 and 2) should be less than 25 per cent of the total. You should have many more supporting sentences (4) than generalizations (3).

The Three Major Influences on My Life

My childhood and early life were quite unusual, and hence the formative influences on my life are not exactly typical. When I was a baby, my father and mother were put in prison for their political views, and I can only remember seeing them once before I was eight. I was raised by a fiercely independent old couple who were unconcerned by the social and political risks of caring for me and who were as intelligent as they were strange. But from this sensitive couple I learned the value of discipline, hard work, concern for the environment, and faith in one's own principles. I had a lot of freedom and time to myself, but "Mom" and "Dad" also spent hours with me, showing me how to do things with my hands; pointing out the details of ideas, nature, and music; discussing the advantages and disadvantages of different behaviors, and helping me utilize my free time to the greatest advantage. Near the beginning of my third year in elementary school, the political climate changed abruptly, my real parents were freed, my stand-in parents moved away, and I found a place in "normal" society. "Mom" and "Dad" are still alive, but I rarely see them anymore.

I eventually got to high school, and surprisingly enough, the most positive influence on my life was a group of wild friends that I met there. In my country most people were very conservative and believed that getting along with others, even if it meant ignoring one's own feelings, was of primary importance. The friends that I made, I believe fortunately, were considered rebellious. They studied, but instead of accepting the moderate and uninteresting interpretations of the teachers, they asked questions that often irritated those in charge of the school. Rather than following all the socially accepted norms, like dressing prettily and saying all the polite things, we developed more honest friendships and were quite frank, sometimes almost insulting, when we disagreed with people. We had our own styles of dress, music, and entertainment, and there were enough of us so that we did not feel lonely. Most of those old friends are doing very well today.

A third influence on my life has been my hobby, for it has taught me an appreciation of nature; it allows me to be outside; it requires me to read, study, and talk with others; and it has given me a real impetus in choosing my career as an entomologist. My hobby is collecting insects, all kinds of insects, but mostly beetles. I have over two thousand specimens, representing about three hundred species. Some are grotesque and some are gorgeous, but all are fascinating and give me a deep respect for the enormous diversity and individuality of all forms of life. This respect, I believe, more than anything else represents the effects of all the influences on my life and characterizes the kind of person I am.

❧ Unit 9 ❧

How to Make Something

Writing form: Process
Writing skills: Avoiding redundancy; avoiding rambling sentences

INTRODUCTION

Telling others how to do something is the purpose of much of what is written: indeed, it is the basis of much of what we call education. A popular topic that clearly illustrates this form of writing is telling someone how to prepare food. Other popular topics are listed at the end of this unit. The focus is on the chronological steps. (In the next unit, another type of writing that tells how to do something, one that emphasizes the *principles* rather than the steps, will be introduced.)

TIP

Imitation is one of the most common and effective ways of learning. You can use this method easily in learning to write by reading what others have written and noting their organization, style, and use of words.

WARMUP I: AVOIDING REDUNDANCY

Redundancy means repetition. A certain amount of repetition is useful, even necessary, but if there is too much, your writing will seem immature and monotonous. There are several types of redundancy, including using the same word over and over, explaining an idea that is already clear, giving examples that are not needed, and using the same structures excessively.

INSTRUCTIONS:
Underline all the parts of the following paragraph that are unnecessary (redundant).

Texas is famous and well known for its chili. People have heard about

42

Texas chili everywhere. There are almost as many recipes for chili as there are Texans. That means that almost every Texan has his or her own recipe.

Mine is fairly simple and easy. It is not hard at all. You must have some ingredients (food) and equipment (pots and utensils) in order to cook chili.

The ingredients and equipment that you should have assembled and in one place before beginning and commencing include the following things that I will list. Ingredients: a pound (16 oz.) of ground beef (beef that is ground up), a small onion that is not too large, two and a half cups of cooked red beans that have already been boiled, a can of condensed tomato soup that you will have to open, some chili powder, flour made from ground wheat, and salt for seasoning.

WARMUP II: AVOIDING RAMBLING SENTENCES

The following exercise provides additional practice in avoiding rambling sentences, a frequent problem for advanced writers.

INSTRUCTIONS:
Break the following run-on paragraph into at *least* three separate sentences. Add transition words, change the sentence structure, or make other stylistic or wording changes as necessary.

We can divide the actual cooking into three stages which all together take about an hour and a quarter of which the first is to chop the onion finely, cook it together with the meat in the skillet until the meat is browned and a loose

mixture of small pieces and in which the second stage is to add the beans and

the tomato soup, letting the mixture boil over low heat for ten minutes until

the final and longest step, which is to mix about two tablespoons of chili

powder, a tablespoon of flour, a teaspoon of salt, and three tablespoons of

water in the cup until the mixture resembles a smooth paste before stirring it

into the mixture in the skillet.

EDITING

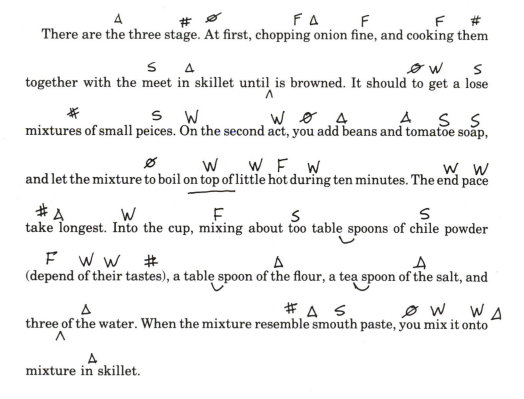

There are the three stage. At first, chopping onion fine, and cooking them together with the meet in skillet until is browned. It should to get a lose mixtures of small peices. On the second act, you add beans and tomatoe soap, and let the mixture to boil on top of little hot during ten minutes. The end pace take longest. Into the cup, mixing about too table spoons of chile powder (depend of their tastes), a table spoon of the flour, a tea spoon of the salt, and three of the water. When the mixture resemble smouth paste, you mix it onto mixture in skillet.

PLANNING AND CHOOSING

Pick one of the following topics:

1. How to prepare a type of food.
2. How to play a game or sport or an instrument.
3. How to do your hobby.
4. How to buy something expensive, such as a house, car, or business property.

Before beginning to write, carefully think through all the steps that your reader needs to understand, and arrange your steps into two or three paragraphs. Avoid unnecessary redundancy and rambling sentences. Read the sample composition to gain ideas on organization and to find useful words.

How to Make Chili

Texas is famous for chili, and there are almost as many recipes for it as there are Texans. Mine is fairly simple. The ingredients and equipment that you should have assembled before beginning include the following. Ingredients: a pound of ground beef, a small onion, two and a half cups of cooked red beans, a can of condensed tomato soup, some chili powder, flour, and salt. Equipment: a skillet (frying pan), a large spoon, some measuring spoons, a cutting board, a sharp knife, a can opener, and a cup.

We can divide the actual cooking into three stages, which all together take about an hour and a quarter. First, chop the onion finely, and cook it and the meat in the skillet until the meat is browned. The meat should be loosened into small pieces. For the second stage, add the beans and the tomato soup and let the mixture boil over low heat for about ten minutes. The final step takes the longest. In the cup, mix about two tablespoons of chili powder (depending on your taste), a tablespoon of flour, a teaspoon of salt, and three tablespoons of water. When the mixture resembles a smooth paste, stir it into the mixture in the skillet. Turn the heat down very low and let the chili just simmer for forty-five minutes. You will have to stir it frequently to keep it from burning. Cover it partially to keep it from splattering all over the top of your stove.

When the chili is done, serve it in soup bowls. Some people like to grate cheese over the top; others add tomato relish or hot sauce. A perfect accompaniment is hot flour tortillas, though any kind of bread goes well. As you eat the chili, enjoy the wonderful fragrance as well as the delicious flavor. Do not be surprised if your neighbors follow their noses to your door and ask you for your recipe.

❧ Unit 10 ❧

How to Succeed

Writing forms: Analysis; process
Writing skills: Omitting unnecessary sentences; improving sentence
  variety

INTRODUCTION

In many types of writing, the author tells the reader how something is done
without giving exact or complete steps. The writing is more of a general analysis
than a recipe. In this unit you will study a composition about how to make
friends in a foreign country, and you will write an analysis of how you do
something, such as learning a language, finding a boy/girl friend, earning
money, or making good grades.

TIP

Be realistic about how much time you should spend writing. You will not
improve much if you spend too little time. On the other hand, since you will
never produce a perfect product, you must learn when to say realistically, "I've
done enough."

WARMUP I: OMITTING UNNECESSARY SENTENCES

A persistent challenge for a good writer is eliminating ideas or details that have
made their way into the first draft of a composition but that do not significantly
contribute to the writer's purpose.

INSTRUCTIONS:
1. Read the paragraph to determine the main idea. 2. Identify and cross out sentences that unnecessarily repeat, that give insignificant information, or that are
uninteresting or tedious. Don't be concerned here about the shortness of the sentences
and the many repeated words: you will correct these in the next exercise.

I think I have discovered three rules. The rules are about making friends in a foreign country. I would not want to tell my friends what the rules are. I had many friends when I was younger. My friends would be surprised if I told them my rules. These are just my rules. I will mention my first rule first. My first rule is this. You should say the opposite of what you really feel. If you feel one thing, say the opposite. For example, when I first arrived I was tired and uncomfortable. Most people get tired when they travel. I realized that when people asked me how I was getting along, they really only wanted to hear some things. People wanted to hear how excited I was. People wanted to hear how pleasant everything was. Maybe I do the same thing with foreigners in my country too. We have a lot of tourists in my country. It is good for our economy. People smiled and asked me about the food. How did I like the food? They really only wanted me to tell them a lie. The lie was that I liked hamburgers. I don't know why Americans like hamburgers. Maybe it is because people are lazy. People passed me on the street. They asked me, "How are you?" The streets are not very crowded here compared with other places.

They don't really want to know about my health. The *last* thing people

wanted was for me to tell them I had a headache. I sometimes have head-

aches. My friends don't seem to care. So my rule became: Say the opposite of

what you mean. I think it is a good rule. Do you?

WARMUP II: IMPROVING SENTENCE VARIETY

After you finished Warmup I, your paragraph still needed a lot of refinement. In
other words, the paragraph is now like a rough first draft. It has too many simple
sentences, and some words are repeated over and over. You can combine and
simplify sentences in a variety of ways. You can also avoid repeating words by
choosing a synonym, using pronouns, or combining the two parts of the sentence
in which the word is used.

INSTRUCTIONS:
Circle the words *rule, rules,* and *people* each time they appear. Combine the sentences
(using words like *as, when, although, but,* or *however*) so that in the revision you have
only one or two simple sentences, and so that you have at least two sentences that
include three clauses. (A clause is a group of words with a subject and verb.) At the
same time, eliminate at least half of the occurrences of the circled words.

I think I have discovered three rules. The rules are about making friends in

a foreign country. I would not want to tell my friends what the rules are. My

first rule is this. You should say the opposite of what you really feel. For

example, when I first arrived, I was tired and uncomfortable. I realized that

when people asked me how I was getting along, they really only wanted to

hear some things. People wanted to hear how excited I was. People wanted to

hear how pleasant everything was. People smiled and asked me about the food. How did I like the food? They really only wanted me to tell them a lie.

The lie was that I liked hamburgers. People passed me on the street. They

asked me, "How are you?" The *last* thing they wanted was for me to tell them I

had a headache. So my rule became: Say the opposite of what you mean.

EDITING

Third rule is assume that the people knows anything about me or my home

city, I grew tired to tell peoples that I do not rode horse to the work, that I keep

the food in refrigerator. I have electricity in my house and that there are the

streets and traffic lights in my town. And I just frequently pretend to be

surprising from "modern" inventions they show me. I met few people who can

ask intelligent issues and comment in depth over my country's issues. But I

see him as happy exception, and am content to being around anothers who is,

quite frankly, well meaning but ignorants.

PLANNING AND WRITING

Choose one of these topics:

1. How to learn a foreign language.
2. How to find a friend (such as a boy friend or girl friend).
3. How to earn money.
4. How to make good grades.

Each of these will require you to do more than provide a simple step-by-step recipe. The process is too complex and too controversial for there to exist a simple formula. Rather, you will need to analyze what you consider to be the underlying principles, factors, or stages in a way that will be clear to your reader. You probably will have each major principle, factor, or stage in a separate paragraph. In the first paragraph as well, you should state clearly what you are describing and how many principles or steps you are going to describe. Include in your last paragraph any concluding or summarizing comments you feel are necessary.

How to Make Friends in a Foreign Country

I think I have discovered three rules for making friends in a foreign country, although I would not want to tell my friends what the principles are. My first rule is that you should say the opposite of what you really feel. For example, when I first arrived I was tired and uncomfortable, but I realized that when people asked me how I was getting along, they really only wanted to hear how excited I was and how pleasant everything was. When acquaintances smiled and asked me how I liked the food, they really wanted me to tell them the lie that I loved hamburgers. And when they passed me on the street and asked, "How are you?" the *last* thing they wanted was for me to tell them I had a headache. So my guideline became: Say the opposite of what you mean.

My second rule is never to show enthusiasm for anything until after I find out if it is fashionable. I used to remark about how clever the political leaders were, and how well organized the schools were, and how exciting a television program was until I realized that everyone around me seemed to hate the politicians, thought the schools were terrible, and were sick of watching television. I made the mistake once of cheering for a football team, only to find the person sitting next to me was a fan of the other team; of buying a delicious steak for an acquaintance who turned out to be a vegetarian; and of telling some friends how good looking they were, only to be told that I was sexist. Anyway, I have learned to watch others carefully before expressing my enthusiasm.

My third rule is to assume that people know nothing about me or my home city. I have grown tired of telling people that I do not ride a horse to work, that I keep my food in a refrigerator, that I have electricity in my house, and that there are streets and traffic lights in my town, and I frequently just pretend to be surprised by the "modern" inventions they show me. I have met a few people who can ask intelligent questions and comment in depth on issues in my country, but I see them as the happy exception and am content to be around others who are, quite frankly, well meaning but ignorant.

❧ Unit 11 ❧

Revising

Writing form: Review of forms used in Units 1–10
Writing skills: Revising; rewriting

INTRODUCTION

One of the four major steps in effective writing mentioned in Unit 1 was evaluating and revising. Even though you planned carefully and wrote in the most accurate way possible, you probably did not spend more than an hour or so writing each composition. You did not have, therefore, at the time you turned it in, the perspective of several days, and you could not, therefore, have adequately revised or written it. In this unit you will have the opportunity to go back to one of those compositions, take a fresh look at it, and revise it.

TIP

Few people can make significant or rapid improvement in writing without feedback from others. Sometimes this feedback is flattering, but sometimes it is painful. In either case, it is your main road to progress and you should attend to it whenever it is available.

WARMUP, PLANNING AND WRITING: THE ROLE OF REVISING AND REWRITING

One key to effective writing is proper planning. Another is skillful use of language. A final key, which is too often neglected or underrated, is rewriting. Writing is a creative activity, an act of invention. What you write is rarely, if ever, perfect when it is first produced. Several useful things happen when a writer comes back to something he or she has written.

1. The writer more closely takes on the role of an outside *reader* and sees the writing more objectively.
2. The writer realizes that he or she needs to add information, clarification, or support.

51

3. The writer realizes that some of the material is weak, irrelevant, or repetitious and should be omitted.

4. The writer sees better ways of organizing the details.

5. The writer thinks of clearer or more elegant ways of constructing the sentences and selects more precise words and phrases to convey the meanings.

6. The writer detects errors or weaknesses in paragraphing, appearance, spelling, or punctuation.

Revising can take place to a certain extent even while you are writing the first draft. For example, you can reorganize, erase, or insert information. Similarly, by using a checklist and rereading your work, you can make last-minute improvements. Real revising and rewriting, however, is most effective after a few days have passed, after you have developed some "distance" from your composition.

INSTRUCTIONS:

1. Reread all the compositions you have written for the first ten units and take brief notes of the major or common problems you have had. 2. Pick *one* of the compositions for rewriting and, using the checklist, the notes your teacher has made, and your own evaluations, make notes of the types of changes you intend to make. 3. Make an outline of the composition as you *intend* to rewrite it. 4. Using a fresh sheet of paper, write the composition over, using the new outline. 5. Using the checklist again, make final changes and turn in your paper. This composition should represent what you consider to be a *good* piece of work.

❧ Unit 12 ❧

Evaluating My Progress

Writing form: Any of those from Units 1–10
Writing skills: Using objective scales for evaluating writing; writing
  under pressure for a grade

INTRODUCTION

Do you ever wonder how well you write compared to some objective standard or how much your writing is improving? You will have a clearer answer to these questions after you study the information introduced in this unit and after you write a composition that the teacher will grade.

TIP

Try to view tests as challenges that can stimulate you to do your best rather than as threatening barriers that will trip you up.

WARMUP: USING OBJECTIVE SCALES FOR EVALUATING WRITING

A common method of evaluating writing is grading a short composition that has been written extemporaneously within a short period of time. A major focus in such evaluations is likely to be sentence structure and vocabulary, although organization, content, paragraphing, and matters of mechanics and appearance should also be considered. Clearly, skill in writing cannot always accurately be assessed on such an examination. The content, setting, pressure, time limitations, and purpose are all apt to be different from normal. Nevertheless, being able to do well in such situations is a useful skill which is worth practicing.

INSTRUCTIONS:

1. Read the descriptions in Appendix II of the levels of writing that you feel represent your present level; then read those that represent the level you would

like to achieve. Use the following scale to guide you in using Appendix II:

A. 90–100 represents skills close to those of an educated native speaker.
B. 80–89 represents skills of very advanced writers who need little, if any, further training in English as a second language.
C. 75–79 represents the skill of advanced writers who are capable of doing academic work in an American university but who have a weakness in writing that for most academic fields requires further part-time coursework.
D. 65–74 represents an advanced level of writing in an intensive English-as-a-second-language program.
E. Below 65 represents an upper intermediate level.

2. Select and read a composition in Appendix II that corresponds to what you believe, on the basis of the preceding descriptions, to be your level.
3. Reread the checklist and see how many weaknesses you can identify and correct in the composition you have read.

EDITING

The following composition was written during a test. The writer did not know in advance what the topic would be and had only 30 minutes to write. The grade given was 70. There are many mistakes in selection of content, in organization, in paragraphing, and in language and mechanics. Correct the mistakes that are marked above the lines (mistakes in language) and consider how you might solve the mistakes indicated in the margins and in the comments (mistakes in content and organization).

Title?

Everyone has his own opinion about many things such as smoking, politics

(too informal)

and what have you. I have my own opinion about knowledge, and how can we

get the knowledge.

In this report I intend to tell the reader if the knowledge we get it from the

classroom is more than what we get from out of classroom.

I entirely agree with this statement. I think the classroom deson't give us

all what we need it maybe give us definite kind of knowledge not all the kind

of knowledge.

Weak Introdu
Omit
of it

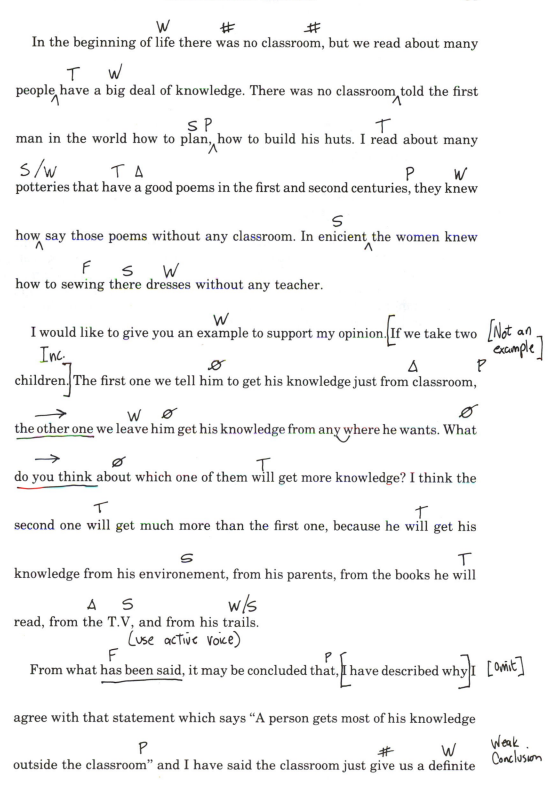

In the beginning of life there was no classroom, but we read about many people have a big deal of knowledge. There was no classroom told the first man in the world how to plan, how to build his huts. I read about many potteries that have a good poems in the first and second centuries, they knew how say those poems without any classroom. In enicient the women knew how to sewing there dresses without any teacher.

I would like to give you an example to support my opinion. If we take two children. The first one we tell him to get his knowledge just from classroom, the other one we leave him get his knowledge from any where he wants. What do you think about which one of them will get more knowledge? I think the second one will get much more than the first one, because he will get his knowledge from his environement, from his parents, from the books he will read, from the T.V, and from his trails.

From what has been said, it may be concluded that, I have described why I agree with that statement which says "A person gets most of his knowledge outside the classroom" and I have said the classroom just give us a definite

P

kind of knowledge but we can get all kinds of knowledge outside the

classroom.

A suggested answer to the editing exercise is listed in Appendix I under the example for 90–100.

PLANNING AND WRITING: WRITING UNDER PRESSURE FOR A GRADE

Your teacher will choose three topics that can be written about by using one of the writing forms you have studied so far (chronology, spatial order, classification, and so on). Think quickly but carefully before you begin to write, and before you finish, take a few minutes to read over the composition and make last-minute changes. Write as much as you can as well as you can in 30 minutes on *one* of the three topics. Do not use a dictionary.

❧ Unit 13 ❧

Similarities and Differences

Writing form: Comparison/contrast
Writing skills: Listing similarities and differences; arranging details in comparison and contrast; using expressions of contrast and similarity

INTRODUCTION

Our ability to recognize and describe the similarities and differences between events, objects, and feelings underlies many of our technical and aesthetic achievements. Writing that compares and contrasts, therefore, ranks among the more common and important forms and is the basis of this and several subsequent units.

TIP

Even experienced writers have "off" days. Don't be surprised if you have days when it is difficult to write and when what you say seems worthless. Better days lie ahead.

WARMUP I: LISTING SIMILARITIES AND DIFFERENCES

Before you can organize or write about similarities or differences you must begin by thinking of and organizing your ideas on the topic.

INSTRUCTIONS:

1. Individually or in a group, think of all the possible differences for each of the following topics. Use no more than five minutes on each, but try to list more points than anyone else. You will probably be more successful if you first designate *categories* (such as physical appearance, personality, or activities) before listing individual features (taller, heavier, more handsome, for example).

   1. The differences between me and another member of the family.
   2. The differences between this class and other classes.
   3. The differences between student life and "normal" life.

2. Individually or in a group think of all the possible *similarities* for each of the three preceding topics. Use five minutes or less on each. Use general categories to help you identify the points.

WARMUP II: ARRANGING DETAILS IN COMPARISON AND CONTRAST

As you will study in more depth in Unit 26, there are several ways to organize details. In this unit use the common pattern outlined here:

I. First paragraph. Introduce the topic in the first sentence. In the remainder of the paragraph, introduce a major category: for example, physical appearance and clothing.
  A. List and discuss all the similarities in the category: for example, similarities in physical appearance when people are dressed alike.
  B. List and discuss all the differences in the category: for example, differences in the styles of clothing.
II. Second paragraph. Introduce another major category.
  A. List and discuss the similarities in the category.
  B. List and discuss the differences in the category.
III. Third paragraph. Continue in the same pattern.

INSTRUCTIONS:
Arrange the following sentence elements into a paragraph that would fit into the outline just given. (The elements have been taken at random from the third pararaph of the sample composition, which you should consult only *after* you have completed the exercise. The transition words such as *but* and *and* have been omitted.)

1. _____ I like to keep things neat and orderly.

2. _____ We agreed on the color we liked best and the kind of furniture we wanted.

3. _____ My twin doesn't seem to have any definite habits and often goes to bed very late.

4. _____ My twin acts as if there were a servant around to pick up all the things that get thrown on the floor.

5. _____ Finally, I like to go to bed early and get up early.

6. _____ We have tried to live in the same room at times.

7. _____ My twin wants to sleep late the next day when I want to get the day started.

WARMUP III: USING WORDS OF CONTRAST AND SIMILARITY

INSTRUCTIONS:
Fill in the blanks with appropriate words from the following list. There may be more than one correct answer. Note the punctuation carefully.

alike   both   however   in contrast
on the other hand   the same   similar   whereas
while

1. I prefer parties to libraries, and my twin feels _____ .

2. We have very similar features. _____ , we like very different styles of clothing.

3. My twin is always with friends, _____ I like to be alone at times.

4. My twin and I look _____ .

5. When we are _____ dressed up we have _____ features.

6. I like to go to bed early. _____ , my twin doesn't seem to have any definite habits.

7. I like to keep things neat and orderly, _____ my twin acts as if there is a servant around.

8. I prefer informal clothes, _____ my twin dresses like a model.

9. My twin likes loud music, _____ I find that night clubs give me a headache.

See the following sample composition for answers. Note also that in items 3, 7, 8, and 9 *while* or *whereas* can be used. (*Although* might be used by some native speakers in these sentences as well.) In item 6 you could use *however, in contrast,* or *on the other hand*.

EDITING

We has such similar temperaments in most of the ways. I don't get angrily easily, I am like to be around with peoples own ages, and young childrens are found by me a little bit irritating, and I would rather to spending the times at the party that in library. My twin feel the same like me. But my twin like music loud and moderns dances, while, I find the night clubs to give me one headache. But, my twin always with the friends, a favorite with all teachers, and wants never have childs. Whereas, I want to be lonely at sometimes, I

→   ∅   W   W   Δ
really not want to try impress the teachers, and attempt someday to have the

＃   F
families of mine.

PLANNING AND WRITING

Choose one of the topics and follow the procedure introduced in Warmup I. That is, determine general categories and then think of relevant similarities and differences within them. Then use a separate paragraph to describe each of the categories you decide to use. Use the outline suggested in Warmup II, first listing all the similarities within a subcategory, then the differences. Use the words of similarity and contrast introduced in Warmup III.

Select one of these topics:

1. The similarities and differences between me and another member of my family.
2. The similarities and differences between this class and other classes.
3. The similarities and differences between the *specific* aspects of two countries. Limit your topic to something you are very familiar with, something that is narrow enough to write about in a short composition. Your topic should be one for which you can provide specific and interesting information.

Before turning in your paper, use the checklist and correct as many of your mistakes as you can.

My Twin and I

Twins are supposed to be very much alike, are they not? Well, my twin and I do *look* alike. Some of the time when we are both dressed up, which is not often, or when we go to the beach, which is not really often either, people recognize the similarity of our features. However, we like very different styles of clothing. I prefer informal clothes, whereas my twin dresses like a model, always wearing the latest fashions.

We have very similar temperaments in most ways. I do not get angry easily, enjoy being around people my own age, find young children a little irritating, and would rather spend time at a party than in a library. In these respects my twin feels the same. But my twin likes loud music and modern dances, while I find that nightclubs give me a headache. My twin is always with friends, is a favorite with all the teachers, and never wants to have children, whereas I prefer to be alone at times, don't really try to impress my teachers, and intend someday to have a family of my own.

We have tried to live in the same room several times, and even agreed on the color we liked best and the kind of furniture we wanted. But I like to keep things neat and orderly, while my twin acts as if there were a servant around to pick up all the things that get thrown on the floor or over the edge of the chair or into the bathtub. I like to go to bed early and get up early. In contrast, my twin doesn't seem to have any definite habits, often goes to bed very late, and then wants to sleep late the next day when I want to get the day started.

What is perhaps most surprising about the two of us, however, is that when people try to compare us or criticize what the other has done, we are very similar: we immediately defend the other one and insist that there is nothing wrong. Despite all our differences, we are very close, even though obviously I am the normal one and my twin is unusual.

(Note: If you write a composition like this, put in a real name, use the pronoun *she* or *he,* and add details to indicate your cultural background.)

🌿 Unit 14 🌿

Advantages and Disadvantages

Writing form: Comparison/contrast
Writing skills: Identifying advantages and disadvantages; arranging
advantages and disadvantages into paragraphs

INTRODUCTION

Showing advantages and/or disadvantages is a common method of developing comparison and contrast (the form introduced in Unit 13). Many of our decisions, both academic and personal, revolve around recognizing similarities and differences and then determining in which ways the options are good (advantages) or bad (disadvantages). As a way of practicing this useful form of writing, you will have an opportunity to write about the relative merits or liabilities of going abroad to study, of owning a car, or of getting married.

TIP

Don't try to imitate a style of writing that is beyond your capabilities or that does not suit your own taste. The happy fact is that most of your readers *prefer* a simple and clear style, not a complex or literary one.

WARMUP I: IDENTIFYING ADVANTAGES AND DISADVANTAGES

Discussing the advantages and disadvantages of something is slightly more complex than merely noting the points of similarity and difference. You should have broad categories in mind (as you did in the warmups in Unit 13), and you need to think of specific details; but more than that, you need to weigh your points, carefully considering their overall positive or negative value. In addition, you need to decide if each point is important or minor. Finally, you need to determine in which way you are going to group your points—which ones you are going to mention first and which last. You will practice these skills in this and the following warmup.

INSTRUCTIONS:
Read the phrases to determine whether they represent an advantage of being married (A) or a disadvantage (D).

Example: __A__ Not having to pay rent to live in two separate apartments.

1. _____ Having someone to talk with.

2. _____ Waking up in the night to feed a baby.

3. _____ Feeling loved.

4. _____ Watching your children grow.

5. _____ Buying an expensive house to suit the family's needs.

6. _____ Spending time finding reliable babysitters who are not too expensive.

7. _____ Arguing over which TV program to watch.

8. _____ Paying for the children's haircuts.

9. _____ Having less freedom to come and go as you please.

10. _____ Sharing physical affection.

11. _____ Walking your children to school on cold mornings.

12. _____ Eating most of your meals at home instead of in restaurants.

13. _____ Not having to pay rent in two places.

14. _____ Learning to cook and wash dishes for the family.

15. _____ Buying expensive clothing for your children, who only wear it a few months.

16. _____ Feeling that your life has meaning and purpose in a family.

17. _____ Trying to get along with in-laws.

18. _____ Being with your children on happy occasions.

19. _____ Going on wonderful vacations.

20. _____ Seeing your old friends less (because you are with your family).

WARMUP II: ARRANGING ADVANTAGES AND DISADVANTAGES INTO PARAGRAPHS

The form of the composition in this unit is more complex than any you have studied so far, and there are many possible variations. The form used in the sample composition and practiced in this warmup is perhaps the best form for you to use unless you already have experience using it. It follows this basic outline:

    I. The advantages of one of the options.
    II. The advantages of the other option.
    III. The disadvantages of both options and the overall conclusion (if any).

INSTRUCTIONS:

1. Group the 20 items in Warmup I into the following categories. You may wish to list an item in more than one of the categories.

   1. Items related to economic issues in marriage.
   2. Items related to having children.
   3. Items related to personal or interpersonal issues.

2. Some of the 20 items are relatively unimportant. Cross them out.
3. Add some items to your list, particularly in those categories that you feel are not well supported. Try to have approximately equal numbers of items showing the advantages and disadvantages of being married.
4. Arrange your items into an outline, placing the most important items first or last and the least important items in the middle. Use this outline:

   I. The advantages of being single.
      a. Economic issues.
      b. Issues related to children.
      c. Personal or interpersonal issues.
   II. The advantages of being married.
      a. Economic issues.
      b. Issues related to children.
      c. Personal or interpersonal issues.
   III. The disadvantages (not already mentioned) of being single and being married and the overall conclusion (if any).

You will notice that in many cases an advantage for one is simply a disadvantage for the other, stated in different words. Try to design your outline, however, so that the advantages are stated *positively,* not negatively, and so that your last paragraph introduces disadvantages not previously considered.

EDITING

TRYING TO DECIDE WHICH COLLEGE TO ATTEND

University in the little town, on the contrary, has a more clear focusing and the orientation on their academic programs: the broad, balancing education cover many careers. Their proffesors are more better paid from those in the city and are be expected that they are excellent like teachers. Classes are small, and it allowing a lot of contact between the all members of community, after class often in the professor home. The library's collection is more small,

W   S   F
in spite of the library building itself is impressive, quite, and comfortably;

            # #   F
and books and material is easy to find and be used.

PLANNING AND WRITING

Choose one of these three topics:

1. The advantages and disadvantages of being married.
2. The advantages and disadvantages of having a (large) car.
3. The advantages and disadvantages of going abroad to study.

If you use Topic 1, you can use the outline you developed in Warmup II. If you do not, select two or three broad categories for your topic and think of advantages and disadvantages within each. Consult the sample composition before beginning.

Trying to Decide Which College to Attend

I will soon have to choose between two universities that have accepted me. The first is a large school in a big city, the other a small school in a little town, both offering some real benefits and drawbacks. Going to the large school appeals to me not only because it has more professors and more courses, but also because in the city I would have access to all kinds of entertainment, social life, job opportunities, and so on. This university has a large department in my field of interest, many books in the library, good laboratory facilities, and many courses, both directly in the department and in related fields. Both the university itself and the city also have many other opportunities. For example, there are several museums, a public library, a swimming pool, many nightclubs, several major athletic teams, and many interesting people to meet. While I do not consider myself wild or radical, I think the freer atmosphere in the city would make me feel more comfortable.

The university in the small town, in contrast, has a clearer focus and orientation in its academic programs: a broad, integrated, balanced education bridging many areas. The professors are paid better than those in the city and are expected to be excellent teachers. Classes are small, allowing a lot of contact among all the members of the community, often in the professor's home after class. The library collection is smaller, but the library building itself is impressive, quiet, and comfortable; and books and materials are easy to find and use. There are fewer opportunities for an exciting night life, but there are many student groups and clubs and places for outdoor activities. Sports are emphasized within the college, and the townspeople often invite students to do things with them.

Unfortunately, some disadvantages in both schools concern me. The city university is not in a very good part of town, and many poor and unemployed people live in the area. Many of the professors have off-campus jobs and appear to be too busy. The smaller school similarly has its limitations. The protective attitude of the administration and the way they watch over the students disturb me. While the reputation and academic standards are high, it is very expensive and the work is hard. Sometimes I wonder if it is worth going to college at all, but then again, I know I would be unhappy if I did not attend. Maybe I will just toss a coin to help me make my decision.

❦ Unit 15 ❦

A Fantasy About the Future

Writing form: Chronology
Writing skills: Using present conditional verb forms; avoiding repetition of words

INTRODUCTION

Imagine yourself in the following situations. What would you do?

1. An eccentric millionaire becomes curious about how you would spend $150,000 if you received it as a gift. In order to get it, you must only promise to spend it entirely on yourself or your immediate family and to get rid of it or invest it within two weeks.
2. While you are watching TV late one evening, the picture suddenly fades and you see mysterious shapes and hear this secret message: "We are friendly visitors from outer space who have selected you from among all the humans we have surveyed. We wish to land our spacecraft near your house and make contact with you. In return we will share our knowledge and invite you to take a trip with us. We will contact you again in an hour to see if you accept."
3. While listening to the radio before going to class one morning, you hear the special bulletin that a new war has broken out in the world. As you listen carefully, you come to the horrible realization that *your* country is one of the participants.

The main purpose of this unit is to provide you with extensive practice in using an important grammatical structure that is difficult even for most advanced students.

TIP

Find a balance between using the same structures over and over and using new structures you are not sure are correct. A ratio of 90 percent familiar and 10 percent new may be a satisfactory combination that will help you learn without appearing careless or inaccurate.

WARMUP I: USING PRESENT CONDITIONAL VERB FORMS

A verb form that can be troublesome even for very advanced writers is the conditional form, which is used to indicate that the sentence is not in fact true but is only being imagined. This unit will treat the present conditional and Unit 16, the past conditional.

If a condition is possible or real, use this form:

1. If I still have $15.00 after buying my books, I'll go to a movie.

The following are examples of the types of present conditional forms you will use in this lesson to indicate that the condition is *not* possible or real:

1. If someone *gave* me $150,000, I *would spend* it.
2. If I *were watching* TV and *heard* this announcement, I *would feel* nervous.
3. If my brother *were* still at home when the war *broke* out, I think I *would be* concerned that he *would be drafted* into the army.

Note these features:

a. The part of the sentence that expresses the condition (the part with *if*) does *not* use a form of *will* but rather a PAST form of the verb.
b. The part of the sentence that expresses the result uses *would* plus the SIMPLE form of the verb.
c. In the condition, the form of the verb TO BE that is preferred in formal writing is *were* for all cases (as in the preceding example 2). In informal use, both *was* and *were* are used.
d. If in a conditional sentence something is mentioned that is *true,* the appropriate tense (such as the PRESENT *think* in example 3) is used.

INSTRUCTIONS:
In the following sentences, select the correct form to fit in the blank. You may need to add *would* or other forms.

1. I (BE) _____ sure that if I (HEAR) _____ a voice from my TV I (BE) _____ very surprised.

2. If they (BE) _____ still (TRY) _____ to communicate with me after a few minutes, I probably (BE) _____ able to think more clearly.

3. After they (STOP) _____ talking with me, I (BE) _____ sure I (WANT) _____ to investigate the source of the message.

4. I (CALL) _____ someone I could trust, in case I (DISAPPEAR) _____ .

5. When I (FEEL) _____ that I really (BE) _____ being visited by aliens, I (SIT) _____ down and (THINK) _____ deeply.

6. If it (SEEM) _____ dangerous, I probably (NOT GET) _____ close to it.

7. If the aliens (BE) ＿＿＿＿＿＿ too large or too small, I (DECIDE) ＿＿＿＿＿＿ to back away.

8. I (GET) ＿＿＿＿＿＿ a lot of satisfaction from being with them.

9. I (BE) ＿＿＿＿＿＿ disappointed if they (TRY) ＿＿＿＿＿＿ to take me as a souvenir.

You can find the answers by studying the sample composition that follows.

WARMUP II: AVOIDING REPETITION OF WORDS

Repeating the same word over and over, unless it is done for a particular dramatic effect or unless there simply is no other alternative, is a sign of immature writing. There are at least three ways of solving the problem.

1. Use another word that has the same meaning (*funds* for *money*).
2. Use a pronoun instead of the noun (*it* for *money*).
3. Change the sentence structure so that the word appears only once (for example, by combining two sentences so that the word appears only once instead of twice).

INSTRUCTIONS:
Rewrite the paragraph so that the words *money* and *spend* occur only half as many times and so that other words are not repeated.

If a rich man gave me a lot of money, I would spend the money on several

things. First, I would spend the money on traveling. I would spend about ten

percent of the money to buy tickets for a round-the-world trip. I would spend

another ten percent of the money to stay in the best hotels. In the hotel I

would spend the money freely to have room service for every little thing. I

would spend the money to use the sauna. I would spend the money to have my

hair shampooed and cut. I wouldn't want to spend all the money, of course, because I would like to invest some of the money in a business so I would have

some more money to spend later on.

(A suggested answer is given in the answer section after Unit 20.)

EDITING

In this editing exercise, there are only verb errors, and they are not marked. You must decide *if* there is a mistake, and if so, what it is and how to correct it.

When the spacecraft actually land, I try to keep control over my emotions

and trust my intuition. If it seems dangerous, for example, I will probably not

get close to it, but if it would not, I get as close to it as possible and tried to

make contact. If the aliens would seem threatening, or if they would be too

terrible looking, or if they had been too large or too small for me to have been

compatible with them, I might have decided to back away. The chances were I

went into the spaceship with them, alone, and asked them to take me for a

ride. Quite honestly, I was sure I got a lot of satisfaction known I were the only

human chosen.

PLANNING AND WRITING

Select one of the three situations outlined in the introduction. Think carefully before writing about two or three general things you would do, and develop each into a paragraph. Be as specific as you can and feel free to use your wildest imagination.

Since a major purpose of this unit is to practice the conditional, use it whenever it is required. In other words, do *not* write your story in the future tense and do *not* write it as if it had really happened. Make sure it is clear that you are merely imagining what *would* happen.

My Visitors from Outer Space

I have always been intrigued by the thought of having someone come from outer space to visit me, but I am sure that if I heard a secret message I would be very surprised and perhaps even terrified. I would undoubtedly have to try very hard to stay calm, check to see that it wasn't some type of trick, and look around for a way to escape or to defend myself. Afterwards, if the voice were still calling me, I would possibly be able to think clearly enough to listen attentively and write down some notes and instructions.

After the mysterious guests had stopped talking with me, I am sure I would want to investigate the source of the message, but I would not want others to know right away what I was up to. I would probably call someone I could trust who would be able to give me scientific or at least rational information, and who would know what I was doing in case I disappeared or got into trouble. For example, I would call some of the neighbors and ask innocently if they had experienced any interruption in their TV programs. I would look through the house carefully for hidden microphones or speakers, check around the outside of the house, ask a few of my friends questions to determine if they were somehow involved, and so on. When I felt satisfied that I was in fact really being visited by aliens, I would sit down in a quiet place and think deeply for a long time.

When the spacecraft actually landed, I would try to keep control over my emotions and would trust my intuition. If it seemed dangerous, for example, I would probably not get close to it, but if it did not, I would get as close to it as possible and try to make contact. If the aliens seemed threatening, if they were too horrible looking or if they were too large or too small for me to be compatible with them, I might decide to back away. The chances are that I would go into the spaceship with them, alone, and would ask them to take me for a ride. Quite honestly, I am sure I would get a lot of satisfaction knowing I was the only human chosen.

I think I would have much larger objectives than just going for a ride. I would feel like an ambassador for the whole world and would try to establish a bond of friendship and confidence. I would be polite but also very cautious and would try to find out as much as I could. I would try to provide them with the opportunity of meeting other important humans if they were willing. If they decided to leave the earth without establishing contact with others, I know I would be disappointed, though not as disappointed as if they tried to take me as a souvenir back to their planet.

❧ Unit 16 ❧

A Fantasy About the Past

Writing form: Chronology
Writing skills: Using past conditional verb forms; keeping structures parallel

INTRODUCTION

We often look back and wish that things had been different or that fate had treated us more kindly. In this unit you will be given a chance to daydream a little about what might have happened if you could have done anything you wanted last week. Would you have gone home to visit your family? Would you have spent the time with a special friend, or at some favorite place, or finishing an important project?

The special focus of this unit is principally grammatical. You will get extensive practice using the past conditional verb forms. You normally do not write an entire composition using this tense, but you will certainly need to have control over this structure, no matter what type of writing you expect to do.

TIP

As time goes by, you should be able to write more and better in the same amount of time, depending on the difficulty of the topic. Once in a while you should count the number of words you write in a thirty-minute composition, and if the number is staying the same, put some pressure on yourself to write faster. Speed will become important to you in your academic program.

WARMUP I: USING PAST CONDITIONAL VERB FORMS

The past conditional verb forms, like those used for the present and future and reviewed in Unit 15, reflect something that exists only in your imagination, something that never happened.

The following are examples of the types of conditional forms you will use in this unit:

1. I wish I *could have gone* home last week.
2. If I *had gone* home last week, I *would have seen* my fiancé(e).
3. We *would have taken* a trip to the beach if the weather *had been* nice.

Note these features:

a. In the condition (the part with *if*), use the PAST PERFECT, not *would.*
b. In the result (the part saying what would have happened), use *would have* plus the PAST PARTICIPLE. (*Could have* or *might have* are also used.)
c. If you use *wish,* use the PAST PARTICIPLE or *could have* (as in the preceding example 1).
d. Sometimes in a conditional sentence something that is true is referred to, and the conditional forms are not used. For example,
    "They would have asked me what I *was learning* in my classes." (The form *had been learning* should not be used since it is true that I *was learning.*) *From the sample composition:* "I *feel* very lucky to be marrying into such an interesting family." (The present form *feel* is used because that is true, and it is happening in the present.)
e. In certain subordinated sentences within a conditional sentence, the simple past, and not the conditional, is used. For example,
    "I would have stood a few moments alone with Rosana before I *had* to leave, and I would have felt sad."

INSTRUCTIONS:
In the following sentences, select the correct form of the verb to fit in the blank. You may need to add *would* or other forms. All of these sentences should be seen as part of a paragraph imagining what would have happened if the writer had gone back to visit his fiancée, Rosana, and spent some time with her family.

1. Last week (BE) _____ long and lonely. (This is true.)

2. I (LOVE) _____ to be with my fiancée if just for two days. (Imagined.)

3. If I (BE) _____ with her we (CAN DO) _____ many things.

4. I (FEEL) _____ very lucky to be marrying her. (This is true.)

5. Her parents already (HEAR) _____ about all the things that I (BE DOING) _____ .

6. I (ASK) _____ them about the latest news.

7. I (DECLINE) _____ to do things with them in order (HAVE) more time with Rosana.

You can find the answers by studying the sample composition.

WARMUP II: KEEPING STRUCTURES PARALLEL

Symmetry, consistency, and balance are features of good music, architecture, and writing in most Western cultures. To achieve these features, keep sequences of recurring structures within the sentence parallel in form. In other words, if you have a sequence of two nouns in a series of three items, the third item should also be a noun, not an infinitive, adjective, or other form. See the following example and exercises for further clarification.

INSTRUCTIONS:
Following the pattern given in the example, correct the faulty constructions. The symbol used to indicate an error in parallel structures is //.

Example: I would have eaten a lot of food, slept half the day, and many parties would have been given for me.

Error: The first two verbs in the series are active verbs (*eaten* and *slept*), but the third is PASSIVE (*been given*).

Correction: I would have eaten a lot of food, slept half the day, and gone to many parties given in my honor.

1. If I had gone home last weekend, I would have visited my girl friend, eaten my favorite food, and the weather would have been enjoyable.

2. I would have sat down with my mother, and she would have told me what my sister had done, how my father missed me, and did I know where my cousin was living.

3. If I had had the choice of going home, visited my cousin in Egypt, or attending the World's Fair, I think I would have visited my cousin.

4. Going to see the Mayan ruins would have been relaxing, enjoyable, and educated me a lot.

5. The old folks would have welcomed me, fed me well, and made that I felt good.

EDITING

In this editing exercise, the only grammatical mistakes are in the verb forms. However, there are also other mistakes indicated in the margins by the following symbols. Correct *both* types of mistakes. The context of the editing exercise is the same as that in Warmup I (an imaginary visit to see Rosana last week.)

1. ¶   (faulty paragraphing).
2. ‖   (error in parallel structure).
3. *Omit*   (unnecessary or repetitious sentence).
4. *Combine*   (phrases or sentences that should be combined).

I also like to get together with friends our own age. [A party seemed like a   [*Combine*]

good idea. And we most likely met in one of my friend's houses][Some of my   [*Omit*]

friends have large houses, whereas some of them have small ones.] We called

‖ up a lot of people, quickly some good food was gotten up, play a lot of great

music, and I completely forgot about the English language.

¶ [I hadn't thought I had gotten much sleep, especially that night. The next   [*Combine*]

day as I stand alone with my sweetheart. Before I had to leave I felt a deep

sadness.] Well, it was worth it.

PLANNING AND CHOOSING

Choose one of these topics:

1. What would you have done if you had gone home last week for a few days?
2. If you could have done anything you wanted last weekend, what would you have done?

Before beginning to write, think over the two or three main ideas that you intend to develop and plan to form a paragraph around each. Use the past conditional whenever it is required. Do not put your composition into the simple past or simple present.

If I Had Seen My Fiancée Last Week

Last week was long and boring, but more than that, it was lonely. I missed my fiancée more than ever. I would have loved to be with her, if just for two or three days. If I had been with her, we could have done so many things together. First, of course, I would have wanted just to be with her, alone, away from all the interruptions and barriers we have had since I left. We would have whispered sweet words to each other, laughed, cried, sighed, and shared our feelings.

As much as I would have liked to spend my whole time just with Rosana, I think I would have spent some time with her mom and dad, mostly talking. They have heard, naturally, secondhand about all the things that I am doing, but they would have wanted a lot more detail. For my part, I would have asked them about the latest news concerning the family, their jobs, local news, and general gossip. We could all have had a big meal together, and then her dad and I might have gone down to his shop and looked at all the latest equipment or gone out on a wild ride on his motorcycle. He would have invited all four of us to go out for a round of golf, but I probably would have declined in order to have more time with Rosana. I feel very lucky to be marrying into such an interesting family.

I would also have liked to get together with friends our own age. A party seems like a good idea, and we most likely would have met in one of my friend's houses, called up a lot of people on the spur of the moment, quickly gotten some good food, played a lot of that great music we have in our country, and completely forgotten about the English language for several wonderful hours. I don't think I would have gotten much sleep, especially that night, and the next day as I stood alone with my sweetheart for the last few minutes before I had to leave, I would have felt a very deep sadness and aching. Well, it would have been worth it. In fact, maybe I just will go home next week. May I miss class?

❦ Unit 17 ❦

Explaining an Opinion or Decision

Writing form: Argumentation
Writing skills: Supporting general statements; improving sentence
variety

INTRODUCTION

A type of writing that cuts across many formats and academic disciplines is
what is labeled *argumentation* in this unit. The purpose is to convince the reader
that some past action, decision, or point of view is logical and correct. Other
types of argumentation will be covered in Unit 18 and other units. Normally the
reader is presumed initially to be unconvinced or at least uninformed.

A common use of this form of writing is on essay examinations. The professor
wishes to determine whether the student can state a point of view and defend it
logically. Your answer will not likely persuade the professor to change his or her
opinion. In fact, the professor may totally disagree with your thesis yet give you
a good grade if your argumentation is acceptable.

TIP

If you are tired, worried, or under stress, you will probably have difficulty
concentrating on your writing. Try to identify and resolve the sources of
pressure before beginning to write.

WARMUP I: SUPPORTING GENERAL STATEMENTS

As you will study in greater detail in future units, effective argumentation
requires the writer to present support that will convince the reader. As we all
know, however, convincing other people is one of the most difficult and subjective of all arts. Salesmen, politicians, professors, and even parents are largely
concerned with trying to influence the opinions of others, and they often do not
succeed. It would therefore be impossible to provide simple rules on how to

convince. You will have to use your previous experience, your understanding of human nature, and your knowledge.

Two useful concepts might be worth reviewing, however. First, convincing someone often depends more on using human reasoning, "common sense," or emotional arguments than it does on using strictly mathematical or symbolic logic. In advertising, for example, the advertiser often tries to convince you, usually indirectly, that if you use the product you will become as handsome, witty, or popular as the person in the ad. The more logical aspects of quality of product, price, and durability are often not even mentioned.

Second, in argumentation it is usually necessary to have sufficient information about the reader's present opinion, about the issue, and about alternative opinions and to present these with clear examples, clear explanations, or by referring to the opinion of someone the reader respects. In other words, the argument has to be well supported.

INSTRUCTIONS:

The sample composition in this unit is an example of argumentation. Its purpose is to convince the reader that the woman who wrote it was justified in not marrying George. If you look at it carefully, you will find in each paragraph one sentence that states an opinion about George. This statement is then carefully supported by examples, explanations, or analysis. The human reasoning, however, is not directly stated. First, find the general statement in each paragraph. List some of the supporting detail and discuss how it supports the general statement. Identify, in your own words, the principle of human reasoning that makes the statement and the support convincing.

Example (from the topic "Why I Went to Gladrock"):

1. General statement: "The people welcome newcomers from other countries."
2. Supporting detail: They have parties for newcomers; they like to learn foreign languages; they invite strangers to their homes; they have movies and festivals about other countries.
3. Human reasoning: If people in a place show an interest in you and your background and make you less uncomfortable when you go there, you will be more likely to want to go there.

Now supply the general information about the sample composition as outlined in the three steps just enumerated.

PARAGRAPH 1

General statement:

Supporting details:

Human reasoning:

PARAGRAPH 2

General statement:

Supporting details:

Human reasoning:

PARAGRAPH 3

General statement:

Supporting details:

Human reasoning:

WARMUP II: IMPROVING SENTENCE VARIETY

INSTRUCTIONS:
Rewrite the following paragraph according to these guidelines:

1. Have a balance of short and long sentences.
2. Use a variety of sentence patterns.
3. Avoid rambling sentences.
4. Avoid using *it* or *there* as subjects where another noun can be used as the subject.
5. Avoid using the passive form of the verb and switching from active to passive voice within the same sentence.
6. Avoid unnecessary repetition of the same word.

George had a very promising start in a business career. He was making a lot of money. The confidence of his employers was had by him. It would have been possible without doubt for him to provide a comfortable income. I would have been offered great flexibility in following my own aspirations. I look at him from my present perspective, however. I perceive how dull he really was. He read a newspaper. The newspaper was exciting to him. It was more exciting than anything else he read. Most of his books were directly related to his work. Outside of these it appears he had no curiosity or interest. Whenever science or even politics was talked about by me he would chat for a while. I would be told sooner or later how much I was loved. He would suggest that it would be good to do something. Apparently to him it was doing nothing to talk.

(The answers can be found in the sample composition.)

EDITING

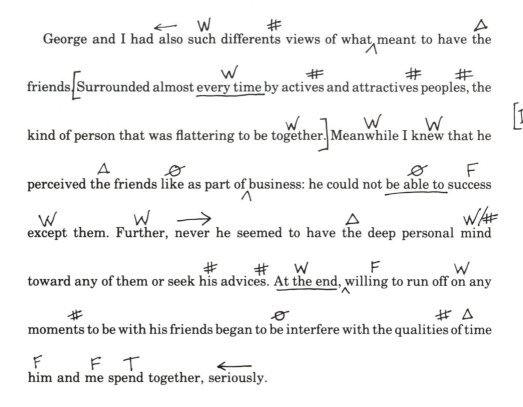

George and I had also such differents views of what meant to have the

friends. Surrounded almost every time by actives and attractives peoples, the

kind of person that was flattering to be together. Meanwhile I knew that he

perceived the friends like as part of business: he could not be able to success

except them. Further, never he seemed to have the deep personal mind

toward any of them or seek his advices. At the end, willing to run off on any

moments to be with his friends began to be interfere with the qualities of time

him and me spend together, seriously.

PLANNING AND WRITING

Choose one of these topics:

1. Why I came to this place to study or live.
2. Why I got a large or small car (or house).
3. Why I got married (divorced or separated).
4. Why I support a political party (social cause or religion).
5. Why I believe _____ (name of person) is the most important person in _____ (name of country).

If you choose one of the first three topics, you may wish to review Unit 14 before beginning. Notice that in this composition you wish to emphasize the *positive* reasons (advantages) and minimize or ignore the negative ones.

In your composition, identify two, three, or perhaps more factors that, according to human reasoning, support your central idea. Be sure you have clarified your assumptions in your own mind and that they are those that would be shared or accepted by your reader. Furthermore, be sure that the many supporting details are specific, clear, and sufficient.

Why I Decided Not to Get Married

In the year since I told the handsome, successful, and popular man I was engaged to that I did not want to get married, I have had many opportunities to reflect on the decision. I now know I made the right choice.

George had a very promising start in a business career, was making a lot of money, and had the confidence of his employers. Without doubt he would have provided a comfortable income, offering me great flexibility in following my own aspirations. As I look at him from my present perspective, however, I am aware of how dull he really was. A newspaper was the most exciting thing he ever read, for most of his books, manuals, and magazines were directly related to his work; and outside of these he appeared to have no curiosity or interest. Whenever I tried to talk about science, art, or even politics, he would chat halfheartedly for a while; but sooner or later he would tell me how much he loved me and suggest that we "do" something. Apparently, to him talking about interesting topics was doing nothing.

George and I also had very different views of what it meant to have friends. Surrounded almost constantly by active and attractive people, he was the model of charm and generosity, the kind of person that it was flattering to be with—for a while. Eventually I realized that he perceived friends as part of his business: he couldn't succeed without them. Furthermore, he never seemed to have deep personal feelings toward any of them or seek their advice or emotional support. Finally, his willingness to run off at any moment to be with his so-called friends and the constant buzz of activity began seriously to interfere with the quality of the time he and I spent together. When I came to realize that my friends and I felt uncomfortable when he did spend time with us, I knew something was seriously wrong.

Finally, I came to resent the self-satisfied way in which George treated me as if I were less important or less intelligent. He would frequently ask me to do him a favor, like fixing him some coffee, buying a gift for one of his clients, or typing one of his reports, but he never offered to pay me back. He became upset when I talked about continuing my education. He knew nothing about cooking or managing a house, assuming, apparently, that that was work for a woman to do. Overall, I do not think we would have been happy together for very long, and while I still worry about being alone, I am sure now that I would rather be lonely than live in a frustrating and unhappy marriage.

❦ Unit 18 ❦

Persuading Someone to Do Something

Writing forms: Argumentation; persuasion
Writing skills: Stating positions; using appropriate support

INTRODUCTION

Could you persuade Ali or his family to do something to resolve the following dilemma?

Ali is the oldest son in a family of successful hotel and restaurant owners. Everyone seems to expect Ali, a bright and outgoing youth resembling his business-minded parents in many ways, to study in a program related to their enterprise and then move in as partner and eventual manager. Several new hotels are being planned by competing firms in the area, Ali's father is no longer as energetic as he used to be and needs help, and the disloyalty of several key executives within the company makes Ali's help seem imperative. Accordingly, Ali has enrolled in a program of hotel and restaurant management and is already becoming proficient in English and Japanese—languages he will need in communicating with customers and suppliers.

Unfortunately, Ali does not find any personal satisfaction in any of his courses. When he is in the hotel, he finds dealing with typical problems irritating and tiring. More and more his thoughts turn to other possibilities. He often considers himself particularly suited to life as a scientist or agricultural researcher, based on his brief but gratifying experiences on a cousin's farm and in elective courses at school. He realizes that he has never really allowed himself to pursue these other interests because he was convinced that his family would be frustrated and angry, and until recently he has not felt strongly enough about it to take that risk. But now he knows that he is approaching a crisis in his emotions and soon will have to do something: either put these "rebellious" thoughts out of his mind and accept his family's expectations wholeheartedly, or follow his own interests.

Your purpose in writing in this unit will be to use reasons in order to persuade or advise. Can you persuade Ali, for example, to follow his own needs in a way that will not leave him feeling guilty? Or can you persuade him that indeed following his family's wishes is in both his and others' interests?

TIP

A piece of writing that you can be proud of is developed over a period of time, rarely at one sitting. If you have something important to write, start on it as soon as possible to give yourself the maximum planning time.

WARMUP I: STATING POSITIONS

In reading most academic, business, and even personal material, the native speaker of English expects the writer clearly to state the point, preferably at or near the beginning. This principle is particularly important when using argumentative forms, since if your point of view is not clearly stated, the reader will be unable definitively to agree (or disagree) with you. Use these guidelines:

1. Directly state your position, preferably near the beginning.
2. State only those issues that you intend to support in your writing.
3. List briefly but clearly all your *major* premises.
4. Be concise and direct, if possible using no more than two or three sentences.

Example:

Since neither going into the family business nor pursuing his own interests in science would give Ali the peace of mind he desires, he should perhaps consider another alternative. He should fall in love with a highly capable woman who is an expert in the hotel and restaurant business, make sure that she is entirely acceptable to his family, marry her, and let her run the business. Shortly after that, he can go back to school and find his own mission in life. This plan has several advantages for everyone.

This statement (even if not intended seriously) would give the reader a very clear idea of exactly what the writer's opinion was and would give the writer the basis on which to provide examples, explanations, and reasons.

INSTRUCTIONS:

1. Read each of the following statements and decide if they are effective as position statements.
2. If not, use the preceding guidelines and try to correct them. If you feel the statement cannot be revised (because it has so many mistakes), write HOPELESS in the left margin.

1. Issue: "Should criminals be punished more severely?"

A topic that everyone is concerned about is crime. It occurs all around

the globe. Many people from all different professions are discussing the causes and cures for crime. My title gives the answer, and I have many

reasons.

2. Issue: "Should elementary school teachers be friends with their students?"

Teachers in elementary school should be friendly with their students in

order to create a positive environment, to allow the children to feel free to

confide in the teacher, and to give the teacher greater access to the feelings

and needs of the children.

3. Issue: "Should children watch violent programs on TV?"

Everyone agrees that TV programs are immature and appeal only to

the entertainment needs of children. If advertisers were not so interested

in making money, they would provide programs of real educational value,

free from violence. In fact, violence has been proven to be dangerous and

should be banned during times when children watch TV.

4. Issue: "Should mothers with small children have careers?"

Women with small children need the stimulation of meaningful em-

ployment outside the home in order to stay healthy emotionally, but they should also have the children's welfare as their primary concern. They can

do so by always leaving the children with a loving and capable person and

being available to the children at the critical hours of getting up, going to

bed, and eating.

5. Issue: "Should the population of the world be controlled by law?"

The world is desperately in need of additional medical services. There

should be a doctor available within twenty-four hours for every citizen. A

good doctor can insure that a newborn baby will receive the protection it

needs, and when it grows up it will become even a greater advantage to

mankind than if it had not been born. Abortion is wrong and should be

prohibited.

WARMUP II: USING APPROPRIATE SUPPORT

In argumentation the following types of support (among others) may be used:

1. Giving an *example* of what you mean so that it becomes vividly clear.
2. Using *data* that prove that you are correct.
3. Using *reasoning* or *logical principles* to make your position seem indisputable.
4. Referring to an expert *authority* whom the reader is apt to believe.

You may fail to convince, however, if you use these incorrectly. If your examples, data, or reasoning are wrong, or if you cite an "authority" the reader does not accept, you will fail to support your idea. In fact, you may lead the reader to believe that the *opposite* of what you say is true.

INSTRUCTIONS:
Consider for each of the following items the types of support (*examples, data, reasoning,* or *authority*) the author attempted to use or should have used. If the support is not used effectively, explain why. Consult Warmup I to determine the issues of each of the five items.

1. _____ Criminals should be punished severely. As Napoleon is said to have exclaimed, "A good enemy is a dead enemy."

2. _____ Fifth-grade teachers in the Cedar River school system, who were firm, but not unkind, had students who scored above average on standardized mathematics exams. In other words, being strict helped raise the scores.

3. _____ The very people who claim that TV helps children learn about the world, adjust to their environment, and have greater self-confidence also claim that watching violence on TV has no effect. Can that be so? For if TV teaches understanding, can it not also teach hate?

4. _____ Mothers who work outside the home run the real risk of neglecting the wellbeing of their children. Harvey Oswald killed John Kennedy, for example, and we can suspect that his mother neglected him.

5. _____ Those who are so urgently pressing for greater control over population growth are ignoring several basic facts. First of all, there is a direct correlation between population growth and economic development. In the U.S.A. the Gross National Product has roughly correlated with the increase of the population. Second, many countries that have succeeded in controlling population growth have not experienced any major improvement in the standard or the quality of living.

EDITING

Ali's family should sold the hotels and restaurants business in order for

give Ali chance to enjoy studying his own career. My first reason is based on

the business environment in nowadays. According to a well-known professor

and business expert in my country, the profit of restaurant decreases when

the total of the prospectives clients is fewer than two thousands per each restaurant. Since new restaurants will founded, Ali's family has to compete

more and more hard to make a profit. Second, the disloyalty of several of key

bosses indicate that the management need extensives changings which will

be very expensive. Last year, as example, one of largest restaurants in my

country try to reorganize itself, but was so confusing that it was a failure.

(Consult the answers section after Unit 20 only after you complete the exercise.)

PLANNING AND WRITING

Write a letter of advice to Ali or to Ali's parents, trying to convince him or them to resolve the problem in the way *you* think is best. (Or you may prefer to write on one of the topics used in the warmup exercises.)

Carefully write your position statement and put it at the beginning (or if you feel the reader would immediately disagree with it, put it at the end, after you have given your reasons). Be sure it states completely and clearly the main features of your opinion. Divide your argumentation into two, three, or four paragraphs, using each to support one major point. Use examples, data, reasoning, or authority as the means of support.

While you are trying to use good argumentation, do not forget also that you are dealing with human beings with feelings. Try to see the problem, therefore, from the reader's perspective. Be tactful, kind, and supportive as well as honest, logical, and forceful.

Use the following format:

Today's date

Dear Ali,

Body of your letter

Sincerely,

Your name

❦ Unit 19 ❦

Revising II

Writing forms: Review of forms used in Units 1–18
Writing skills: Revising; rewriting

INTRODUCTION

This unit offers you the opportunity to reread all of your previous compositions, generalize about your strengths and weaknesses, and do what any good writer must do: revise and rewrite. Since this unit has the same purpose as Unit 11, you should look back at the discussion of the role of revising and rewriting.

TIP

It is fascinating, and probably useful, to understand how you write. Try as an impartial observer to note the processes you use, and continue to ask, "Is there a better way to write?"

PLANNING AND WRITING

Reread the compositions that you have written. They should be corrected by now and in your folder. Review the notebook or the sheets suggested in the introduction to this textbook and in the tip in Unit 6, and bring your comments up to date. You should be able to tell from the pattern of mistakes whether you are making progress (that is, eliminating earlier errors and attempting new constructions).

Choose one of your old compositions that you think needs to be rewritten and look it over carefully, taking notes on improvements that you feel you can make. Read the checklist for additional suggestions.

When you are satisfied that you have carefully thought about the content, theme, and organization, make a simple outline before you begin to write. Then write the composition, reuse the checklist, and make any final changes. Turn in your outline, folder, and your rewritten paper.

❧ Unit 20 ❧

Evaluation II

Writing forms: Any of those from Units 1–18
Writing skill: Writing under pressure for a grade

INTRODUCTION

In this unit you will write on one of three topics the teacher selects. You will not have time to prepare for the topic in advance, and you will not be able to use a dictionary or other aids.

The purpose of this exercise, as of that in Unit 12, is to help you write under the kind of pressure you may experience in your academic coursework. It will also give your teacher an opportunity, under conditions that are equal for all the students, to evaluate how well you can communicate in English, organize a new topic, and select and present facts, events, and ideas.

The teacher will use Appendix II in evaluating your work, so before you begin to write, look again at the appendix, particularly at the description and sample of the level you hope to reach on this evaluation.

WRITING UNDER PRESSURE FOR A GRADE

INSTRUCTIONS:
The teacher will choose three topics from the teacher's manual that fit the writing forms that you have studied. Be sure to plan before writing and to check your work after writing. Write as much as you can as well as you can in 30 minutes on *one* of the three topics. Do not use a dictionary.

❦ ANSWERS TO ❦ EXERCISES IN PART I

Unit I—Warmup II

1. The paper used should be white, lined, and large (8½ inches by 11 inches, the standard size in the U.S.A.).

2. There should be about 2.5 centimeters (about 1 inch) on the right, left, and bottom margins and about 3.0 centimeters at the top.

3. There should be about 19 lines on the page, and every other line should be blank (so you or the teacher can write there later).

4. The author's name, date, and title should all be at the top of the page.

5. There are four paragraphs.

6. The first paragraph introduces the thing being described and gives the *expected* impression.
The second paragraph describes the first thing the author encountered: the hotel.
The third paragraph describes the next thing the author encountered: the city around the hotel.
The fourth paragraph describes the first impression of the university campus and summarizes the overall impression.

7. There are many details in each paragraph that support the theme of the paragraph. In the second, the details are the poor location, the uncooperative clerk, the high price, the unpleasant room, the noises, and the inconsiderate workers.

8. In most of the paragraphs there is a variety of sentence types and lengths.

9. The last sentence is a good summary of the major idea.

The answers to the editing exercises in Units 1–19 can be found in the sample composition for each unit.

Unit 7—Warmup I

1. In the first place, there were the numerous details that I had to take care of.

2. My personal affairs also made the planning hard.

3. I have several other interests in addition to horticulture.

4. For me the water itself is the most exciting part of the scene, at least once we get into it.

5. I love to be outdoors, to participate in sports, and to do somewhat daring things.

6. I also like to be around my friends, and I get bored if I have to sit at home with nothing to do for more than a few hours.

Unit 8—Warmup I

Unit 4 is primarily chronological, although the information at the end may be considered the most important and hence reflect recency.

Unit 5 is spatial and uses order of recency (since the details are arranged more or less from least to most important).

Unit 6 is spatial, chronological, and also shows the order of recency (since the last part of the description is the most important).

Unit 7 appears to emphasize saliency, since the most important information comes first and the least comes last.

Unit 15—Warmup II

If a rich man gave me a lot of money, I would spend it on several things. First, I would use about $15,000 to buy tickets to travel around the world. Another similar amount would go for staying in the best hotels. There I would freely have room service provide me with every little thing. I would enjoy the sauna and have my hair shampooed and cut. Some of the sum, of course, I would invest in a business so that later on I would still have funds at my disposal.

Unit 16—Warmup II

1. If I had gone home last weekend, I would have visited my girl friend, eaten my favorite food, and enjoyed the wonderful weather.

2. I would have sat down with my mother, and she would have told me what my sister had done, how my father missed me, and where my cousin was living.

3. If I had had the choice of going home, visiting my cousin in Egypt, or attending the World's Fair, I think I would have visited my cousin.

4. Going to see the Mayan ruins would have been relaxing, enjoyable, and educational.

5. The old folks would have welcomed me, fed me well, and made me feel good.

Unit 17—Warmup I

Paragraph 1
Statement: "I am aware of how dull he really was."

Details: They are listed in the paragraph and include his reading habits and his conversational abilities.

Reasoning: Most people would agree that if a woman is married to a dull man, she will become frustrated and unhappy.

Paragraph 2

Statement: "George and I had very different views of what it meant to have friends."

Details: They are given in the paragraph and include his treatment of friends as part of his business, his lack of personal feelings, and his neglect of his fiancée when his friends were around.

Reasoning: Most people would agree that if a man and woman have conflicts over friends, they will not be happy.

Paragraph 3

Statement: "George treated me as if I were less important or less intelligent."

Details: The paragraph includes details about his treating her like a servant, his being unwilling to return favors, his lack of interest in her education, and his disinterest in doing work in the home.

Reasoning: Most people would agree that marriage should be a relationship of mutual respect and trust, and if a man does not respect his wife, the relationship will not be adequate.

Unit 18—Warmups I and II and Editing

Warmup I

Numbers 2 and 4 are adequate as they are.

Numbers 1, 3, and 5 are *very* weak. Number 5 seems hopeless, since it is not even clear what the writer's position is.

Warmup II

Number 1 uses authority ineffectively. In other words, Napoleon is not considered a good authority, the quotation may or may not be accurate, and it has little to do with crime anyway.

Number 2 uses data but draws an invalid conclusion.

Number 3 uses logic rather well.

Number 4 uses a false, or at least uncertain, example.

Number 5 uses reasoning and data rather effectively.

Editing

Ali's family should sell the hotel and restaurant business (in order) to give Ali the chance to follow his own interests. My first reason is based on the business climate these days. According to a well-known professor and business expert in my country, the profits of a restaurant decrease when the total number of prospective clients is smaller than two thousand per restaurant. Since new restaurants will be built (are being planned), Ali's family will have to compete harder and harder to make a profit. Second, the disloyalty of several of the key executives indicates that the management needs extensive changes, which will be very expensive. Last year, for example, one of the largest restaurants in my country tried to reorganize, but the problems were so complex that the business failed.

PART

II

Introduction

Part II serves to bridge the gap between the skills outlined in the introduction to Part I and the demands of academic writing. Part I is not a prerequisite for a class that already possesses some degree of writing fluency and an ability to recognize and correct most errors marked on their compositions. A relatively advanced class can begin the course with Unit 21 without losing any basics, as the most common organizational forms of writing are presented again in Part II but with a more formal rhetorical focus. In keeping with the aim of preparing students for academic writing, topics are generally less personal and more abstract than in Part I.

Units 21–30 present a progression of composition planning and developmental skills that includes brainstorming, classifying, organizing/outlining, paragraphing, selecting a form of development appropriate to the topic, and writing introductions and conclusions. In these same units the most basic rhetorical forms are also presented, including explanation, illustration, comparison/contrast, process, analysis, argumentation, and extended definition. By Unit 30, a student should have learned how to take any academic writing assignment and brainstorm it, narrow it, organize it, and choose an appropriate developmental form.

Units 35–38 continue the progression of argumentative skills begun in Units 27 and 28. Units 33–34 focus on the development and manipulation of vocabulary, while 31–32 make students aware of differences between sophisticated sentence structure and nonnative or immature sentences that are not necessarily acceptable for being free of actual errors. The topic in Unit 33 forces students to practice modality, a grammatical form they often avoid or use incorrectly.

As in Part I, each unit's format of warmup exercises, editing, and occasional sample compositions prepares the students for both the content and the skills pertinent to the composition assignment. The difficulty of concepts or skills presented in some units may prompt the teacher to devote more than one class meeting to each. In cases where the term is too short for inclusion of all the units, the teacher should select those that best suit the needs of a particular class. Units 23–30, 32, 35–37, and 39 contain information and exercises essential to the development of academic writing skills; as such, they should be covered even if other units are omitted. Flexibility is the keynote in utilization of the text, and the teacher is urged to experiment with combining lessons in whatever way suits the needs of the class and the time available. While frequent writing is strongly recommended, an occasional alternative would be to take the class through all the exercises leading up to but not including the actual composition assignment.

❧ Unit 21 ❧

A Mixed Marriage

Writing forms: Explanation; advice
Writing skills: Brainstorming; paragraph coherence

INTRODUCTION

Recently you visited your younger brother in the American city where he is studying. He introduced you to his friends, one of whom was an American woman who was intelligent, pretty, and well educated. She was neither over-bearing nor shy, and you liked her because she got along so well with people from your country. Your brother mentioned that she was divorced but had no children and that she hoped to have a career in computer science. The night before you left, your brother asked you how you liked this woman, then confessed that they were very much in love and wanted to get married. He said she was willing to live in your country and adjust to your customs. But he was frankly worried about the difficulties they would face and whether your parents would accept her as a daughter-in-law. He asked you to think the situation over, then advise him. What should you say?*

WARMUP: BRAINSTORMING

For many people, the biggest problem in writing is thinking of something to say. One of the best ways to generate ideas is to "brainstorm," which means to make a list of as many things as possible that pertain to the topic. When brainstorm-ing, a writer doesn't stop to evaluate or edit these ideas; the value of the list lies in its length and variety, not its quality, organization, or coherence. In the following exercise, you will brainstorm ideas for a letter advising your brother/sister on the dilemma presented in the introduction.

INSTRUCTIONS:

1. Working together as a class, for each of the categories below, think of as many disadvantages as possible for this proposed marriage. Follow the pattern given

*If you prefer, you may change the situation so that it is your sister who wants to marry an American man and stay in the United States with him.

95

in the example. Have someone write the disadvantages on the chalkboard so that all of you can see them. Here are the categories:

Customs	Religion	Relationships with families
Male–female roles	Where to live	Daily life
Professional life	Rearing children	

Example (disadvantages):

Religion
Each spouse might pressure the other to convert.
The families might oppose the marriage on religious grounds.
The husband and wife might keep worshipping separately instead of together.
One or both spouses might have to worship in a foreign language.
There might be conflicts over deciding on which religion to rear the children in.

2. Now brainstorm to discover as many solutions as possible for each of the disadvantages you have just written.

Example (solutions):

Religion
Each spouse could take an active interest in the other's religion.
The spouses could be patient with their families and could try to inform them and develop their religious tolerance.
The husband and wife could take turns worshipping together.
One or both spouses could conduct private devotions in their native languages.
The children could be reared to respect both religions and could make their own religious choices when they are old enough.

EDITING*

The following exercise is an opportunity for you to practice correcting errors that are commonly made by students at your level. Your goal should be to become aware of your own most common errors so that you can correct them on your own compositions, and so that eventually you will not make them at all. The correction symbols used to mark the errors in this exercise are the same as those presented in Part I and listed on the inside back cover.

In addition to correcting the errors, in this exercise you will also have to put the sentences into the correct order so that the paragraph will be *coherent*.† This

---

*Answers to some of the exercises in this part of the book can be found in the answers section between Units 40 and 41. Other answers are in the Teacher's Manual.

†The principle of coherence in a written piece deals with the relationships of information and language. If there is no clear relationship, the piece is said to be incoherent and poorly written. Coherence may be achieved through proper sequencing of information and ideas (as in this exercise), through the use of transitional expressions (see Appendix III), through the use of words and expressions (such as pronouns) that refer to information and ideas in other parts of the piece, and through repetition of words or language structures. You will practice applying this principle in this and upcoming units.

paragraph is easiest to understand when the sentences are presented in chronological order, that is, in the order in which the events happened.

Dear Mama and Papa:

You know that I passed the spring holidays with Gerardo in Boston. That's why he asked me write you first and explain you the situation. The night before I left, he told me a wonderful news: they are in love with themselves and would like get married. I'm sorry that I didn't write since a couple of weeks, but I've been struggling with something so important, and I didn't know how to approach you about it. But while Gerardo knows how happy you must be to hear that news; he is reluctant to tell you by himself because he is afraid, you might be worry about couple of things. During I was there, he introduced to me a very attractive, personable young woman whom I liked her too much.

PLANNING AND WRITING

Choose one of the following topics:

1. Write a letter to your brother/sister, advising him/her on what to do.
2. Write a letter to your parents, explaining the situation and telling how both you and your brother/sister feel about it.

After you pick your topic, use your brainstorming list to provide you with material on which to write. Don't try to write about the whole list: concentrate on the strongest parts of it. Select only the two or three categories that seem most important to you, and under each category, select only the disadvantages or solutions that you consider most important. Each category should be the basis for a separate paragraph, as follows:

    I. First paragraph: State the purpose of the letter, and present the first category with its most important advantages or disadvantages, depending on your point of view.

    II. Second paragraph: Second category and its most important advantages or disadvantages.

    III. Third paragraph: Third category and its most important advantages or disadvantages.

    IV. Conclusion, telling your overall advice (for example, marry or don't marry) or opinion (for example, "I support my brother and hope you will too, Mother and Father").

Audience

Notice that what you write is going to depend not only on which topic you choose, but also on whether you are writing to your brother/sister or your parents. What and how you write is determined largely by your choice of the reader, your "audience." What is your relationship with your audience? How much information does your audience already have on your topic? What is your purpose in writing for this audience? You must adjust your level of formality, the kind of information you give, and the nature of your advice with this person in mind. In writing a paper to persuade or advise someone, you will address your audience more directly than in other, more impersonal writing forms.

Personal Letter Form*

Today's date

Dear Charles,
Dear Mr. Atkinson,
Dear Mom and Dad,

The "greeting," using the name you call the reader, followed by a comma

The message or "body" of the letter

The "complimentary closing," chosen according to the level of intimacy between you and the reader

Yours truly,
Warmly,
Love,

Carol
Carol Black

Your signature, using the name you expect the reader to use

*See also Unit 18.

❧ Unit 22 ❧

Adapting to Another Country

Writing forms: Explanation; illustration
Writing skills: Brainstorming; classifying

INTRODUCTION

If you received a letter like the following from a friend who was coming to visit you from another country, how would you answer?

Dear Aicha,

As the time draws nearer for me to visit you and your family in Morocco, I feel more and more excited, but I have to admit that I'm a little nervous too. I'm sure that life there is quite different in many regards from life here. I do want to get along well on my visit, and I don't want to embarrass anyone, including myself, by doing or saying the wrong thing. You've told me a little about the adaptations you had to make when you were living here, and that experience puts you in a good position to advise me. Before I come, please write and tell me what to expect and how to adapt to Moroccan customs and behavior.

Love,
Maryann

WARMUP I: BRAINSTORMING

In this exercise you will practice "brainstorming," or making a long list of everything you can think of that is related to your topic. When brainstorming, you shouldn't worry about the practicality or reasonableness of these ideas; you should just open your mind to the great range of possibilities available.

INSTRUCTIONS:
Together, think up a long list of specific things a person must do differently when visiting another country. One way to do this is to remember what differences you may have encountered in other countries and how you dealt with them. As you think of things, have someone write them on the chalkboard.

Examples:

> Reading a menu
> Making local telephone calls
> Making conversation in a foreign language
> Being "on time"
> (Now you continue. Make the list as long and specific as you can.)

WARMUP II: CLASSIFYING

After brainstorming or collecting ideas, the next phase of getting ready to write is classifying. There are two steps to this process.

1. The first step is dividing the brainstorming list into groups of related items. Each group must have a unifying idea or heading that shows what all of its items have in common.
2. The second step is omitting items that do not fit readily into any group, then going through each group and crossing out all but the most important items. The resulting list should provide strong, pertinent material for the composition.

INSTRUCTIONS

1. Working together, divide your brainstorming list into groups of related items.
2. Give each group a heading or title that shows what the items are about.
3. Omit any leftover items that do not fit into the existing groups and are not centrally related to your theme.
4. Working individually, omit all but the most important items within each group.

You should end up with four or five groups, each with from three to five items. Each of these groups can provide you with material for a well-unified and detailed paragraph in your composition, though you will not have time to write about all the groups.

Example: Shopping

> Locating stores
> Determining hours stores are open
> Communicating needs to salesclerks
> Using different clothing measurements
> Making change in foreign currency

EDITING*

The editing exercise is taken from a letter written to someone who is going to visit the writer's country.

1. Correct the errors that are marked.
2. Find and cross out a sentence that weakens the paragraph because it doesn't explain or illustrate adaptations.

*Do the exercise before checking the answers in the answers section between Units 40 and 41. Any answers to exercises in Part II that cannot be found in this answers section are in the Teacher's Manual.

Of course you must adapt our customs concerning be a guest, because all my relatives and freinds will expect you to visit their. You'll need taking taxi from airport to the my village, as it doesn't go there any bus. It is not too much different between the behaviors of a guest in your country and in mine, but let me give you some advices they will help you enjoy your staying. First, always take a gift your hostess: candy, flowers, wine are the most appropriat present. Second, never insist to help in the kitchen like you make in your country; your hostess would be offended. Except this, just relaxing and do whatever you feel like to do, I'm sure you have good time.

PLANNING AND WRITING

Today you may choose either of the following topics:

1. Write a letter to a foreign friend who is planning to visit your country. Tell what important adaptations he or she will need to make in order to have a good visit.
2. Write a letter to a friend who is planning to come from your country to visit you abroad. Tell what important adaptations he or she will need to make in order to enjoy the visit.

Keeping your topic in mind, return to the list you made in the warmup exercises and choose the three groups or the three stages of the visit that seem most important to you. Your choice of what is important will naturally depend on the type of person you are writing to, what your friend is going to do during the visit, and how he or she is going to travel. Each of the groups or stages you choose should be discussed in a separate paragraph. Within each group, select only a few of the most important examples to include in your paper. Be sure that all of the sentences in each paragraph contribute directly to your purpose of explaining and illustrating adaptations that should be made.

I. First paragraph: State the purpose of your letter. Present your first group of adaptations, with examples and explanations.

II. Second paragraph: Present your second group of adaptations, with examples and explanations.

III. Third paragraph: Present your third group of adaptations, with examples and explanations. Conclude, telling your friend not to worry or expressing how eager you are to see her or him.

Follow the format for a personal letter given at the end of Unit 21.

In the answers section you can find a sample list of adaptations to supplement yours in Warmup I.

Corrections

Every time your writing teacher returns a composition to you, correct all the errors that you made. If there are any that you don't understand, ask for help. Make a list of the kinds of mistakes you make most often, and copy examples from your compositions on it. Then use this as a "personal checklist" to help you correct these types of errors before turning in your compositions in the future.

❧ Unit 23 ☙

Two Countries

Writing form: Comparison/contrast
Writing skills: Brainstorming; classifying; organizing; paragraph coherence

INTRODUCTION

Living in another country, as you may be doing now, provides you with a new perspective on both your new and your old environments. As you discover another culture's institutions, systems, and patterns of behavior, the contrasts also make you aware of aspects of your own culture that you may never have noticed before. Today you will draw on your powers of observation and reflection to write a composition that compares and contrasts some aspect of your own country and another country that you have visited.*

WARMUP I: COMPARISON/CONTRAST

The ability to observe and clearly express similarities and differences is a skill that will serve you well in your academic career, no matter what major field you pursue. The first principle involved in comparing and contrasting is to choose subjects that are comparable.

INSTRUCTIONS:
Decide which of the following pairs could be compared. After each pair, write "Yes" or "No" and defend your decision.

Examples:

Texas and Alaska	Yes	(Both are states of the United States.)
Texas and Houston	No	(One is a state, the other a city within that state.)

---

*If you have never traveled abroad, you may write instead on two cities, two areas of your country, or two ethnic or professional groups. But choose a topic you know about through first-hand experience: don't write about a city or area you have never visited.

104

1. Swahili and Fortran.

2. Biology and botany.

3. Swimming and a winter vacation.

4. Classical music and a rock group.

5. American Indians and college professors.

6. Classical music and rock music.

7. American Indians and Chinese Americans.

8. Influenza and blindness.

9. Deafness and blindness.

10. Your country and the United States.

WARMUP II: BRAINSTORMING AND CLASSIFYING

After choosing the subjects for a comparison/contrast, the next step is to select the characteristics on which they will be compared and contrasted. These are called the *bases of comparison,* and they have to be points that both subjects possess.

INSTRUCTIONS:
Working together, make a list of five or six bases of comparison that could be used in comparing and contrasting any two countries.

Examples:

Climate
Form of government
Economic base

1.

2.

3.

4.

5.

6.

While such a general list is a good starting point, it still does not provide a sound basis for specific writing, so you need to narrow your list and brainstorm on an even more specific level.

INSTRUCTIONS:

From the preceding list, choose the basis of comparison that you know most about. Be sure to choose one for which you can think of both similarities (comparison) and differences (contrast) between the two countries. You may wish to work with other students who are writing about the same countries in order to exchange ideas and specific data.

Example (U.S. and West Germany):

Basis of comparison: Population
Similarities: Much German influence in U.S. population, because many German immigrants settled in U.S. in the past
Many foreign immigrants in both countries today, resulting in similar political issues
Differences: Much greater ethnic variety in the U.S.
U.S. has a native population (Amerindians) that predated European settlement
Size (U.S.: over 230 million people; W. Germany: around 62 million people)
Density (U.S.: 20.5 people per square kilometer; W. Germany: 249.4 people per square kilometer)

WARMUP III: ORGANIZING

After selecting the content of a comparison/contrast composition, the next step in planning is to organize it effectively. There are two common ways to do this. The first is as follows:

Example 1   **I.** United States' population
   A. Size
   B. Density
   C. Ethnic makeup
II. West Germany's population
   A. Size
   B. Density
   C. Ethnic makeup

Although this method of organization is obvious, it is not considered as clear or sophisticated for a short paper as another way:

Example 2   **I.** Population size
   A. West Germany
   B. United States
II. Population density
   A. West Germany
   B. United States

III. Ethnic makeup of population
    A. Similarities between West Germany and United States
    B. Differences
        1. West Germany
        2. United States

Because the reader can follow the development of the points so easily, the second method of organization is recommended for essay examinations and academic papers that require development through comparison/contrast.* Use it as the basis for your outline for today's composition. Substitute the countries of your choice and your own bases of comparison, using the similarities and differences you listed for Warmup II. When you have finished, you will have gone through all the steps of planning a composition—brainstorming, classifying, and organizing—and you will be ready to write, using your outline as a guide.

EDITING

INSTRUCTIONS:

1. In the following model paragraph, correct all the errors that are marked.
2. Then fill in the blanks with the expressions listed at the end of the exercise. You will notice that the paragraph is much easier to understand after these expressions are added. Their purpose is not to add content, but to make the paragraph more *coherent* by showing the relationships between the items of content.†

_____ Germany and the United States

are like in some respects. _____ Germans

and their American counterparts value the hard work and the monetary

rewards it brings. _____ Germans, like

Americans, stereotype as being rather distant and cool but in reality both

*See the sample composition at the end of Unit 13 for an example of this organizational approach.

†Review the note on coherence in the editing exercise in Unit 21 on page 96. The exercise you are about to do deals with achieving coherence through the use of transitional expressions, some of which are listed under various forms of development in Appendix III at the end of this book.

countries are generally friendly and helpful, even to strangers. _____

_____ I have to say that the differences about the two

nationalities are more marked as the similars. _____

_____ Germans are always concerned to do things by a best way, and

they like to advise to each other when they know to do something a better

way. Americans, _____ have a so strong

sense of individual, that they may begin angry if someone offers advice they

have not asked for it.

Now put each of the following expressions into one of the blanks:

> one of the most notable differences is that
> where the national character is concerned,
> but speaking as a German in the United States,
> another similarity is that
> in contrast,
> both

Vocabulary and Grammar Note

For transitional expressions used in comparing and contrasting, see Comparison/Contrast in Appendix III.

PLANNING AND WRITING

Write a composition comparing and contrasting some aspect of your country and another country, following the outline you prepared in Warmup III. Your writing time is too limited to make this an in-depth study, so concentrate on clear organization and expression of the points you have chosen to cover.

In this composition, unlike the previous two, your "audience" is your teacher. As the basis of your relationship is academic rather than personal, you should concentrate on your task of giving information clearly, not on relating personally as you did in Units 21 and 22.

Before handing in your composition, check it against your "personal check-list," the list of your own most frequent errors. Remember to add to this list every time your teacher hands back one of your compositions for you to correct. Study your corrections of these errors so that you can recognize and correct them before handing in future compositions.

❧ Unit 24 ❧

A Specialized Process

Writing forms: Process; explanation
Writing skills: Preparing to describe a process; paragraphing

INTRODUCTION

A patient facing heart surgery asks his doctor to describe what is going to happen, not in such detail that he could perform such an operation himself, but well enough to understand the process and feel satisfied that the doctor is competent. The patient's confidence in the surgeon rises in direct proportion to the surgeon's ability to explain the operation in language that he can understand. In the same way, you should develop the ability to describe specialized processes in your major field of study so clearly that an outsider to your field could grasp the steps and general principles involved.

WARMUP I: PREPARING TO DESCRIBE A PROCESS

One of the most commonly used forms of analysis is describing how something is done. In order to describe a process clearly, the writer must

1. Break the process down into its component steps.
2. Explain the steps and their relationships to each other.

Although the process is described chronologically (that is, in the order in which the steps occur), there is also a great deal of development through explaining (giving reasons, examples, definitions or specialized terms, and so on). In this exercise you will prepare to describe a specialized process in your major field of study.*

---

*If you have not decided on a major, you may write a description of any specialized process with which you are familiar. If you feel you lack the expertise to do this, you may write on another process-related topic such as how to do something official (for example, obtaining a passport); how to break a bad habit; how to train an animal; or how to play a game or sport.

INSTRUCTIONS

1. Choose a process related to your major field of study as your topic. Although it doubtless requires a certain amount of expertise and/or specialized equipment, do not try to explain it in such detail that your reader could perform it. Choose a process that you feel confident you can explain so that your reader can understand the general idea.

Write your topic here:

2. Make a detailed list in chronological order of the specific steps involved in your process.

3. Organize your list by grouping your steps under headings that seem natural. For example, the steps involved in heart surgery can be divided into the three groups of . . .

   I. Preparing the patient
   II. The actual operation
   III. Recovery from the operation

Begin making a formal outline by numbering each of these main headings with a Roman numeral, as has been done here. You should not have less than two or more than four main headings.

4. Expand your outline by filling in supporting details of the process and by listing reasons, examples, exceptions, and other important information. Observe both the information and the numbering system in the following example from a formal outline. Follow this numbering system in making your own outline.

   I. Preparing the patient
      A. Should be as strong as possible
         1. Better chance of survival and recovery
         2. Emergency surgery may not permit waiting to build up strength
      B. Should be well informed
         1. Of the procedure
         2. Of the risks

WARMUP II: PARAGRAPHING

Dividing a paper into paragraphs makes it easier to read and shows the reader how the topic has been organized. Each paragraph consists of information or ideas that are closely related, either by a main idea (which may or may not be expressed in a "topic sentence") or by a specific purpose (such as classification, analysis, explanation, illustration, definition, logical proof, description, and so on). When the writer finishes developing this main idea or purpose and moves on to another one, he or she signals the change to the reader by starting a new paragraph.

INSTRUCTIONS:

The following composition, which describes the process by which an oil company leases mineral rights, should be divided into three paragraphs, each of which has a separate focus and function. Indicate where the divisions should fall by writing in the symbol for "paragraph," ¶ .

LEASING MINERAL RIGHTS FOR OIL PRODUCTION

One might think that producing oil is just a matter of locating a promising field and pumping the crude out of the ground, but in fact between the first act and the second an extremely complex legal process takes place. Before drilling can begin, the oil company must obtain the mineral rights to the land from all the various landowners involved. This process is handled by a specialist called a "lease hound." The lease hound's first task is to find out who owns the mineral rights, and if the oil field is large, literally hundreds of owners may be involved. Identifying them means spending countless hours of research in county courthouse records of land transactions and wills. Sometimes a landowner dies without a will, and the lease hound has to track down the heirs, who may not even know about their inheritance. Some of the owners may have left the area and moved far away. Others may have died and further divided their rights among their own heirs. But if the company is to have access to the entire oil field, all these owners of portions of the mineral rights have to be located. The next step is to persuade all the owners to sign leases permitting the oil company to drill on their land. The lease hound or another representative of the oil company may have to correspond with people or travel to see them in distant areas. Problems may arise when one owner demands a "royalty," or payment, that is out of proportion to the terms of the other leases before he will sign. Delays are caused if owners of key tracts of land refuse to sign. The lease hounds have to be very thorough, because the oil company wants legal access to the entire field before they commence drilling. Because of the complicated nature of the process, whole years could conceivably elapse between the signing of the geologists' recommendation of the field to the company and the actual commencement of drilling.

As you can see, the composition is hard to read because it is all printed together instead of being divided into paragraphs. Once you have properly divided it, note that each paragraph has a separate contribution to make to the composition:

1. The first paragraph introduces the topic and the specialized term "lease hound."
2. The second paragraph explains, mainly through examples, the first step of the process.
3. The third paragraph explains the next step, also through examples, then concludes the composition with a general statement related to the whole process.

In other words, each paragraph is restricted to one basic function in the composition (two can be combined if one is very short, as is done in the third paragraph) or to exploring one aspect of the topic.

WARMUP III: FAULTY PARAGRAPHING

Some common problems in paragraphing are:

1. Not developing an important idea that is mentioned.
2. Making paragraphs too short.
3. Dividing paragraphs in the wrong places.
4. Including sentences that do not contribute to the paragraph's function or main idea.

In this exercise you will focus on the fourth of these problems.

INSTRUCTIONS:
In the following composition on the disposal of radioactive waste:

1. Identify the main idea or function of each paragraph.
2. Cross out a sentence in each paragraph that does not belong there.

DISPOSAL OF RADIOACTIVE WASTE

The process of disposing of radioactive waste can be divided into two parts: preparation and storage. Preparation consists of packaging the waste into protective containers. This presents technology with the challenge of finding or developing materials that will not corrode over a period that may last up to ten thousand years. However, since civilization will probably not last that long, worrying over this problem may be a waste of time that could be spent on other scientific pursuits. In addition to being noncorrosive, the packaging materials must withstand the heat generated by their radioactive contents and must not enter into any chemical reaction that would damage the container. Clearly, modern technology is more capable of producing radioactive waste than of packaging it safely.

The second step is storage of the waste containers. A third step might be retrieval of the materials after they have lost their radioactivity, but that step can be worked out by future generations. While numerous storage methods have been proposed, including disposal at ground level, in the sea bed, in polar ice, and even in outer space, the method that currently seems to offer the best possibilities is geological isolation far below the surface of the earth. But while the technology already exists for burying waste containers in mined vaults, melted rock chambers, or "superdeep holes," research cannot yet provide enough information to assure the safety of underground disposal. For one thing, we do not have a clear enough understanding of the effects of such construction and of the heat generated by the waste on the "host rock." In addition, we are not yet knowledgeable enough to predict accurately the geological behavior of an area over a period of hundreds to thousands of years.

In short, while the process of radioactive waste disposal may be readily identified as a matter of preparation and storage, the current limitations of technology and research make it clear that our attempts in the near future will be only temporary measures until a final solution can be developed.

Accidents like the Three Mile Island incident make the whole world reconsider the desirability of using nuclear energy at all.

EDITING

In this passage from a composition on test-tube fertilization of human embryos, complete the following steps:

1. Correct the errors that are marked.
2. Be prepared to explain why:
   a. One sentence is marked "omit."
   b. Another sentence is marked "add."
   c. "¶" has been written between two sentences.
   d. "No ¶" has been written at the start of the second paragraph.

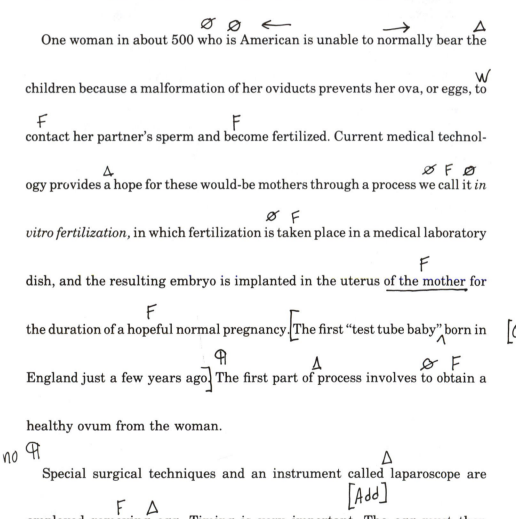

One woman in about 500 who is American is unable to normally bear the

children because a malformation of her oviducts prevents her ova, or eggs, to

contact her partner's sperm and become fertilized. Current medical technol-

ogy provides a hope for these would-be mothers through a process we call it *in*

vitro fertilization, in which fertilization is taken place in a medical laboratory

dish, and the resulting embryo is implanted in the uterus of the mother for

the duration of a hopeful normal pregnancy. The first "test tube baby" born in   [Omit]

England just a few years ago. The first part of process involves to obtain a

healthy ovum from the woman.

Special surgical techniques and an instrument called laparoscope are

[Add]

employed removing egg. Timing is very important. The egg must then

F   Δ   F

maintain in special solution that permits it retaining its potency until
                                                 ∧

fertilization takes place.

Vocabulary and Grammar Note

For transitional expressions used in describing a process, see Chronology/ Process in Appendix III.

PLANNING AND WRITING

Use the outline you developed in Warmup I as the basis for today's composition. Each group of steps should be described in a separate paragraph. But in addition to telling what the steps are, you may also need to explain why certain steps are important, to define special terms you use, or to tell what problems might arise if a step is left out or not done correctly. Refer to the models in Warmups II and III and the corrected editing exercise to observe how this may be done. Review and follow the guidelines in Warmups II and III concerning paragraph divisions and faulty paragraphing. Assume that your audience is composed of people with a good general education and an interest in your topic but without specialized knowledge of it.

When you finish writing, use both the checklist on page 289 and your own personal checklist before handing your paper in.

Unit 25

The Disadvantages of Being Rich

Writing forms: Explanation; illustration
Writing skills: Writing introductions and conclusions

INTRODUCTION

A couple of weeks ago, I ran into my boyhood friend David Oglesby for the first time in twenty years. I had heard that David had made a fortune on the stock market, so I was surprised he wasn't driving a Mercedes or wearing a designer outfit. As a matter of fact, he looked a lot like me, wearing an inexpensive suit that looked a couple of years old and driving a car with a few dents and a little rust around the edges. I asked him what he was doing these days, and he said he was teaching business at the local community college. "Teaching business?" I exclaimed. "I thought I heard you were in New York, making a killing in stocks and bonds." David smiled. "Yeah, I did that until about five years ago, but I got out. The stress was giving me an ulcer and a bad heart. Besides, once I got into that rat race, I had to run just to keep up. I never had any time to spend with my family. We're all much happier now."

I shook my head. Every man's ambition, and he had achieved it—only to give it up. I had always dreamed of having money, but it had never occurred to me that there might be disadvantages to being rich.

When people dream of things they don't have, they seldom stop to consider the drawbacks that may accompany the more obvious advantages. Today you will exercise your imagination by thinking and writing about the disadvantages that go hand in hand with such desirable situations as being rich, living on a beautiful tropical island, marrying a beautiful or handsome person, or growing up in a country that is an industrialized world power.

WARMUP I: WRITING INTRODUCTIONS*

As the first thing your reader sees, the introduction is one of the most important parts of a composition. Because of this, a good writer should be aware of several things that an introduction should do and several others that it should not.

*See also Unit 6.

116

An introduction *should:*

- Catch the reader's interest.
- Announce the topic.
- State the purpose of the composition (such as classification, comparison, analysis, and so on).
- Be short, direct, and relevant to the topic.

An introduction *should not:*

- Simply quote the title.
- Be more general than the topic.
- Promise more than you will actually do.

Here are some suggested ways of opening a composition. The examples are related to the topic "The Disadvantages of Being Rich."

1. Start with a short anecdote related to your topic:
    See the introduction to this unit, although that anecdote would be too long to introduce a thirty-minute in-class composition.
2. Start by announcing your topic in an interesting way:
    It's a good thing the upper class has a lot of money, because they need it to pay the high cost of being rich.
3. Start with a quotation or proverb related to your topic:
    "They were probably sour anyway," said the fox when he couldn't reach the grapes. This "sour grapes" attitude is a great comfort to the poor when they observe the rich. Surely all that money just brings on endless misery.
4. Start with an interesting fact or statistic:
    As a person's income rises, so does his susceptibility to certain physical, psychological, and social ills, according to a recent study published in Health Today.
5. Start with a statement or belief that is just the opposite of the point that your composition is going to make:
    Although all my friends dream of becoming millionaires, you couldn't pay me to be rich. I am convinced that the burdens of wealth are far harder to bear than the burdens of a moderate income.

After catching the reader's attention and identifying your topic in a sentence or two, continue your introduction by telling the reader something about the purpose of the composition and/or the way you are going to organize it. This is important because the clearer your purpose and organization are, the more easily the reader will be able to grasp your ideas. Here are some examples related to various topics:

- This process follows three major steps.
- While these two countries have significant similarities, their differences are even more striking.
- We can compare the populations of these two countries on the basis of size, density, and ethnic makeup.
- The members of this large group can be classified into the subgroups of

_____ , _____ , _____ , and _____ , each of which has its own distinguishing characteristics.

• Despite the popularity of this notion, it can be readily disproven by the following argument.

In this exercise you will apply these guidelines in writing an introduction for today's composition.

INSTRUCTIONS

1. Choose a topic for today's composition from among those suggested in the introduction to this unit.
2. Write an introductory paragraph for your composition, following these steps:

    1. Review the *shoulds* and *should nots* in this warmup.
    2. Follow one of the five opening methods suggested.
    3. Continue your opener with a sentence or two about the purpose and organization of your paper, as previously indicated.

    Your whole introductory paragraph for a thirty-minute composition should be no more than four sentences long.

WARMUP II: WRITING CONCLUSIONS*

Every composition needs some sort of closing. Simply stopping after developing your last main point makes the composition seem weak and unfinished. As with introductions, there are several points to keep in mind for writing conclusions.

A conclusion *should:*

• Be short.
• Refer to the whole topic, not merely to the last main point.

A conclusion *should not:*

• Simply repeat the wording of the introduction.
• Introduce additional main points or supporting material.
• Apologize for the composition.
• Give exceptions or objections to what has been written.

Here are some good ways to conclude a composition, with examples related to various topics on the disadvantages of otherwise desirable conditions.

1. Finish by summarizing (However, a thirty-minute in-class composition is so short that a summary is unnecessary, as your reader can easily remember your main points.):
   In short, a person who cares about his health and family life would do well to pursue a modest lifestyle rather than a wealthy, extravagant one.
2. Finish by referring to something said in the introduction (an anecdote, quotation, fact, or statistic):

*See also Unit 6.

I have concluded that my friend David was right. He certainly is much happier now. Maybe I too am better off than I realized.

3. Finish by giving a quotation:
   If these pitfalls are so widespread and obvious, and if they contribute to both physical and social unhealth, then why, we may ask, does almost everyone who doesn't have money dream of having it, and a lot of it? Perhaps the answer lies in humorist Sheldon Arbuckle's insight: "Money may not buy happiness, but poverty can't buy anything."

4. Finish by asking a question:
   So the next time you envy a person from an industrialized nation, a person with "all the advantages" of "the good life," you would do better to ask yourself, "Is his life really worth more than mine? Shouldn't he be envying me instead?"

5. Finish by looking to the future, perhaps recommending a course of action to solve a problem described in the composition:
   In light of all the problems delineated here, we may well ask ourselves if marriage is worth going into. My answer is that it is, but only if we go into it aware of the dangers and prepared and determined to overcome them. Two mature adults who are committed to succeeding in their relationship can surely overcome anything.

There are several expressions called "conclusion markers" that signal your reader that you are ending your paper. These do not have to be used, but you may find them useful. They include:

finally	in conclusion
last	then
it seems then	in short
so	in light of

In this exercise you will apply these guidelines in writing a conclusion for today's composition.

INSTRUCTIONS:
Use these guidelines to write a conclusion for today's composition. Imagine that the introduction you wrote for Warmup I is the one that you will be using; you may want to refer to it in your conclusion.

1. Review the *shoulds* and *should nots* for writing conclusions.
2. Choose one of the five closing methods given and write a two- or three-sentence conclusion.

PLANNING AND WRITING

First, brainstorm a list of disadvantages for the topic you chose in Warmup I. You might work individually or with other students who have chosen the same topic. Once you have a rather long list, work individually to classify and organize it. Choose three of the items on your list as the main points of your composition. Then brainstorm several specific supporting details (examples, reasons) for each one.

Example: Topic: Disadvantages of Being Rich
                Main point: Health
                              Support: Stress leads to ulcers, heart condi-
tion; rich food results in gout, heart
condition; lack of exercise leads to
obesity, heart condition

When you have finished listing the specific details that will develop each main point, organize your list in the order in which you want to present it. Although there are various principles by which this can be done, the most common format is to save your most important point until last, in order to end your composition on a strong note.

Be sure to use your personal checklist before turning your paper in. In addition, check your paper against the checklist on page 289.

❧ Unit 26 ❧

Changes

Writing form: Analysis
Writing skill: Supporting with examples

INTRODUCTION

Recently I went to visit my grandmother on her eightieth birthday. In good health and surrounded by her family, she should have been more than content; however, I found her miserable. Instead of the happy stories she used to tell, she recounted all the grisliest and most depressing items she had read in the newspaper lately: a man going berserk and murdering his whole family, then himself; an isolated farming couple terrorized by a motorcycle gang; children abused by their own parents; hitchhikers victimized, or robbing the people who picked them up; a policeman run over by car thieves, then robbed by passersby as he lay in the street. It was clear to me that my grandmother was frightened at the changes in values that had taken place in the world since her retirement.

Changes of various sorts, some minor, some major, are a part of everyone's life. What changes have you noticed lately in yourself, in someone else, or in your environment? This is your topic for today's composition.

WARMUP I: ANALYZING

To analyze is to separate a whole into its component parts. For example, when an agronomist analyzes soil, he or she determines what chemicals and particles it is composed of. In almost all cases, however, an analysis is not merely an exhaustive list of all the parts but rather a list of those parts that are significant, that contribute directly to the characteristics of the whole. For example, the agronomist is analyzing soil to determine why certain plants do or do not grow well in it, and he or she is interested only in measuring those parts that significantly affect the plants.

In the composition today you will be analyzing changes. First of all you must narrow your topic to something that you can discuss specifically in a short composition. Suggested topics follow. Second, you must think of numerous examples, characteristics, effects, and causes related to the change you are analyzing. Finally and most important, you must determine which of the details are significant, truly explaining, characterizing, or representing the change.

INSTRUCTIONS

1. Choose one of the following topics for today's composition.
   a. How you have changed since you graduated from high school. Choose a theme such as how you have become wiser, have learned to manage money, have become more independent. This theme will determine the examples that you will select to develop an overall impression.
   b. How an old person you know (such as a grandparent) has changed in the past several years. Again, choose a theme such as changes that have deeply impressed the family or the old person himself/herself.
   c. How daily life in a particular place has changed in the past ten or fifteen years. Again, choose a theme that determines your examples: has the overall change been for the better, for the worse?
   d. How something such as the educational system, attitudes toward women, or family structure has changed in your country in the past several years. Your thesis statement will be some specific statement about how this system has changed: for example, "The advent of television has affected family structure in my country in ways that were undreamed of twenty years ago."
   e. How your goals in life have changed since you were a child. Think of an overall theme. Have you become more materialistic, more idealistic, more practical, more . . . ?
   f. How your goals and ideals about marriage have changed. What statement could you make to sum up these changes?
2. Break your topic down into two or three of the most important *kinds* of changes, which will be the main ideas (paragraphs) of today's composition.

Example

Topic: How life has become faster and more exciting in my home city
      Kinds of changes: More diversity in goods and entertainment
                               More crime and other kinds of danger
                               More employment opportunities

WARMUP II: SUPPORTING WITH EXAMPLES

A composition is usually organized around three or four rather general main points. Then each of these main points needs to be supported or developed with details that are much more *specific*. This support may take various forms,* but without such specific development the composition is considered very weak. In this exercise you will practice supporting a general idea (such as one of the kinds of changes from Warmup I, step 2) by using specific examples.

INSTRUCTIONS:
Choose three of the following main ideas and jot down two or three supporting examples for each.

---

*Some of the more common forms of development are examples, reasons, anecdotes, facts, reference to authorities, narration, instructions, enumeration, suggestion, and cause and effect.

Example

> Main idea: I have become much more materialistic than I used to be in my attitudes toward marriage.
> Example 1: I want my wife to work so we can have two incomes.
> Example 2: I want us to share a comfortable, large home.
> Example 3: I want to be able to send our children to good schools.

1. Life is more dangerous in my hometown than it used to be.

2. My goals in life have become more _____ since I was a child.

3. The kind of person I want to marry is more _____ than the kind I used to want.

4. I have become more independent since I graduated from high school.

5. My grandmother's increasing feebleness has given her a special place in the family in the past several years.

6. Women have greater educational opportunities in my country than they had ten years ago.

7. In the last five years, my hometown has had trouble providing enough city services to keep pace with its rapid growth.

EDITING

In the five years past I went thru radical changes in my mind, behavior. In one thing, I have been so independently and take proud in my capable to managing in my on. I have my apartament, and car support me with part time job. On the contrary, I've lost the feel of close I was use to have with my family. Now I fine I have in common more with my friends here than my own brother at home. These makes my feeling lonely in spite of my accomplishments.

PLANNING AND WRITING

Take the topic you chose in Warmup I, step 2, and make an outline. Each of your two or three *kinds* of changes should be developed into a separate paragraph with supporting examples. If you want to, you can add a sentence or two interpreting what each kind of change means or how you feel about it. Here is a sample outline:

   I. Introduction, stating your overall theme (if short, not a separate paragraph)

  II. One kind of change

     A. Two or three examples

     B. Interpretation (optional)

 III. Another kind of change

     A. Two or three examples

     B. Interpretation (optional)

  IV. A third kind of change (if you are using as many as three)

     A. Two or three examples

     B. Interpretation (optional)

   V. Conclusion (if short, not a separate paragraph)

How do you decide which main ideas, or which examples, to put first and which last? As in your composition for Unit 25, save your most important or most convincing main idea or example until last. This ends your composition on a strong note.

Now write your own outline, then your composition. Before you hand in your work, check it carefully against the checklist on page 289. Also correct your most common errors.

❦ Unit 27 ❦

Coming of Age

Writing form: Argumentation
Writing skill: Supporting with reasons

INTRODUCTION

At what age does a person become an adult? The answer varies from culture to culture and from individual to individual. The responsibilities and privileges of adulthood generally include marriage, voting, employment, military service, driving, buying alcohol (in some cultures), and liability for criminal actions (that is, liability to prosecution as an adult). The ages at which these things are permitted may vary even within one culture: for example, the driving age is generally lower than the voting age. But when one is permitted by law to do all of them, that person is legally an adult. What do you think is an appropriate age for a person to be considered an adult? What are your reasons? This is your topic for today's composition.

WARMUP: ARGUMENTATION: SUPPORTING WITH REASONS

Argumentation is a form of writing in which the writer uses reasons and facts to support a statement of opinion. Here is an example of such an opinion and such support, related to today's topic:

Thesis statement: Before the age of eighteen, people should not be allowed to marry.
Support: Until the age of eighteen most people are still in high school and are still growing biologically and psychologically. Getting married before this age would add pressures and demands that would greatly interfere with their basic education. Furthermore, their physical and emotional immaturity could seriously hinder their making a suitable adjustment to marriage.

Here are some points to keep in mind when writing an argumentative paper. Notice how each point is accomplished in the preceding example.

1. Your thesis must be a statement that can be proved.

125

2. You must prove it by presenting sound reasons and facts—not mere opinions, incomplete evidence, or faulty logic.

3. You must present your thesis and your support as clearly as possible.

INSTRUCTIONS:

Following is a thesis and a list of supporting statements. Before each supporting statement, write the letter *A* or *B* for the following categories:

   A. An opinion, a faulty or incompletely stated reason, or an unrelated statement.
   B. A good reason, clearly expressed.

Be prepared to defend your choices.

   Thesis statement: Fifteen-year-olds should not be allowed to vote.

Examples

   A   They are too young. (opinion)

   A   Age is a good basis for deciding who can vote. (incomplete reason, undeveloped)

   B   Their experience with life is generally limited to matters of childhood and adolescence, while voting issues deal with a much broader and more adult spectrum of life. (good reason, clearly expressed)

1. _____ While some of them may be mature and well informed enough to vote, most are not, and it's easier to have an age limit than to devise a maturity test.

2. _____ I'm an authority because I'm fifteen.

3. _____ I'm an authority because I have a son who is fifteen.

4. _____ I'm an authority because I'm a sociologist, and I have written and published an exhaustive study on this subject based on extensive research and samples taken over a period of several years.

5. _____ If fifteen-year-olds were allowed to vote, some clever person would talk them into voting for whomever he or she wanted, because they are easily led.

6. _____ Even the fifteen-year-olds I know agree that they're too young to vote.

7. _____ They would vote blindly or for the wrong reasons.

8. _____ Anyone who is over the age of eighteen (the legal voting age in some places) is mature and well informed enough to vote.

9. _____ No one who is fifteen is mature and well informed enough to vote.

10. _____ The people who set the voting age at eighteen are wiser than I, and if they felt that was a good age limit, I'm sure they had a good reason.

11. _____ Fifteen-year-olds are not interested in politics. All they are interested in is having fun.

12. _____ Most of them are not experienced with handling such responsibility and could not be depended on to handle it well in the case of voting.

13. _____ None of the fifteen-year-olds I know even read the paper, so how could they vote intelligently if they don't even know what the issues are?

14. _____ If age is to be the basis for deciding which citizens can vote, the limit has to be set according to the supposed maturity of the *majority* of people that age.

EDITING

Why youngs should not allowed to marriage until eighteen years old have important economical reasons. Most of people do not finish their high school before eighteen years. These people need to be as free as possible from pressures and demands. These pressures and demands will interfere with their studies before finish this basic level of their education. Once graduate, they are in a better position. They can find job that pays enough well. They can support a family. If they get marriage before graduate. They can force by financial pressures to drop out of the school and looking for work, almost it is impossible for the high-school dropout to can find good job.

[Combine] [Combine] [Combine]

PLANNING AND WRITING

For your thesis statement (the statement that you are trying to prove), use something like this: "By the age of _____, a person should be considered legally an adult. He or she should be able to _____, _____, and _____." Fill in the last three blanks with three of these categories:

marry   drive
vote   buy alcohol
serve in the military   have a full-time job
be liable to prosecution as an adult for criminal offenses

These three categories will be your three main points, and you should devote a paragraph to each. Develop your paragraphs by using good reasons and, if possible, facts and statistics. For your short conclusion, you may want to refer to the methods of concluding suggested in Unit 25. Before handing your paper in, use your personal checklist as well as the one on page 289.

❧ Unit 28 ❧

Tracing Causes and Effects

Writing form: Argumentation
Writing skills: Expressing cause and effect; choosing forms of
   development

INTRODUCTION

The ingenious human brain is not content merely to observe the present: it seeks
to interpret present events by looking for their causes and by attempting to
predict their results. In writing, cause and effect is a form of argument, because
the writer has to give evidence proving that the relationship between the events
is a causal one. The ability to establish this kind of relationship and to express it
clearly is a skill you will constantly use in university coursework, no matter
what you major in. What is a topic related to your field of study on which you
could write a cause-and-effect composition?

WARMUP I: CAUSE AND EFFECT

Cause and effect is a more complex relationship than it may appear to be. In
assigning cause, the writer must first *be sure* of the facts: Did this event really
cause that event? Second, the writer must *explain* what happened clearly
enough, and in enough detail, to convince the reader that the so-called cause
really did produce the so-called effect. If either of these principles is violated, the
composition (or examination or research paper) will fail. In the following
exercise, you will observe some common fallacies of cause and effect.

INSTRUCTIONS:
Following is a list of questions to test causes and effects.

1. Read the list carefully.
2. Read the statements following it, which are weak, incomplete, or simply wrong.
3. For each statement, tell which question it violated and be prepared to explain
   the statement's weakness.

Questions to help you determine cause and effect:

A. Did the first event really cause the second?

129

B. Were there additional causes that you have failed to notice or mention?

C. Are you sure which is the cause and which the effect? Could their roles have been the reverse?

D. In writing down these causes and effects, have you left out any important intervening steps or events?

Example:

I inherited my poor vision from my father. Before I was born, he impaired his vision by looking directly at an eclipse of the sun.

Weakness: See question A. The two events are unrelated.

1. _____ The current economic crisis is all the fault of the last president's policies.

2. _____ The high crime rate in this neighborhood is the reason why the area is so poor. All the middle-class people have either been robbed into poverty or have moved away.

3. _____ The reason I don't get any exercise is that since I'm so fat, I don't have enough energy to exercise.

4. _____ If the Romans had not become so wicked and immoral, their empire would not have collapsed.

5. _____ Malaria is caused by mosquitoes.

6. _____ The volcano erupted and destroyed the village because the villagers had refused to sacrifice a maiden to the fire goddess.

7. _____ Evolution caused apes to develop into man.

WARMUP II: CHOOSING A TOPIC AND AN ORGANIZATIONAL SCHEME

Whatever your field of study may be, it offers many cause-and-effect topics. In this exercise you will select such a topic for today's composition, and then you will choose one of several possible ways of organizing it.

INSTRUCTIONS:

1. Choose a cause-and-effect topic related to your major field. It should be a topic with enough causes or effects that you can write a well-developed composition about it.* Here are a few topics to give you ideas:

*If you have not yet begun your university coursework and/or you feel you lack the information to write on a topic related to your major, choose a less specialized cause-and-effect topic, such as

A. A cause-and-effect event related to your nation's history (such as causes and effects of a war or other crisis).

B. A cause-and-effect situation in your family or personal experience (for example, causes and/or results of my father's decision to change his career in middle age).

C. Causes and effects related to one of your hobbies or special interests (for example, what causes houseplants to decline or die or the results of "crash" or "fad" dieting as opposed to following a balanced diet to lose weight).

Note: Be sure your topic is cause and effect and not process.

(Computer science)   What can cause a program not to run properly?
(Economics)   What are the causes and results of devaluation of a nation's currency?
(Psychology)   What are some causes and effects of poor mental health?
(Civil engineering)   How has the development of the computer industry affected traffic engineering?

Write your topic here:

2. Examine the following organizational schemes and decide which one best fits your topic.

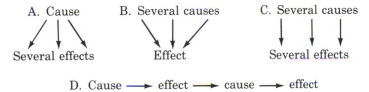

A. Cause — Several effects   B. Several causes — Effect   C. Several causes — Several effects

D. Cause ⟶ effect ⟶ cause ⟶ effect

EDITING

PROBLEMS RESULTING FROM THE SUCCESS OF AMERICA'S NATIONAL PARKS

 F   Δ   S
The overwhelming popular of the America's national parks has lead to

             F   F   F
numerous unexpecting results. Wanted to preserve and protect particular

 F   Δ   S   T
beautifully natural spots, goverment set them a part so that visitors can

 T   Δ F   S   S   W
enjoyed them in careful controled enviroment. But such many people have

         #   F   P   F   ref
flocked to this famous areas in annual increased numbers that they have

            S   F
become victims of there own succeed. Now shelters, souvenir shops, lodges,

                                              F   P   P
restaurants, laundromats, post offices have been constructing, in the parks,

 W   P   W   Δ
for providing for the visitors' necessaries. Are necessary the reservations at

F /→

many campgrounds in summer because of the record campers' numbers. And

P   #

long lines of sightseers cause massive, traffic jams along the narrow parks

Δ   Δ   F

roads as they come from all over world to enjoy spectacular beautiful of the

Grand Canyon, Yellowstone, and Yosemite.

Vocabulary and Grammar Note

For transitional and other expressions of cause and effect, see "Cause and Effect" in Appendix III.

PLANNING AND WRITING

First make an outline for the topic you chose in Warmup II. How are you going to develop your paragraphs? You have a variety of options, including the following:

1. Schemes A and B. If you have several causes or several effects, you could devote a paragraph to each, developing it through examples, through reasons, by explaining a process, or by showing the reader *how* this cause produces this result.
2. Scheme C. If you have several causes and several effects, you could devote a paragraph or two to discussing the causes thoroughly and then a paragraph or two to discussing the effects thoroughly.
3. Scheme D. If you have a cause that leads to an effect that then causes another effect, you could devote a paragraph to each cause–effect action.

Once your outline is complete, write your composition, keeping the following points in mind:

1. Ask yourself the questions in Warmup I to test the validity and clarity of your causes and effects.
2. Present the facts, and then convince your reader that one (or some) really *caused* another (or others). Be sure you present this relationship convincingly to your reader, who is not a specialist in your field.

❧ Unit 29 ❧

As You Liken It

Writing forms: Comparison; explanation
Writing skills: Writing analogies; choosing forms of development

INTRODUCTION

In many ways, learning a foreign language is like learning to dance. You begin by memorizing the "steps," or short segments of the language. In both language learning and dance, you have to train your body or your mouth to master the new positions and sequences required. The more you practice and become familiar with the new material, the more meaning it comes to have for you, until you begin to see the foreign language, like dancing, as an artistic means of self-expression. Gradually you develop your ability to improvise, using the "steps" you have learned to create your own unique "dances." In the end you have learned a new and creative way of communicating. Every conversation and composition is like a performance on stage, and you are rightfully proud of yourself, the "artist."

The preceding paragraph is an analogy, or a comparison between two things that seem quite different on the surface. For today's composition you will practice using analogies as a means of comparing and explaining ideas.

WARMUP I: WRITING ANALOGIES

If you compare a heart to a pump, or the human eye to a camera, you are able to explain how the heart or the eye works by comparing it to something more familiar to your reader. This kind of comparison, in which the two things being compared are really in quite different categories, is called an analogy. Analogies are very useful in writing, but there are several points to keep in mind when you write them:

1. Because it is only a comparison, no analogy can *prove* anything.
2. Because the two things are categorically different, no analogy is perfect; that is, the two things are alike only in some regards, not all.
3. An analogy is different from a literal comparison in that the two things being compared are in different categories. In a literal comparison, they would have to be categorically the same (for example, they would both have to be countries or both animals, and so on).

133

4. Because analogies are used to explain concepts that might otherwise be difficult to understand, the analogy chosen must be familiar to the reader.

In this exercise you will practice developing analogies.

INSTRUCTIONS:
Working in pairs or in groups, make a list of as many different answers as you can think of to each of the following questions. Keep in mind the guidelines just given.

1. How is marriage like a relationship between two countries?

2. How are universities like factories?

3. How is a person's mind like a house?

4. How is being poor like being stranded on a desert island?

WARMUP II: SELECTING FORMS OF DEVELOPMENT

The purpose of today's composition will be to explain an idea you will choose in this exercise. Explaining is a form of writing that can be developed in numerous ways, including:

- Analogies
- Anecdotes
- Definitions
- Enumeration (listing) of details
- Examples
- Facts
- Reasons
- Reference to authorities
- Specific events
- Statistics
- Suggestions or associations

When you are assigned a topic for a composition, research paper, or examination, that topic is seldom so clear-cut that there is only one way of developing it. You need to learn to *choose* appropriate types of development as a crucial part of the process of planning your paper. In this exercise you will choose today's topic, then decide on two or three types of development for it.

INSTRUCTIONS

1. Choose one of the following topics for today's composition.
   - Capitalism (or another economic system)
   - Democracy (or another political system)
   - Growing up
   - Life for a foreign student
   - Marriage
   - My family
   - My life
   - Poverty
   - Raising a child
   - Student life (in general, not just for foreign students)

2. Narrow your topic, which is so general that whole books could be written on it, to a *thesis* (a statement of your position on the topic) specific enough to be developed in a thirty-minute composition.

Examples

Democracy is a very inefficient form of government.
Growing up is a painful process.
Marriage is what everyone wants—until they get it.
My family is chaotic but very loving.

Your thesis:

3. Look at the list of methods of development at the beginning of this warmup and choose two methods in addition to analogy to use in developing your thesis for today's composition. Write down your methods and, under each one, make a little list of what you could include.

Example

Thesis: Growing up is a painful process.
1. Analogy: Adolescence is like a disease—you often don't feel good (socially); you experience pain because you always seem to do the wrong things; adults often don't want to be around you, as though you might be contagious; people seem to think they're specialists and prescribe courses of action for you to take.
2. Specific events and anecdotes from my life: the times I tried so hard to make a big impression that I acted nervous and unnatural; all the useless advice my parents gave me on how to be popular.
3. Conclusion through return to the analogy and further reference to specific events: But adolescence is fortunately not a terminal illness, and we all outgrow it in time. Events and anecdotes: Gradually I became more confident and seemed to do fewer embarrassing things. I found that as I relaxed and enjoyed life more, other people enjoyed me more too.

Your thesis:

1. Analogy:

2.

3.

EDITING

Learning English Is Like Growing Up

For me, learn English was like grow from a baby into an adult. When I first

arrived to U.S., I knew any English at all. I got an apartment with two

American students, they tried talk with me, but I couldn't. I joined with them

at the parties, but everyone made me always feel as a baby. [Because I could

not talk. So they ignored me or talked about me each with others] In almost

[Combin

cases people didn't treat to me like as an adult because of I can't com-

municated at their level. Really this affected to me too much. Only in the my

English class, which all the person has the same ability like me, do I felt like

an adult.

After a while that I lived here, I found the more I developed ability, the

more I could communicate better. I could talk, but because my English was

still poor, other people thought my ideas must be not better than a child, so

they treated me as one. Gradually my proficiency of english has grown up, and now I can express better. When I talk to people they realize that I am real

person with interested ideas, experiences, etc. Now I feel myself like if I have

grown up at last.

This passage, when corrected, provides a short sample composition developing an analogy. See the answers section between Units 40 and 41.

PLANNING AND WRITING

Using the developmental outline you wrote in Warmup II, write your composition. Be sure to include your thesis statement in the first paragraph with your analogy. Each of the other two methods of development you have chosen will be represented in a separate paragraph. Don't forget a short conclusion, which can be part of the third paragraph. When you finish writing, use your personal checklist and the one on page 289.

❧ Unit 30 ❧

Education

Writing form: Extended definition
Writing skill: Developing extended definitions

INTRODUCTION

When my family took me to the airport to see me off to the university in another city, my father took me aside just before I got on the plane and gave me some very strange advice: "Don't let your studies interfere too much with your education." The plane was leaving, and there was no time to ask him what he meant. I thought about his words throughout the trip and off and on for the next four years. What exactly is *education,* if it is not just studying? Is our usual concept of it too limited? By the time I graduated from the university, I had formulated a pretty good definition, and it was not the same one I had had when I graduated from high school. I had also gotten a good education by my definition, and as much of it took place outside the classroom as within.

What does the term *education* mean to you? Today you will develop your answer to this question into a composition that is an *extended definition,* a common and important form of academic writing.

WARMUP: DEVELOPING EXTENDED DEFINITIONS

Whenever a writer uses a term with which the reader might not be familiar, he or she must define the term clearly. This definition may simply be copied from the dictionary, or it may take up several pages of explanation. The latter form, an extended definition, is the basis for today's composition on education (or on one of the alternative topics suggested in the third step of this warmup).

The purpose of a definition is to *limit* the meaning of a term in such a way that the reader cannot confuse it with any other meaning. In other words, the definition must include all relevant features and exclude all others. In order to accomplish this purpose, the writer must adhere to several principles:

1. Try to put yourself in the place of the reader, who does not understand the term as you do.

2. Keep in mind that the purpose of the definition is to clarify the term for the reader.
3. Don't use the term being defined in the definition itself. "Education is the process of being educated" is called a *circular definition* because it puts the reader back where he or she started.
4. Provide specific detail. If "a school is a building where people learn," then how is a school different from a library, where people also learn?
5. Define the term using vocabulary that your reader will understand.

There are many methods that can be used to develop an extended definition, and in this exercise you will choose the ones you want to use in today's composition. Here is a list of forms of development:

1. Giving the dictionary definition, which may be useful but is not adequate. Continue by using one of the other strategies.
2. Giving the etymology, or origins and history of the word itself. As with the dictionary definition, the etymology is inadequate for an extended definition but can be a useful starting point.
3. Analyzing or classifying the components of the term. (What are its ingredients? Examine and discuss them.)
4. Telling what the term is *not*.
5. Giving examples. (This is especially helpful if the term is abstract.)
6. Giving an analogy to help clarify the term.
7. Explaining the functions and effects of the term.

INSTRUCTIONS:
Following is a list of components and developmental ideas that could be included in an extended definition of education. Some are more useful than others, and some will appeal to you more than others.

Step 1. Read them through carefully and identify which of the preceding forms of development each represents.

1. The word *education* comes from Middle English *educaten,* which comes from Latin *educare,* "to bring up, educate," which comes from Latin *e(x),* "out" or "from," and *ducere,* "to lead."
2. The American Heritage Dictionary defines *education* as "1. The act or process of imparting knowledge or skills; systematic instruction; teaching. 2. The obtaining of knowledge or skill through such a process; schooling. 3a. The knowledge or skill obtained or developed by such a process; learning. 3b. A program of instruction of a specified kind or level."
3. In the United States, the components of formal education include nursery school, kindergarten, elementary school, middle school, high school, and the alternatives of specialized trade school or college/university.
4. The function of education is to _____.
5. Education is _____. Education is not _____.
6. The effects of a good education are _____.
7. The process of education can be compared to _____.
8. An example of a good education is _____. An example of a bad education is _____.
9. A description of an educated person is _____. A description of an uneducated person is _____.

10. The dictionary definition of education is inadequate because _____ .

11. Most people think that education is _____ . In reality, it is
   _____ .

12. The components of informal education include _____ ,
   _____ , and _____ .

13. Education does not take place only in schoolrooms. Some other places where
   education occurs are _____ , _____ , and
   _____ .

14. People who are certified and employed to teach in schools are not the only
   teachers. Others include _____ .

Step 2. Read the sample composition at the end of this unit to give you an idea of
what an extended definition can look like.

Step 3. Now that you have an idea of the many alternatives to use in developing
your composition, think about what *your* definition of education is. (If you prefer,
you may choose another term to define. Suggestions include *masculinity, femininity, freedom,* and *success.*)

Your thesis or position statement will serve as the core of your extended definition.
Write it here:

Step 4. Once you have written a thesis for your paper, return to the list of fourteen
examples of developing an extended definition of education (or to the more general
list of seven forms the examples are based on, if you are defining another term).
Read them again, and then mark three or four that would lend themselves best to
developing the thesis you have written down.

Step 5. Finally, make an outline for your composition. Include the three or four
methods you have selected, developing each into a separate paragraph in your
composition. How are you going to develop each paragraph? Which specific reasons,
examples, facts, or anecdotes are you going to use for support in each one? Write
your outline out in some detail.

A Word on Audience

The way you define a term depends on who will be reading your paper. How
much does your audience already know? If you are writing a technical paper for
other scholars in the same field, your definition should of course be technical, as
you can assume that they understand the same specialized vocabulary and have
a good basis in your subject. If you are defining a term for people unfamiliar with
your field, you must explain it in simple terms with which they are familiar. If
you are offering a new or more adequate definition of a familiar term, make sure
the differentiating features of your definition are clear and convincing.

PLANNING AND WRITING

Using the outline you wrote in the warmup exercise, write your composition.
Keep in mind that your thesis statement is a condensed version of your
definition and that everything in the composition must be directly related to the
purpose of explaining and expanding that definition for your reader. Use your
checklists before handing in your paper.

Femininity

"Femininity is back," proclaimed the ad for the boutique's new collection of soft, frilly dresses. Someone evidently thought that in the interval between now and some idealized time in the past, women had somehow ceased to be women but had recently come to their senses again. The distinction seemed frivolous to me, as I had come to a totally different definition of femininity.

In my parents' day, femininity was defined in terms of a woman's appearance and behavior. A feminine woman spent hours on her looks. She wore the kind of dresses in the boutique ad, and she never left the house without putting on makeup and doing her hair. She was very conscious of her posture. She was never loud, never told dirty stories or used strong language. If she worked outside the home, she chose a "suitable" white-collar profession, never manual labor. Such a woman was either imitated or envied by other women, and mothers urged their daughters to follow her example as they grew to womanhood.

While many people still subscribe to this definition, others look beyond appearance and behavior and find the essence of femininity in a woman's attitudes toward herself. These people feel that a feminine woman is simply any woman who enjoys being female. This attitude may lead her to follow the older standards of dress and behavior, but it may not: she may wear no makeup, have a "masculine" haircut, wear jeans, not be very posture-conscious, and violate other items on the old behavioral code. She may be a secretary or she may be a welder. But because she is comfortable with her identity as a woman, people can tell by looking at her and being around her that she is totally feminine. By this definition, we need never fear that femininity will somehow go out of style. As long as there are women who feel good about themselves, femininity is here to stay.

Unit 31

From the News

Writing form: Newspaper style
Writing skills: Presenting information directly and quickly;
correcting misplaced modifiers

INTRODUCTION

From a local newspaper:

At 3:00 A.M. Tuesday, police apprehended a man suspected of robbing the First National Bank at 1530 Commerce Street. Officers D. R. Brightwell and T. E. Czinski said they found the man, who gave his name as Cesar Molina, sitting in a car in front of the bank when they were making their routine rounds. The door of the building was standing open, and bank officials summoned to the scene determined that over half a million dollars had been taken. When questioned at police headquarters, Molina denied any knowledge of the crime and said that the door had been open when he had arrived at the spot around five minutes before his apprehension by the officers, but that he had seen no one and had not gotten out of his car. A search of Molina's person and vehicle yielded no trace of the missing money. Molina was released following extensive questioning. He is no longer considered a suspect in the case, although police have no other leads at this time.

When asked by reporters what he had been doing at the bank at that hour, Molina said that he had gone in response to an ad in the paper requesting a driver who was "reliable, punctual, and discreet." Molina said he called the phone number in the ad and spoke with a person who identified himself only as "Rocky," and who promised Molina $100 if he would pick him up at the corner of Main and Commerce Streets at 2 A.M. Tuesday. Molina said he agreed but lost track of the time because he fell asleep while studying, and he arrived at the address an hour late. He said that he was not aware of the bank's location there, nor did he have any idea where the open door led. He surmised that the person who identified himself as "Rocky" had committed the crime and then fled on foot when Molina was not there to pick him up.

Molina, a Venezuelan, is a student at the English Language Center at Stockford University here. He said he answered the ad because he "needed some extra money." When asked whether he had not been suspicious of "Rocky's" intentions,

142

he said, "No, North Americans do a lot of things I don't understand, and I've learned not to ask questions. It's easier just to go along with them."

Today you will be using a similarly journalistic style of writing to practice presenting information quickly and directly in a "news story" of your own.

WARMUP I: NEWSPAPER STYLE

Newspaper writing is remarkable for its ability to get right to the point. The first sentence or two generally give you the answers to the questions *who, what, where, when,* and *why*. The remainder of the information is arranged in order of lessening importance, so that the reader can find all the most directly relevant information at the beginning and the least relevant at the end. In this exercise you will practice presenting information by this direct method.

INSTRUCTIONS

1. Look back at the "news story" in this unit's introduction. Notice that instead of beginning with the kinds of introductions you have been using in compositions, the opening of a news story gives you as much information as possible. Find and underline the answers to the questions *who, what, where, when,* and *why* in the first two sentences.
2. Now plan a news story of your own by making an outline–list. For the *who,* select a classmate or classmates, or even your teacher. For the *what,* think of several possible events, preferably humorous or interesting, and then choose the one you like best, perhaps an accomplishment, an adventure, a crime. (For ideas, think of the kinds of events you have seen reported in the newspaper lately.) Continue by deciding on a place, a time, and a motive. When you finish, you will be prepared to write today's assignment.

Who:

What:

Where:

When:

Why:

WARMUP II: CORRECTING MISPLACED MODIFIERS

One of the most common problems students have with English sentence structure is misplacing modifiers of nouns. A relative clause, a participial phrase, or a
prepositional phrase should appear immediately adjoining the noun that it
modifies if at all possible. If the modifier appears elsewhere in the sentence, its
meaning may be changed or unclear. Here are examples, with corrections, in all
three categories:

> *Misplaced prepositional phrase*
> Incorrect: A serious problem was identified by the mechanic *in the engine.*
> Correction: A serious problem *in the engine* was identified by the mechanic.

> *Misplaced participial phrase*
> Incorrect: Mr. Molina failed to see the open door *waiting in his car.*
> Correction: *Waiting in his car,* Mr. Molina failed to see the open door.

> *Misplaced relative clause*
> Incorrect: I gave the tickets to a child *that I found lying in the street.*
> Correction: I gave a child the tickets *that I found lying in the street.*

A related problem occurs if the writer neglects to include the modified noun in
the sentence. This leaves the modifier dangling with nothing to refer to.

> *Dangling modifier*
> Incorrect: *Performing an exploratory operation,* the patient was discovered to have a
> tumor.
> Correction: *Performing an exploratory operation,* the surgeon discovered that the
> patient had a tumor.

INSTRUCTIONS:
Each of the following sentences contains a misplaced or dangling modifier. Rewrite
the sentences, making whatever changes are necessary to correct them.

1. I want to explain the differences between my country and the United
States, which is a group of large islands in the western Pacific.

2. Having been sent to the wrong address, I got the letter several days late.

3. The noisy children awakened the old man playing ball in the front yard.

4. When I got to the table, I was so hungry that I ate three platefuls of food
along with my two brothers.

5. Having spent all my money, there was nothing to do but write my parents for more.

6. Another use of boats is for transportation, which can be used for carrying goods and products.

7. I found the letter you left me hanging on the door.

8. My father told me to throw the horses over the fence some hay.

EDITING

From the *Houston News:*

     Yesterday a Houston man who is Mr. Ricardo Silberman, was between fifty

two passengers were released from a jet of the Caribbean Airways after held

at gunpoint during three days for hijackers. Mr. Silberman told to the *News*

this story:

     "Our plane hijacked shortly after took off from the Houston's Interconti-

nental Airport, and the two hijackers, one of them threatened pilot while

another covering the cabin, had demanded to be taken to an unknown

country of Central America. On the contrary, our pilot circled back and landed again in Intercontinental, he hoped hijackers will not dare shooting

him lest the plane crashes. . . ."

PLANNING AND WRITING

Using the list you made for Warmup I, plan and write a news story that is two or three paragraphs long. Include as much specific detail as possible, using information that you think your classmates would enjoy reading. Remember to put the most important information first, the least important last. For this style of writing, you do not need a conclusion.

If time allows, your teacher might read some of your articles to the class next time you meet.

❧ Unit 32 ❧

Revising III

Writing forms: Review of forms used in Units 21–31
Writing skills: Polishing sentence structure; revising; rewriting

INTRODUCTION: WHAT'S IMPEDING YOUR PROGRESS?

You have now completed over half the work in this book, and you have made a great deal of progress. Your papers are longer, better organized, and more fully developed than they were at the beginning of the course. You have learned to identify your most frequent errors and to correct most of them with the aid of your teacher's correction symbols. You are doing so well, in fact, that you are ready to move up to a more sophisticated level of correcting beyond the more obvious kinds of errors you have been trying to avoid. In this unit you will focus on revising sentences to make them more natural and mature in style, and you will apply this skill by rewriting one of the compositions you wrote for the past eleven units.

WARMUP: POLISHING SENTENCE STRUCTURE

There is more to good writing than avoiding actual mistakes, which is why native speakers of English sometimes write perfectly "grammatical" papers that may still be very poor. In your own case, some of your sentences that are technically correct may still sound unnatural or immature by the standards of good academic writing. If you are satisfied simply to be correct, you will make very limited progress beyond this point. But if you really want to improve your writing, you will have to become aware of the sentence structures you are using, and you will have to make a conscious effort to change them.

Three categories of problems in sentence structure at this level are described here, with examples and suggested improvements.

Problem One:

Examples of unnecessary repetition.
1. My country is an industrialized country. The United States is an industrialized country too.

147

2. This process is carried out in a laboratory, and the people who carry out the process have to have a lot of skill in the process, and they also need special equipment there in the laboratory to use when they carry out the process.

Solution: Combine the sentences or clauses* in a way that reduces the repetition.

Examples, Improved:

1. Both my country and the United States are industrialized.
2. This process is carried out by skilled technicians in a specially equipped laboratory.

Problem Two:

Examples of overuse of simple subject–verb–object clauses, either in separate short sentences or strung together with the coordinating conjunctions *and, but,* or *so.* This style is considered immature in academic writing.

1. The American government wanted to protect some natural spots, and these natural spots were particularly beautiful, so they set them apart and now visitors can enjoy them.
2. I have developed a feeling of independence over the past five years. I am proud of it. But I no longer feel very close to my family. I miss that feeling.

Solution: Cut down on the number of independent clauses by converting some of them into dependent clauses, phrases,† or single-word modifiers. This process is called *subordination* and is a mark of mature, sophisticated writing in English.

Examples, Improved:

1. Wanting to protect particularly beautiful natural spots, the American government set them apart so that visitors could enjoy them.
2. While I am proud of the independence I have developed over the past five years, I miss the feeling of closeness I used to have for my family.

Problem Three:

Examples of non-native, unnatural sentence structure that results from translating. People who do this may be avoiding unfamiliar or difficult English structures, particularly modals and the passive voice.

1. It is better that you not marry this woman.
2. Someone removes the embryo from the laboratory dish and implants it in the wall of the mother's uterus.

Solution: Master the unfamiliar or difficult structures. Otherwise your writing will never be quite natural.

Examples, Improved:

1. You should not marry this woman.
2. The embryo is removed from the laboratory dish and is implanted in the wall of the mother's uterus.

---

*A *clause* is a group of words with a subject and a verb. A sentence may be composed of one or more clauses. An *independent clause* can stand alone as a complete sentence (*He became a wealthy man*). A *dependent clause* is not a complete sentence, though it too contains a subject and a verb.
                 independent clause   dependent clause
Example: *He became a wealthy man   when oil was struck on his land.*

†A *phrase* is a group of words that function together as a part of a sentence. A phrase, unlike a clause, does not have a subject–verb combination. Examples of phrases: *The man   in the classy Italian sports car   is going to win   the race.*

INSTRUCTIONS:
The following sentences are grouped according to the categories of problems just enumerated. Revise the sentences as well as you can; then check your answers.

PROBLEM ONE: REPETITION

1. I love my family very much, and they love me in return.

2. If you want to be here three months, you need to bring your winter clothes because of the cold in this place. In this place the temperature in the winter season is lower than 32° F; that's why I told you that it's necessary that you bring your winter clothes.

3. I'm driving a very large car now, but I'm looking for a smaller car, because smaller cars are cheaper to run.

4. It was impossible for me to be there. If I hadn't taken the GRE exam, I would have gone there.

5. I would have seen my parents, I'd have kissed them, and I'd have embraced them.

PROBLEM TWO: IMMATURE STYLE

6. Unfortunately, the test was very difficult and I didn't pass it.

7. I was a freshman at the university in my hometown. I studied engineering.

8. I always hoped I could be a university student. After eight years of hoping, my dream came true.

9. I would have become a full-time housewife. I think I would have cleaned my house every day. I would have cooked nice meals. I would have taken my dog out for a walk every morning. I would have spoiled my dog more.

10. I would have kissed my dad. I would have told him, "Dad, you're a great man, a great father."

11. At that time my mother worked in the fields with my father. They went out before sunrise and came back after sunset.

12. In 1975 I got married. After that I moved to Washington. I lived there for about four years. I moved from Washington to Lansing in 1979.

PROBLEM THREE: UNNATURAL STYLE

13. It's possible that our government will change this policy soon.

14. More and more cars crowd city streets every day.

15. It was necessary that I complete my education before getting married.

Check your answers. If you did well, you should be able to do the same kind of revising on your own compositions. You will have an opportunity to try this in the "Planning and Writing" section.

PLANNING AND WRITING

Reread your compositions from Units 21–31. Look for sentence structure problems from the three categories presented in the warmup in this unit. Review the personal checklist on which you are recording your mistakes and problems and bring it up to date. You should be able to tell from the pattern of mistakes whether you are making progress, eliminating earlier errors, and attempting new constructions.

Choose one of the compositions that you feel needs rewriting and look it over carefully, taking notes on improvements that you think you can make. Read the checklist on page 289 for additional suggestions.

When you are satisfied that you have thought carefully about the content, theme, and organization, make a simple outline before beginning to write. Then rewrite the composition; reuse the checklist; and turn in the outline, the new draft of the composition, and the folder containing your other compositions.

Unit 33

Whatever Happened to the Twentieth Century?

Writing form: Speculation
Writing skill: Using suffixes to change word forms

INTRODUCTION

It is the year 2995. A group of historians, archaeologists, and anthropologists are attending a symposium on a key period of world history: the long-past twentieth century. At the moment the scholars are attempting in a panel discussion to determine whether that century's contributions to humankind brought more good or more ill. Those arguing "for" are mentioning technological achievements, agricultural advances, and organizations devoted to world peace. Those on the opposing side are reminding the others of warfare, genocide, and famine.

If you were on this panel looking back on our century, which side would you take? How do you think the twentieth century will be remembered by future historians, relative to other centuries—a time of peace, war, progress, tragedy, plenty, want, enlightenment, stupidity? A time about which people in the distant future might sigh and say, "I wish I could have lived then," or not?

WARMUP I: SPECULATION

Speculation is the act of predicting that events going on now will produce particular results in the future. Because no one really knows what the future will bring, speculation is uncertain at best, and even the language forms we use to express it reflect this uncertainty: instead of saying "will," we add "if" or "unless"; we use modals, such as "may," "should," "might"; we say "probably" and "it seems likely that." Besides requiring special grammar and vocabulary, speculation requires the same logic that we apply to any expression of cause and effect (see guidelines in Unit 28).

Today's composition is speculative in nature. You may choose either of the following related broad topics, and you will then narrow your choice into some more specific area.

1. Imagine that you are an anthropologist or historian in the year 2995. You have been asked to write an article demonstrating that the contributions of the twentieth century to humankind were either mostly positive or mostly negative (choose one of these positions).
2. Given the state of affairs at the present, what do you think the world will be like one hundred years from now?

INSTRUCTIONS

1. Choose one of the preceding topics.
2. Break into two discussion groups on the basis of topic. Use ten or fifteen minutes to generate as many ideas and as much information as you can on your group's topic, considering the following areas and discussing possible future effects of current conditions and events for each one. Take notes to refer to when you write your composition. You will narrow your topic to a speculation on *one* of these areas for your paper.

your country's government		other countries' governments
the United Nations	population	agriculture and food
war religion	economics	family energy
art transportation	communications	other areas

WARMUP II: USING SUFFIXES TO CHANGE WORD FORMS

In order to have the broad vocabulary you need as a writer, you must know how a word changes to form a noun, a verb, an adjective, an adverb. This knowledge is important because a particular sentence structure requires a particular form of the word.

Most words have several different forms, though not all words occur in all four of the forms previously mentioned. The most common way a word changes forms is by changing suffixes. In addition, many words change internally or in intonation from one form to another. You can expand your vocabulary greatly simply by learning the different forms of the words you already know and by making a point of learning all the forms of new words. Your dictionary is a ready reference for these forms.

INSTRUCTIONS:

In the following pairs of sentences, change the forms of the underlined words in each first sentence to different forms of the same words for use in each second sentence. A list of some common suffixes for each form follows the sentences. When in doubt, use your dictionary to determine which suffixes you need for this exercise.

1. The world atmosphere during the 1980s was extremely tense.

   _____ _____ characterized the world at-

   mosphere during the 1980s.

2. During the twentieth century the <u>economy</u> <u>grew</u> and <u>failed</u> by turns.

   The twentieth century saw repeated _____

   _____ and _____ .

3. What people <u>knew</u> about <u>science</u> increased greatly.

   People's _____ _____ increased greatly.

4. Heart <u>surgery</u> <u>advanced</u> <u>technically</u>.

   Heart _____ made great _____ in

   _____ .

5. Astronauts <u>succeeded</u> in <u>flying</u> to the moon several times.

   Astronauts made several _____ _____ to

   the moon.

6. The superpowers <u>built up</u> enormous <u>arms</u> stockpiles.

   The superpowers engaged in enormous _____

   _____ .

7. Many people went <u>hungry</u> because of poor <u>nutrition</u>.

   Many people suffered from _____ because they couldn't

   obtain _____ food.

8. In some countries the government <u>censored</u> the <u>press</u> from time to time.

   In some countries _____ _____ occurred

   from time to time.

9. Periodic <u>invasions</u> were made during border disputes.

   _____ , nations _____ their neighbors dur-

   ing border disputes.

10. In some societies parents didn't <u>bring up</u> their children very <u>attentively</u>.

    In some societies parents didn't pay much _____ to their

    children's _____ .

Suffixes and Word Forms, with Examples

1. ***Some common noun suffixes***
   State, condition, or quality

nation, tension	aptitude
contentment	jealousy, urgency
quietness	independence, endurance
hardship	average
growth	ministry, mockery
brotherhood	tenure, architecture
realty, reality	

   Belief or condition
   monotheism
   Act or condition

acting	referral

   Person, object or agent

teacher, doctor, liar, engineer, waitress	
specialist	layman
German, Italian, librarian	referent, defendant
Senate	

2. ***Some of the most common adjective suffixes***

jealous, furious	stellar
bountiful	wooden
penniless	picturesque
stretchy	stylish
pensive	economic, realistic, magical
friendly	backward
lenient, reliant	hostile
ornate	sensory, predatory
outgoing	defeated
likable, responsible	venal, partial
manlike	coronary, ornery

3. ***Some of the most common verb suffixes***

generalize, generalise	lengthen
defy, deify	dominate

   Two common verb prefixes

belittle	enlighten

4. The only common adverb ending is -ly, which is also an adjective suffix, but not on the same words.

5. There are other ways of changing the form of a word. Some nouns and verbs use the same spelling but different intonation:

Noun	Verb
cónflict	conflict'
rébel	rebel'

Other words make interior changes instead of or in addition to adding suffixes. These changes are not easy to predict and have to be learned as you encounter them. Still other words change even more and are hardly recognizable as related forms.

Grammar and Vocabulary Note

As you write today's composition, keep in mind that speculation is by its nature uncertain. You will not be able to write a speculative paper effectively or fluently without some mastery of the several forms and meanings of modal auxiliary verbs. Since these verbs are among the last major grammatical points to be mastered anyway, it might be helpful for you to review them in a reliable grammar text. See the list of references at the end of this book for suggestions. Conditional forms and meanings, though somewhat easier to master, might also be a source of problems in such a composition unless you are fairly confident of your ability to use them.

PLANNING AND WRITING

Before you can begin writing today's composition, you must have a statement of thesis based on your topic. If you chose topic 1, your thesis will be either that the twentieth century's contributions to human history in the area of (transportation, communications, or whatever area you chose) were mainly good or that they were mainly bad. If you chose topic 2, what controlling idea will determine all the information and detail in your composition? Do you think the world will become a planet of plenty in terms of agriculture and food? Will it likely be destroyed by war or become more peaceful? Will overpopulation become its most serious problem?

To organize your composition, choose three aspects of the general area you chose from Warmup I. Bear in mind that these three aspects and all the supporting facts and reasons you include *must* contribute to your thesis. Another method of organization would be to choose one of the cause-and-effect organizational schemes suggested in Warmup II of Unit 28.

❧ Unit 34 ❧

Don't Count Your Chickens Before They Hatch

Writing forms: Explanation; illustration
Writing skills: Using a thesaurus and a dictionary

INTRODUCTION

The following sample composition explains and illustrates a well-known English proverb. What are some proverbs from your language? Be thinking of one that you could illustrate for today's writing assignment.

Every native English speaker could tell you that the proverb "Don't count your chickens before they hatch" means "You can't be sure of anything that hasn't happened yet." But although I grew up hearing my mother quote this wise old saying, I never really experienced what it meant until my senior year in high school.

At that time I was the school's champion long-distance runner. Every day when classes were over, I persuaded my friends to run with me for miles through the countryside, and I never seemed to tire. At competitions with other schools, no one could come close to me, and I carried off all the prizes. My bedroom began to resemble a sports shop, with ribbons and medals covering the walls and trophies sitting in every available space.

There was only one more competition to win, and it was against an equally well-known distance runner from a neighboring state. This time the prize was an athletic scholarship to a famous university that I had been hoping to attend. I was so sure of winning that I wrote all my relatives and told them where I would be studying in the fall. I spent hours daydreaming and talking about my brilliant future, which would take me undefeated to the Olympics and maybe even to Hollywood. At such moments my mother would only smile wisely and caution, "You'd better not count your chickens before they hatch, son." Then on the day of the race, sure enough, the winner was—not me, not my rival, but one of my friends who had been training with me every day! I hated to admit that my mother had been right. How embarrassing it was to have to write my relatives and tell them about the change in my "plans."

157

WARMUP I: PROVERBS

INSTRUCTIONS

1. In class discussion, see if you can guess and explain what some of these English proverbs mean:

Rome was not built in a day.
You can lead a horse to water, but you can't make him drink.
Let sleeping dogs lie.
Birds of a feather flock together.
One man's meat is another man's poison.
Don't look a gift horse in the mouth.
You can catch more flies with honey than with vinegar.

2. What are some well-known proverbs in your culture? What do they mean? Explain them to your classmates.
3. Choose a proverb that you can explain and illustrate in today's composition. Write your choice here:

WARMUP II: EXPANDING YOUR VOCABULARY

What would you do if you needed a very specific word but only knew a general one? In this case a practiced writer would turn to a reference book called a *thesaurus,* which lists words in groups related to general concepts. For example, if you look up the general word *harm,* the thesaurus gives numerous nouns, verbs, adjectives, and adverbs, including phrases, idioms, formal and informal words, and slang, all related to the concept of harm. You could then decide whether the specific word you needed was *damage, ruin, hurt, injure, wrong,* or any of about thirty other related verbs.

You would have to consult your dictionary for definitions, as the purpose of a thesaurus is only to provide the words and phrases, not their meanings. But it is a valuable reference book when you want to avoid repetition, to find an exact word, or to learn vocabulary by studying groups of words related to a single concept. In this exercise you will increase your awareness of the variety of vocabulary related to certain general concepts, and you will use your dictionary to expand your own vocabulary.

INSTRUCTIONS:
Following are eight exercises, each dealing with groups of words based on entries in a thesaurus. Follow the instructions and examples for each exercise. Refer to a large English-to-English dictionary for definitions of words unfamiliar to you.

1. The following words are all related to the verb *break.*

| crack | splinter | crush | fracture | shatter |
| sever | rupture | chip | crumble | smash |

Which of the preceding verbs could be used to describe the "breaking" of each of the following items or materials? (*Example:* a plate: crack, chip, shatter, smash.)

a. a bone
b. a blood vessel
c. glass
d. bread
e. a tin can

2. Match these nouns, all related to *land,* with their definitions.

   1. mainland   **a.** a picture of trees and fields
   2. premises   **b.** a piece of land to plant a crop on
   3. mud   **c.** a piece of land and the buildings on it
   4. lot   **d.** the opposite of an island
   5. field   **e.** what you need to grow plants in
   6. landscape   **f.** what wars are sometimes fought for
   7. territory   **g.** earth after a rain
   8. clay   **h.** the solid surface of the earth
   9. ground   **i.** a piece of land to build a house on
   10. soil   **j.** what you make a flower pot from

3. Divide these verbs, related to *harm,* into those that can describe living beings and those that can describe inanimate objects.

   damage   ruin   hurt   injure   wrong   spoil   wound

living beings	*inanimate objects*
Example: wrong	*Example:* spoil

4. The following nouns are all examples of *coverings.* Tell what sort of thing they might cover. (*Example:* veneer ___furniture___ .)

   hood _____   sheath _____
   crust _____   roof _____
   peel _____

5. All of these adjectives could describe a *thin* person, but some are complimentary, while others are somewhat offensive. Categorize them.

   skinny   slender   scrawny   haggard   willowy   slim

compliments	*insults*
Example: willowy	*Example:* haggard

6. What kind of creature has *nails?* _____
   Claws? _____ *Talons?* _____

7. All of these verbs are related to *possess*.

have   own   contain   keep   belong to

Make a sentence using one of the preceding verbs for each of these subjects/objects.

Example:
house (object): I'd like to *own* a *house* someday.
house (subject): That *house* across the street *belongs to* my cousin.

   a. box (subject)
   b. cat (object)
   c. this old desk (subject)
   d. all his letters (object)

8. All these verbs are related to *depart*. Choose one for each of the following sentences. Be careful of tense and form.

> secede   retire   retreat   set out
> resign   abandon   evacuate   pass away

   a. Unable to fight us any longer, the enemy _____ from the battlefield.
   b. I like to _____ on a trip early in the morning when I'm feeling fresh and rested.
   c. In the U.S. Civil War, the Southern states tried to _____ from the Union.
   d. The frightened young mother _____ her baby on someone's doorstep.
   e. After a long and happy life, the old man at last fell ill and _____ .
   f. When she was seventy, my aunt _____ from her job with the company she had helped to found.
   g. Because of the terrible floods, everyone in our little town had to be _____ .
   h. When I was forty-two, I _____ from my job to accept an offer from a better company.

PLANNING AND WRITING

The proverb you chose in Warmup I, step 3, is the thesis for your composition, which will be devoted to explaining and illustrating it. Follow this organization: Your introductory paragraph should state the proverb and explain it. The remaining paragraph or paragraphs should illustrate the truth of the proverb with an event or situation that could be either true or fictional. End the composition with an appropriate conclusion.

❧ Unit 35 ❧

A Question of Honor

Writing form: Argumentation
Writing skills: Identifying issues and taking stands; writing sound
  arguments

INTRODUCTION

Jack Gray and Steve White, who were good friends, were taking the same course in law school. On the day of the final exam, Jack noticed Steve copying answers onto his paper from some notes he had hidden in his sleeve. Their university, like most in the United States, subscribed to an "honor code" that (1) prohibited students from giving or receiving assistance during examinations, and (2) required students to report anyone seen giving or receiving such assistance. Jack sincerely wished he hadn't seen Steve cheating, but having done so, he felt obliged to turn his friend in, even though he knew it would cost Steve a future in law.

Imagine that this case has been brought to the attention of the university policy-making board, of which you are a member. After giving careful thought to the case and the issues it raises, your job is to write a recommendation that the university retain, modify, or abolish the honor code. Which of these courses of action should you recommend, and why?

WARMUP: IDENTIFYING ISSUES AND TAKING
POSITIONS ON THEM

An *issue* is a point of discussion, debate, or public concern, usually presented in question form. The case of Jack Gray and Steve White suggests several issues. To mention a couple:

Should students cheat on exams?
What constitutes cheating?

INSTRUCTIONS

1. Working together as a class, identify as many other issues as you can from the introductory case. Try to think of at least eight. Have someone write them in question form on the chalkboard.

161

Naturally, everyone has an opinion on issues such as these. Your answer to such a question is called your *position* or *stand* on the issue. In the first sample issue, for instance, your position could be that students should not cheat on exams, that cheating on exams is not wrong, or that cheating on exams may sometimes be justified.

2. Write a one-sentence position answering each of the issue questions from step 1. Your position should reflect your actual beliefs.

EDITING: SOUNDNESS OF ARGUMENT

A good professor is less interested in what position you take than in how clearly you can present your argument and how soundly you can support it. Your support must be logical, relevant, objective, and up-to-date. These principles are often violated by writers who make the common mistakes that are given in the following outline, along with advice for avoiding them.

When writing an argument,

1. Don't oversimplify.	Do explore the complexities of your issue.
2. Don't digress.	Do make sure that every detail or argument contributes directly to supporting your position on the issue.
3. Don't argue in circles. Example: "The honor code prohibits cheating because cheating is wrong."	Do give reasons. Example: Instead of saying that the honor code prohibits cheating because cheating is wrong, explain why and how it is wrong.
4. Don't make assumptions that haven't been established.	Do give the reader all the information that he or she needs to understand your argument.
5. Don't try to *prove* anything by using analogies or proverbs, though you can use them to help *explain* things.	Do rely on reasoning and on factual evidence for proof.
6. Don't jump to extravagant conclusions.	Do draw conclusions that you have supported reasonably.
7. Don't apologize for your paper.	Do assume that your arguments merit consideration if you have reasoned them out and presented them carefully.

INSTRUCTIONS

1. Read the following paragraph carefully. Each passage that is underlined violates an item on the preceding checklist. Determine which item has been violated for each underlined passage.
2. On a separate sheet of paper, rewrite the paragraph, correcting the violations. The result should be a strong, well-written argument.

The following paragraph argues that the honor code should be abolished.

One issue raised by this matter is whether the responsibility for preventing cheating is the student's or the teacher's. Of course this is only my opinion, but it seems likely to me that if we made teachers responsible for controlling cheating, fewer students would cheat than do now under the honor code. In the case in question, Jack had no choice but to turn his friend in because the honor code obligated him to do so. Why didn't the professor stop Steve instead of waiting so that Jack had to report his friend? The teacher has authority over the class, just as parents have authority over their children, and everyone knows that if a child damages something, it is his parents who have to pay for it. Accordingly, Jack and Steve's professor is the one who should be suspended, not Steve.

PLANNING AND WRITING

Reread the second paragraph in the introduction to this unit. Your recommendation will be the thesis of your composition. As your main points, choose two or three issues generated in the Warmup exercise or from among the issues given in the answers to this unit. Choose only issues that are directly relevant to your recommendation. Devote a paragraph to supporting your position on each issue through sound logic and/or factual evidence.

Example: (Each Roman numeral refers to a separate paragraph.)

I. Introduction
   A. Purpose of paper: to determine whether to retain, modify, or abolish honor code.
   B. My recommendation: abolish it.
   C. "An examination of three crucial issues supports my position."
II. Issue 1: Most students refuse to turn each other in.
    Support: Friendships mean more to them than the honor code, and so on.
III. Issue 2: It is wrong for a person's whole future to be ruined just because he or she cheated on one examination or paper.
     Support: Punishment is too severe, and so on.
IV. Issue 3: The teacher, not the student, should be responsible for preventing cheating.
    Support: Making the student responsible creates more problems than it solves, and so on.
V. Conclusion: "In the face of these reasons, I can only conclude that the honor code currently in use at this university is cumbersome and ineffective and should be abolished."

Save your best argument for last, in order to end your paper on a strong note. Assume that your reader is reasonable and convinceable and really wants to do the right thing.

When you finish writing, refer to the checklist in the editing exercise and make sure you haven't violated any of its points. Then check your paper for your most common errors.

❧ Unit 36 ❧

Censorship

Writing form: Argumentation
Writing skills: Exploring both sides of an issue; disposing of the opposition

INTRODUCTION

A student writing a paper on comparative government went to her university library to find information but was told that many of the books and journals she wanted had been removed from the shelves since her country's recent change in government. When she explained that she only wanted them for research on her paper, not because she believed in the ideas they contained, she was told that such ideas were too unhealthy and dangerous for the general public to be exposed to and that she should write her paper on a different topic.

The student went home and told her father what had happened. He listened in silence and then told her a story of his own. That morning a government censor had appeared in the newspaper office where he worked and had announced that from then on, all articles had to be approved by her before they could be printed. All the articles for the next edition were submitted to the censor, who rewrote parts of some of them, rewrote others completely, and rejected still others outright. When some of the journalists objected, the censor explained that some of their sources of information were not objective or reliable, and that in addition, certain information or interpretations were not healthy for the general public to have. While some of the edited information was undoubtedly true, she said it was counterproductive to stir up the people by releasing it to them at a time when their government was working against great odds to restore economic and social stability after a period of unrest.

The student and her father were deeply disturbed because they believed that all people always have a right to any information they want, so that they can make intelligent, informed decisions and so that they can know what is happening.

What are your own views regarding censorship? Do you agree with either of these positions, or is your view somewhere in between? Today, after learning more about effective arguing, you will write a paper taking a stand on this controversial topic.

WARMUP I: EXPLORING BOTH SIDES OF AN ISSUE

One of the assumptions you make when you argue is that your reader does not agree with you; otherwise, why would you be arguing? And if the reader disagrees, then you should also assume that he or she has reasons for doing so. Your own argument will be stronger if you are fully aware of the reasons and facts supporting the opposition. In this exercise you will give equal attention to both extremes of opinion on today's topic.

INSTRUCTIONS

1. Imagine that you are the government censor in the introductory situation. Make a list of answers to the following questions:
    a. Why does censorship occur? What does it aim to accomplish?
    b. Under what circumstances should it take place?
    c. What kinds of material should be censored?
    d. Who should be denied access to censored material? Who should have access to it?
    e. Who should censor this material?
2. Now imagine that you are the student or her father. Write down two or three good reasons against censorship.
3. Now be yourself. If your position on censorship lies somewhere between these two extremes, look at everything you have written for this exercise so far and edit it according to your own beliefs.

WARMUP II: DISPOSING OF THE OPPOSITION

A good argument does more than present the writer's own position. It also shows that the writer is aware of the opposite point of view and has thought carefully about it before taking his or her particular stand. The writer accomplishes this by "disposing of the opposition," which means stating and then disproving the most obvious opposing view(s). Usually this is done toward the beginning of the paper and is done briefly, as the majority of the paper should be devoted to supporting the writer's own view(s). In this exercise you will write a paragraph disposing of the opposition for today's argumentative composition.

INSTRUCTIONS

1. Using the ideas you generated in Warmup I, write down the strongest or most obvious argument *against* your own position on censorship.
2. Write down reasons why this argument is incomplete, incorrect, superficial, unreasonable, contradicted by facts, or otherwise unsubstantiated.
3. Write a paragraph disposing of the opposition. Use this form: First, introduce the opposing argument with an opener like any of these:
    a. Many people believe that censorship is a violation of human rights because . . .
    b. One line of reasoning argues against (or for) censorship on the grounds that . . .
    c. Opponents (or proponents) of censorship argue that . . .
    d. Those who strongly favor (or oppose) censorship often argue that . . .

e. A popular notion among proponents (or opponents) of censorship is that . . .

Continue by giving the argument you wrote down in step 1 of this exercise. Then introduce your own response to this argument in one of the following ways:

a. A closer look at the facts reveals the weakness in this argument.
b. While this view is popular, it is incomplete because . . .
c. The attractiveness of this view often satisfies those who are unwilling to test its reasonableness. In fact, . . .
d. Superficially, this view has undeniable appeal. But when we examine it carefully, we find that . . .

Continue by showing how or why the argument is insubstantial, using what you wrote in step 2 of this exercise.

EDITING

An argument stated without specific support will convince no one of its validity. Generalities have to be supported with specifics. The allegations in the following passage are unacceptable because they are not supported with reasons, examples, or definitions of terms.

> I believe that censorship is necessary under certain circumstances, and that some kinds of material should sometimes be kept from certain people. Only qualified persons should be allowed to censor this material.

Rewrite and expand the passage by identifying "certain circumstances," "some kinds of material," "sometimes," "certain people," and "qualified persons." You may change the content of the passage to agree with your own view regarding censorship. If you wish to use these generalities as your main points, you could even use them as the basis for your whole composition today, developing each main point into a complete paragraph with adequate support.

PLANNING AND WRITING

Write a composition giving your own views on censorship. First write a thesis sentence and then plan your paper according to the following general outline:

   I. Introduction, including thesis statement
  II. Disposal of the opposition (as in Warmup II)
 III. First main point supporting thesis, developed with reasons, definitions, explanation, cause and effect, or facts
 IV. Second main point supporting thesis, developed adequately (see III)
  V. Conclusion

Use your checklists before handing your paper in.

❧ Unit 37 ❧

TV or Not TV

Writing form: Argumentation
Writing skills: Exploring both sides of an issue; being objective; relying on authorities

INTRODUCTION

A skill that is highly valued in American academic programs is the ability to argue a variety of viewpoints on the same topic. You may be required to argue on theses that you oppose or are not even interested in. A common form of examination question is to ask students to present the arguments both for and against a thesis. What the student really believes is of less interest to the professor than whether the student knows the material well and can argue equally objectively for either side. Today you will practice this approach to argumentation by presenting both sides of the issue "Is television a bad influence?"

Now that Linda and Hal's baby was beginning to show an interest in television, they found themselves having their first major disagreement. It was about the TV set. Linda insisted that they get rid of it because TV was a bad influence, and she didn't want their baby growing up around it. Hal responded that it wasn't a bad influence, and besides, she just wanted to get rid of it because *she* didn't enjoy watching it, while *he* enjoyed it very much. They argued in circles for a couple of weeks, getting angrier and angrier, but were unable to reach a solution. Finally they decided they would each write down all the reasons for their opinions, and would then read and think about each other's lists before discussing the matter again. Here are their lists:

Hal's List For TV

TV offers educational programs to all levels of viewer age and interest.

TV commercials keep people informed of products and special sales.

TV news informs people immediately of current events. News specials give people in-depth coverage on the scene.

TV provides the entertainment a serious society needs to lift its spirits.

TV offers company to lonely people, and it helps them keep their minds off their problems.

167

TV serves as an electronic babysitter.

Favorite TV programs can be used to reward a child for good behavior or turned off to punish him or her for bad behavior.

TV exposes a child to a broader reality than her or his daily experience can provide. Thus it expands the child's experience and mind.

Linda's List Against TV

Children watch so much TV that it interferes with their homework and with other healthy activities like sports.

Children who grow up constantly watching TV are less likely to develop their conversational and other social skills.

TV exposes children to violence, abusive language, and casual sex.

TV news is superficial, and people who rely on TV for all their news get a distorted view of the world.

Children who are raised on a steady diet of TV may not be able to distinguish between fantasy and reality. They see people break chairs and bottles over each other's heads and not get hurt. A child in Saudi Arabia was killed when he jumped off a roof in order to fly like his favorite TV character.

People who are influenced by TV commercials may spend beyond their means.

TV commercials are offensive. They often offend the intelligence by assuming that the viewer is stupid; they often reinforce stereotypes about women and ethnic groups; and many of them bring such objectionable subjects as hemorrhoids, sanitary napkins, and toilet bowls into the viewers' living and dining rooms.

WARMUP I: BEING OBJECTIVE

Academic writing usually requires that the writer be objective rather than subjective; in other words, the writer is to present the facts and reasons and let them argue the point, instead of presenting her or his feelings about those facts and reasons. Objective writing is impersonal and unemotional in style.

Linda's and Hal's lists against and for television are objective, but some of their feelings on the subject were wildly subjective and had to be reworded. Here are four examples of their original subjective wordings, a brief explanation of how each violated the rules of objectivity, and an objective rewording of each.

1. *Subjective:* "Children who are raised on a steady diet of TV cannot distinguish between fantasy and reality."
   Problem: Linda's sentence is so general that it means *all* children who watch a lot of TV can *never* distinguish between fantasy and reality. She should instead use qualifying words such as *many, may, often.*
   Objective: "Children who are raised on a steady diet of TV may not be able to distinguish between fantasy and reality."

2. *Subjective:* "The people who make TV commercials want us all to spend more money than we have."
   Problem: Linda cannot prove that these people have evil intentions. She can, however, make an objective statement about results.
   Objective: "People who are influenced by TV commercials may spend beyond their means."

3. *Subjective:* "TV has some fantastic educational shows that everyone who claims to be well educated should watch."
   Problem: Vocabulary such as *should, shouldn't, good, bad, fantastic* makes

value judgments, a violation of objectivity. Hal should describe the facts, not evaluate them.

Objective: "TV offers educational programs to all levels of viewer age and interest."

4. *Subjective:* "I just can't believe these kids of the TV generation. They're like zombies! They can't even carry on a conversation."

Problem: Linda is using language in a way that shows her emotional involvement, making the reader doubt her rationality and her ability to be objective.

Objective: "Children who grow up constantly watching TV are less likely to develop their conversational and other social skills."

In this exercise you will convert some of Linda's and Hal's other subjective statements into objective ones suitable for inclusion in a composition.

INSTRUCTIONS:
The following statements are too subjective for use in today's composition because they violate one or more of the four principles just illustrated. Rewrite them to make them more objective.

1. The programs on TV are really stupid, and children who watch them grow up imitating this standard of stupidity.

2. So-called liberal intellectual types are always badmouthing TV, but here's something they never stop to think about. If enough viewers really objected to what they saw on TV, the networks would respond by giving them what they wanted, so evidently most of the public is satisfied.

3. Watching TV is a passive occupation, not an active one. Watchers just sit and stare. They don't have to move more than lifting their Coke cans or potato chips to their lips. They don't have to think or talk. Their bodies get flabby, their brains turn to mush, and their social skills disappear entirely.

WARMUP II: RELYING ON AUTHORITIES

Who is an authority? How can a writer decide which authors to refer to in order to strengthen an argument? Here are some questions to test authority:

1. Is the author an expert in the area? (Does he or she have pertinent training and experience?)
2. Is the author reliable?
3. Is the author objective? (Or, on the contrary, does he or she have something to gain from the conclusions of the report?)
4. Is the author really in a position to know?

If the answer to all four questions is yes, you can safely assume that quoting from the author's work will strengthen your argument. In this exercise you will apply these principles in determining who is an authority on today's topic and who is not.

INSTRUCTIONS
Rank the following sources of information as follows:

    A. Authoritative
    B. Moderately authoritative
    C. Not authoritative

Be able to defend your choices by referring to the preceding questions.

1. A commercial for the Channel Four News says that it gives the most complete, up-to-date coverage of world and local events.
2. Mark Ransom, newscaster for the local ABC channel, says that Dan Rather of the CBS Nightly News is the finest newscaster on TV.
3. John Brandon, president of a major network, says that TV is a reflection of the viewers' tastes and morality rather than an influence on it. In other words, TV presents violence and sex because that is what the viewers demand. If the viewers stopped watching it, the networks would stop showing it. So the viewers, not the networks, are responsible for what is shown.
4. My grandfather watches TV all the time now that he has retired, and he says that the programming is terrible and that TV is a bad influence on children.
5. The findings of a National Institute of Mental Health ten-year study showed that TV violence leads children who watch it to become more aggressive.
6. A sociologist at a local university studied the influence of TV on family dynamics, and after three years of research, she concluded that TV can actually bring families together and stimulate intellectual and communicative activities if parents regulate the amount of TV their children watch and if the families watch TV together and talk about what they are watching.
7. A junior sociology student at the same university studied her family's TV-watching habits for a week and concluded that TV was a bad influence on them.

8. A murderer in Florida argued in his defense that too much TV watching had "brainwashed" him until he was no longer responsible for his actions.
9. A writer for *TV Guide* magazine said that researchers who concentrate on TV's negative effects are just trying to blame TV unfairly for problems really caused by social ills such as poverty and parental neglect.
10. Author Jerzy Kosinski's novel *Being There* tells the story of a man who grew up using TV as a substitute for family, friends, and education. By the time he was an adult, the world on his TV screen was his standard of reality instead of the outside world.

PLANNING AND WRITING

For today's composition, argue both sides of the issue "Is television a bad influence?" Your paper will be divided into two major parts, and each one will have as its thesis a different answer to the issue. Look at Linda's and Hal's lists and choose two or three of the strongest points from each, or you may use other arguments that you think of yourself. You will develop these main points through reasons, facts, appeal to authorities from Warmup II, explanations, causes and effects—any of the methods of support that you have studied and practiced for argumentation in Units 17, 18, 27, 35, 36, 37.

Be as objective as you can. Your reader shouldn't be able to tell which of the viewpoints reflects your own opinion, and each of your arguments should be so well supported that the reader will have difficulty deciding which side is "right."

  I. Introduction to the whole paper, telling its purpose and both theses.
 II. Thesis 1: "Television is a bad influence."
    A, B, and so on: Support
III. Thesis 2: "Television is not a bad influence."
    A, B, and so on: Support
 IV. Conclusion

Before you hand your paper in, check to make sure you have not violated any principles of argumentation or objectivity, and use your checklists.

❧ Unit 38 ❧

A Speech to the United Nations

Writing form: Persuasion
Writing skills: Arguing subjectively; distinguishing between subjectivity and objectivity

INTRODUCTION

War. Famine. Unemployment. Racial tension. Religious mistrust. Uncertainty. Economic failure. What a legacy we have inherited from the previous generation! This is the world we are expected somehow to improve, to raise our children in, and then to pass along to them in turn. Often it seems the people running the planet have the worst motives and plans, do all the wrong things, are leading us down the path to certain disaster. But you—you know better. Inside yourself, you have always known that there is a better way, if only people can be persuaded to put aside their selfish interests and work together for the good of all. Through some miracle, the leaders of the world have recognized the wisdom of your voice and have given you the opportunity to address the world through the medium of the United Nations. So here you stand today, facing the microphones, looking out over the roomful of anxious faces at the General Assembly as you collect your thoughts. The world is your audience, and somehow you must persuade them that your plan is their—our—only hope. The room quietens. You begin to speak, confidently and urgently.

WARMUP: PERSUASION AND SUBJECTIVITY

Argument, as you have learned in the past several units, is a form of writing in which you give proof or evidence supporting a belief or conclusion. The success of the argument is entirely dependent on your ability to support it through logic and facts. Persuasion is a form of argument and as such should not violate any of the principles of argumentation. The distinctive feature of persuasion is that it is *subjective,* whereas other forms of argument are *objective*.

The essence of subjectivity is appeal to emotion, whereas objectivity is characterized by its absence of such an appeal. A subjective argument makes your reader *want* to agree with you. It persuades him. Although most academic writing is required to be objective, today's subjective assignment, a speech to the United Nations, will help you become aware of the distinctions between the two approaches by focusing your attention on subjectivity.

The following are some methods of subjective argument:

1. Address the reader directly: *Your life is in these people's hands.*
2. Identify with the reader so that the reader will identify with you: *This is the world that you and I are raising our children in.*
3. Appeal to specific emotions in the reader: *We are completely alone in this nuclear nightmare. There is no one to call out to. There is no one to help us.*
4. Use specific details, which evoke a stronger emotional response in the reader than generalizations: *After the radiation dies down, the rats will invade the ruins of your home, fighting and breeding and dying and rotting in what used to be your fragrant kitchen and in the nursery where your baby once lay.*
5. Use vocabulary that evaluates and to which people react emotionally: *These narrow-minded tyrants have deceived us long enough.*
6. Ask your reader questions to involve him or her emotionally: *What will you tell your children when they ask you why you have to go off and fight someone else's war?*
7. Tell your reader that he or she agrees with you: *Fortunately, you and I can see through their lies.*
8. Praise the reader: *You are too intelligent to be deceived.*

INSTRUCTIONS

1. Read the sample composition at the end of this unit.
2. In it, identify as many of the previously listed methods of subjectivity as you can.

EDITING

Correct the marked errors in the following passage on today's topic.

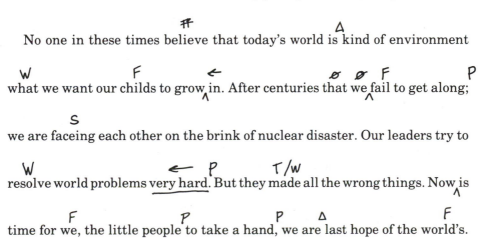

No one in these times believe that today's world is kind of environment

what we want our childs to grow in. After centuries that we fail to get along;

we are faceing each other on the brink of nuclear disaster. Our leaders try to

resolve world problems very hard. But they made all the wrong things. Now is

time for we, the little people to take a hand, we are last hope of the world's.

As we all know our problem most big is not that no one has a solution but

everyone do and this solutions are all conflicting generaly benefiting only the

ones which think of them. That is why other people can not agrees with they.

That we need is a generation of people enough far-sighted to give up his own

selfish imediate ends for ends they will benefit all mankind. I believe that we

are that generation.

PLANNING AND WRITING

Your assignment today is to write a speech to the United Nations suggesting a way or ways to improve the world situation. Think carefully about what you want to say, and then fill in this outline:

I. In your first paragraph, persuade the listeners that some current world situation is unacceptable. Be very specific.
II. In your second paragraph, persuade your listeners that your alternative or alternatives would improve that situation.
III. In your last paragraph, persuade your listeners that if your suggestion is not followed, the situation will worsen.

Use your checklists before handing your paper in.

A Speech to the United Nations

My friends, I thank you for inviting me here today. We are gathered here because we are all extremely worried about the state of our world, and we are looking for help. Our problems seem insurmountable. Each country seeks only its own good and mistrusts its neighbors. Our leaders serve only the limited interests of their parties, their religions, their ethnic groups, or their countries. Millions are being spent on military might while the world goes hungry and unschooled.

Last night my precious little daughter asked me what would happen to our family when the bomb hit.

I said, "What bomb, little one?"

She said, "You know, the nuclear bomb."

I did not know what to say. Tell me, what would you have said? What do bombs have to do with childhood, which should be a time of growing and sharing and innocence? Instead, we see our children growing up in an atmosphere of fear and hate. Who can we turn to? We have no reason to turn to our leaders, because so far their policies and actions have not improved the world at all, and in many cases have only made it worse. The answer, my friends, lies within us. Only we can solve our problems.

What we must do is change our citizenship. We can no longer afford to attach our loyalties to individual countries. We are citizens of the world, and our first loyalty must be to the world. The reason for this is that what affects one part of the world affects the rest as well. We each have something to offer the global community, which cannot afford to ignore any of its members' gifts or needs. How shall we do this? First, by replacing our leaders with people who recognize that our survival is totally dependent on our working together for the good of all, and who will work toward that end. Second, we must ban all weapons as threats to our goals of cooperation and peace. The money now being spent on arms must be invested in education and agriculture. We must encourage multilingualism and travel as our passports to understanding.

This is a formidable task. Some will say it is impossible. But consider the alternative. Our nuclear capabilities will increase as technology advances and ever more money is spent building up military preparedness. Future leaders will react to the global atmosphere of selfishness and paranoia and will become even more selfish and paranoid. Our children will grow up in this environment and cannot help but be affected by it. And finally, our children will be the leaders of tomorrow, and having grown up in such a world, they will be even more corrupt, more limited, more suspicious and fearful. The finger that pushes the button detonating the final bomb may be that of your child or mine. That is why we cannot wait.

❧ Unit 39 ❧

Revising IV

Writing forms: Review of forms used in Units 21–38
Writing skills: Revising; rewriting

INTRODUCTION

This unit offers you the opportunity to reread your previous writing, to gain an overview of your strengths and weaknesses, and to do what every good writer must do: revise and rewrite.

PLANNING AND WRITING

Reread the compositions in your folder that you have not previously reread and bring your personal checklist up to date.

Choose one of your old compositions that you feel needs to be rewritten and look it over carefully, taking notes on improvements that you think you can make. Read the checklist on page 289 for additional suggestions.

When you are satisfied that you have thought carefully about the content, theme, and organization, make a simple outline before you begin to rewrite. Then rewrite the composition, reuse the checklist, and finally turn in the outline, the new draft of your composition, and your folder.

❧ Unit 40 ❧

Evaluation III

Writing form: Any of those previously introduced
Writing skill: Writing under pressure for a grade

INTRODUCTION

In this unit you will write on one of three topics your teacher suggests. You will not have time in advance to prepare for the topic, and you will not be able to use a dictionary or other aids.

The purpose of this exercise is to help you write under the kind of pressure you may experience in your academic coursework. It will also give your teacher an opportunity, under conditions that are equal for all the students, to evaluate how well you can communicate in English; organize a new topic; and select and present facts, events, and ideas.

Your teacher will use the guide included in Appendix II to evaluate your work. Before you begin to write, look again at this appendix, particularly at the description and the sample of the writing level that you hope to reach on this evaluation.

WRITING UNDER PRESSURE FOR A GRADE

INSTRUCTIONS:
Write as much as you can as well as you can in 30 minutes. Choose only *one* of the topics your teacher gives you. Read your composition over completely and correct any obvious mistakes or omissions before turning it in.

❧ ANSWERS TO ❧ EXERCISES IN PART II*

Unit 21

Editing Exercise

Dear Mama and Papa,

I'm sorry that I haven't written for a couple of weeks, but I've been struggling with something very important, and I didn't know how to approach you about it. You know that I spent the spring holidays with Gerardo in Boston. While I was there, he introduced me to a very attractive, personable young woman whom I liked very much. The night before I left, he told me some wonderful news: they are in love with each other and would like to get married. But while Gerardo knows how happy you must be to hear that news, he is reluctant to tell you himself because he is afraid you might worry about a couple of things. That's why he asked me to write you first and explain the situation to you.

Unit 22

Warmup I: A Sample List of Adaptations

understanding a foreign language	following different meal schedules
determining hours stores are open	eating new foods
understanding drinking customs	using different table manners
finding out where things are	bargaining when shopping
meeting people	using public transportation
using manners expected of guests	obeying traffic laws
adjusting to different weather	using different restroom facilities
making change in foreign currency	using different laundry facilities
locating stores	making conversation in a foreign language
using different kitchen facilities	using a map
exchanging money	using different clothing measurements
making local telephone calls	using different methods of payment
using the postal system	being "on time"
reading a menu	communicating needs to salesclerks
ordering in a restaurant	finding entertainment
finding and making new friends	coping with emergencies
wearing appropriate clothes	pronouncing a foreign language

*Answers not included in this section may be found in the Instructor's Manual.

Editing Exercise

Of course you must adapt to our customs concerning being a guest, because all my relatives and friends will expect you to visit them. (Omit the next sentence.) There is not too much difference between the behavior of a guest in your country and in mine, but let me give you some advice that will help you enjoy your stay. First, always take your hostess a gift: candy, flowers, and wine are the most appropriate presents. Second, never insist on helping in the kitchen as you do in your country; your hostess would be offended. Besides this, just relax and do whatever you feel like doing, and I'm sure you'll have a good time.

Unit 23

Warmup II: A Sample List of Bases of Comparison

degree of industrialization   national character   population   form of government
climate   economic base   history   educational system   religion
architecture   calendar system   marriage customs   crime   natural resources

Editing Exercise

Where the national character is concerned, Germany and the United States are alike in some respects. Both Germans and their American counterparts value hard work and the monetary rewards it brings. Another similarity is that Germans, like Americans, are stereotyped as being rather distant and cool, but in reality the people in both countries are generally friendly and helpful, even to strangers. But speaking as a German in the United States, I have to say that the differences between the two nationalities are more marked than the similarities. One of the most notable differences is that Germans are always concerned with doing things in the best way, and they like to advise each other when they know a better way to do something. Americans, in contrast, have such a strong sense of individuality that they may become angry if someone offers advice they have not asked for.

Unit 24

Editing Exercise

One American woman in about 500 is unable to bear children normally because a malformation of her oviducts prevents her ova, or eggs, from contacting her partner's sperm and becoming fertilized. Current medical technology provides hope for these would-be mothers through a process called *in vitro fertilization*, in which fertilization takes place in a medical laboratory dish, and the resulting embryo is implanted in the mother's uterus for the duration of a hopefully normal pregnancy.

The first part of the process involves obtaining a healthy ovum from the woman. Special surgical techniques and an instrument called a laparoscope are employed to remove the egg. Timing is very important, because the egg has to be obtained at the moment when it is ready for fertilization. It must then be maintained in a special solution that permits it to retain its potency until fertilization takes place.

2a. The sentence marked "omit" is irrelevant to the description of the process. It thus violates point 4 in the guidelines in Warmup III.

2b. "Add" means that the writer should not say timing is important unless he or she is prepared to explain why. This sentence violates point 1 in the guidelines in Warmup III.

2c. "¶" means that a new paragraph should begin here because this sentence introduces a new idea. See point 3 in the guidelines in Warmup III.

2d. "No ¶" means that this is the wrong place to begin a new paragraph. This information (all of which concerns the first step of the process) should be in the same paragraph as the previous sentence, which introduces the step. See point 3 in the guidelines in Warmup III.

Unit 26

Editing Exercise
In the past five years I have gone through radical changes in my thinking and behavior. For one thing, I have become very independent and take pride in my ability to manage on my own. I have my own apartment and car and support myself with a part-time job. On the other hand, I've lost the feeling of closeness I used to have with my family. Now I find I have more in common with my friends here than with my own brother at home. This makes me feel lonely in spite of my accomplishments.

Unit 27

Editing Exercise
There are important economic reasons why young people should not be allowed to marry until they are eighteen years old. Most people do not finish high school before they are eighteen, and they need to be as free as possible from pressures and demands that would interfere with their studies before finishing this basic level of their education. Once they graduate, they are in a better position to find a job that pays well enough to support a family. If they get married before graduating, they can be forced by financial pressures to drop out of school and look for work, and it is almost impossible for a high-school dropout to find a good job.

Unit 28

Editing Exercise
The overwhelming popularity of America's national parks has led to numerous unexpected results. Wanting to preserve and protect particularly beautiful natural spots, the government set them apart so that visitors could enjoy them in a carefully controlled environment. But so many people have flocked to these famous areas in annually-increasing numbers that the parks have become victims of their own success. Now shelters, souvenir shops, lodges, restaurants, laundromats, and post offices have been constructed in the parks to provide for the visitors' needs. Reservations are necessary at many campgrounds in summer because of the record numbers of campers. And long lines of sightseers cause massive traffic jams along the narrow park roads as they come from all over the world to enjoy the spectacular beauty of the Grand Canyon, Yellowstone, and Yosemite.

Unit 29

Editing Exercise
For me, learning English was like growing from a baby into an adult. When I first arrived in the United States, I knew no English at all. I got an apartment with two American students who tried to talk with me, but I couldn't. I joined them at parties, but

everyone always made me feel like a baby. Because I could not talk, they ignored me or talked about me with each other. In almost all cases people didn't treat me like an adult because I couldn't communicate at their level. This really affected me very much. Only in my English class, where everyone had the same ability as I, did I feel like an adult.

After I had lived here a while, I found the more ability I developed, the better I could communicate. I could talk, but because my English was still poor, other people thought my ideas must be no better than a child's, so they treated me like one. Gradually my proficiency in English has grown, and now I can express myself better. When I talk to people they realize that I am a real person with interesting ideas and experiences. Now I feel as if I have grown up at last.

Unit 31

Editing Exercise

Yesterday a Houston man, Mr. Ricardo Silberman, was among fifty-two passengers released from a Caribbean Airways jet after being held at gunpoint for three days by hijackers. Mr. Silberman told this story to the *News:*

"Our plane was hijacked shortly after takeoff from Houston's Intercontinental Airport, and the two hijackers, one of whom threatened the pilot while the other covered the cabin, demanded to be taken to an undisclosed Central American country. Instead, our pilot circled back and landed again at Intercontinental, hoping the hijackers would not dare shoot him lest the plane crash. . . ."

Unit 32

Warmup: Polishing Sentence Structure (suggested answers)

1. My family and I love each other very much.

2. If you want to be here three months, you should bring your winter clothes because the temperature in winter is lower than 32° F.

3. I'm driving a very large car now, but I'm looking for a smaller one that's cheaper to run.

4. I couldn't be there because I was taking the GRE exam.

5. I would have seen my parents, kissing and embracing them.

6. Unfortunately, the test was so difficult that I didn't pass it.
Unfortunately, the test was too difficult for me to pass.

7. I was a freshman engineering student at my hometown university.

8. After eight years of hoping to attend the university, I realized my dream.

9. I would have become a full-time housewife, cleaning my house every day, cooking nice meals, taking my dog out for a walk every morning, and spoiling him more.

10. I would have kissed my dad, telling him, "Dad, you're a great man and father."

11. At that time my mother worked in the fields with my father from sunrise to sunset.

12. In 1975 I got married and moved to Washington, where I lived for about four years until I moved to Lansing in 1979.

13. Our government may change this policy soon.

14. City streets become more crowded every day.

15. I had to complete my education before getting married.

Unit 35

Warmup: A Sample List of Issues
Should students cheat on exams?

Should students turn in friends who cheat?

Should students turn in anyone?

Is it fair to require students to turn each other in?

Is cheating sometimes justified?

Who is responsible for preventing cheating, the student or the teacher?

Is an honor code a good idea? If so, how should it work?

What constitutes cheating?

Is it right for a person's whole future to be ruined because he or she cheated?

Do examinations encourage cheating?

Editing Exercise
The first underlined passage violates point 7.

The second underlined passage violates point 2. It is not related to the issue under consideration in this paragraph.

The third underlined passage violates point 4. It has not been established whether the professor saw Steve cheating.

The fourth underlined passage violates point 5. The similarities between parents and teachers do not extend to include the comparison stated in this statement.

The fifth underlined passage violates point 6. It is an extravagant conclusion.

Unit 38

Editing Exercise
No one in these times believes that today's world is the kind of environment in which we want our children to grow up. After centuries of failing to get along, we are facing each other on the brink of nuclear disaster. Our leaders try very hard to solve world problems, but they do all the wrong things. Now it is time for us, the little people, to take a hand. We are the last hope of the world.

As we all know, our biggest problem is not that no one has a solution, but that everyone does, and these solutions are all conflicting, generally benefiting only the ones who think of them. That is why other people cannot agree with them. What we need is a generation of people far-sighted enough to give up their own selfish, immediate ends for ends that will benefit all mankind. I believe that we are that generation.

❧ PART ❧
III

Introduction

Whereas Parts I and II teach the basic forms and skills of writing compositions, Part III requires students to apply these principles in presenting factual information on job and graduate school applications, in lecture notes, on examinations, and in reports and research papers. Because the skills of choosing and following a developmental form, organizing, outlining, and paragraphing are presupposed, Part II (if not Part I as well) is a prerequisite to Part III. Students should not attempt the more sophisticated level of material in this section of the book unless they are capable of self-correcting most major errors in grammar and sentence structure and can express the same ideas and information in a variety of ways.

As in the previous two sections, the units in Part III can be grouped on the basis of related skills or forms: specifically, Units 41–42 deal with the differences between formal and informal English; 43–44 use biography as a context for selecting, summarizing, and presenting factual information; 45–46 provide guidelines for taking lecture notes and examinations; 47–49 lead the students through a progression of skills (summarizing, paraphrasing, and synthesizing information) preparatory to Units 51–58, which focus on the entire research procedure, including selecting an appropriate topic from the student's own field of study, finding and using source material, taking and utilizing notes, citing references, developing an outline, and writing a paper.

Most of these units cannot be completed within a fifty-minute class session. Each could be presented over two sessions, or some of the material could be assigned as homework. If time does not permit covering all the units, the teacher should take into account the particular needs of the class. Unit 41, for example, addresses the exclusive needs of students who intend to work in the United States, whereas Unit 42 deals specifically with graduate school admissions. The other units have direct applications to all academic work but can be telescoped into the groups just mentioned so that all the exercises in a group could be covered but only one writing assignment given. Teachers who wish to explain the term paper without requiring their students to write one should cover Units 51–54, "Understanding the Term Paper"; Units 55–58 apply this information in actually producing a research paper.

As in Parts I and II, the warmup and editing exercises serve to prepare students for both the content and the skills required in the writing assignments. Samples are included as needed. Although the answers to some exercises are located at the end of this section, answers apt to require explanation are included in the Teacher's Manual. Answers are not provided for Units 48 and 49 because of the multitude of correct possibilities; in these cases the teacher should check students' papers and give appropriate feedback.

❧ Unit 41 ❧

Applying for a Job

Writing forms: Résumé; cover letter to accompany a job application
Writing skills: Using formal and informal English

INTRODUCTION

3/29/84

Dear Les,

Just a note to say thanks for letting me know about the chance for a job with your company. I wrote to Owens, the man you told me about, & said I was interested, & he gave me the name of the dept. mgr. I needed to send my application to. (Man named Graves—know him?) I tried phoning but he wasn't in, so I sent my résumé with a routine cover letter—mentioned your name, gave a lot of background on my education & experience, & ended up asking a few questions, etc. Think I'll get it? Hope so—from what you've told me, I know I'd really enjoy working there. And thanks for putting in a word for me.

Best wishes,

JoAnne

This is obviously an informal letter from one friend to another. In what ways would it be different if it were a formal business letter between two people who did not know each other well? In this unit you will learn what vocabulary, grammar, and sentence structure are appropriate for formal English, and you will use them in writing a formal cover letter to a company you would like to work for. You will also learn to write a résumé suitable for presentation to prospective American employers.

WARMUP: USING FORMAL ENGLISH

Standard English can be divided roughly into three categories: informal English, which is generally spoken; formal English, which is generally written and is used in business, public, academic, and other "official" functions; and "general" English, which is neither distinctly formal nor informal, and which makes up the bulk of English vocabulary and sentence structure. Because formal English is required in business letters, statements of purpose on graduate school applications, and most academic work, students need to know how to write formally when the occasion requires. Some conventions of formal English follow.

Vocabulary

Two-word verbs and words that came from Old English (the Anglo-Saxon language) are generally less formal than single-word synonyms based on Latin, French, and Greek. There are other words that are also considered informal, though there may be no "rule" to help you categorize them. Here are some examples from the letter in the introduction:

Informal or General English	Formal English
just	only
let someone know	inform someone
about	concerning
chance	opportunity
job	position
company	firm
tell	inform
a lot of	a great deal of, quite a bit of
end up	finish by
ask questions	request information, inquire, make inquiries
get	acquire, obtain, receive, comprehend, contract
really	very much
put in a word for	recommend

Abbreviations and short forms are generally considered informal. Write out the longer forms in the following blanks.

thanks	_____
&	_____
phoning	_____
dept. mgr.	_____

Sentence Structure and Grammar

Formal English grammar and sentence structure also vary in several respects from that of informal and general English. In the first place, formal English requires complete sentences. Complete the following "sentences" from the letter.

Just a note to say thanks.	_____
Man named Graves—know him?	_____
Think I'll get it?	_____
Hope so.	_____

The sentence structures of informal and formal English also vary in other ways. Informal English is likely to be stated in loosely connected clauses, whereas in formal English some of the information is subordinated into other grammatical structures, leaving fewer clauses in the sentence. Look at the following examples and then make similar changes of your own.

Informal or General English	*Formal English*
I told him I was interested.	I informed him of my interest.
I tried phoning but he wasn't in, so I sent my résumé with a routine cover letter.	When I was unable to contact him by telephone, I sent my résumé with a routine cover letter.
I sent a routine cover letter—mentioned your name.	_____ _____
Gave a lot of background on my education & experience, & ended up asking a few questions.	_____ _____ _____
Think I'll get it? Hope so—from what you've told me, I know I'd really enjoy working there.	_____ _____ _____

Further notes: Certain connecting and transitional words and phrases are considered formal and are used most often in writing, not in conversation. A few examples follow:

Expressions of Chronology or Addition	*Expressions of Contrast*	*Expressions of Cause and Effect*
moreover	however	consequently
furthermore	nevertheless	hence
subsequently	while	therefore
afterwards	whereas	as
eventually	yet	due to
		for
		thus

Notes on punctuation: Semicolons are used more often in formal than in informal English. Dashes and parentheses, on the other hand, are more commonly informal than formal. For example:

Informal or General English	*Formal English*
He gave me the name of the department manager I needed to send my application to. (Man named Graves—know him?)	He suggested that I send an application to the department manager, Mr. Graves, whom you may know.

Final notes on grammar: The word *whom* is used only in formal English; and formal clauses do not usually end with prepositions. Both rules are illustrated in the following sentence:

He gave me the name of the man I needed to send my application to.	He gave me the name of the man to whom I needed to send my application.

The following sentence could be improved by using *whose:*

I wrote to Owens, the man you told me about.	I wrote to Mr. Owens, whose name you mentioned.

Impersonalness

Formal English is generally less personal than informal English. Personal pronouns referring to the writer and the receiver of the letter (*I, we, you*) are used less often than in informal and general English. One way to avoid such personal references is to use the passive voice more frequently. In addition, personal feelings are not generally expressed in formal English.

Informal or General English	*Formal English*
I have received your application.	Your application has been received.
You haven't answered my letter.	I have not yet received a reply.
Thanks for putting in a word for me.	I very much appreciate your recommendation. (Even more formal: Your recommendation was greatly appreciated.)
I know I'd really enjoy working there.	The position interests me greatly.

Business Letter Form

An example of personal letter form is given at the end of Units 18 and 21. Basic business letter form is as follows:

Sender's address

Date (no abbreviations)

Receiver's name and title

Address

Dear Ms. Applegate:
Gentlemen:
Dear Sir or Madam:

(The "body" of the letter goes here.)

Yours sincerely,

Your full name

Your full name

Finally, business letters should be typed if at all possible.

EDITING

Rewrite the letter in the introduction, making it more formal. Imagine that you are the sender and that you are writing to a man named Leslie Cash, who is a systems analyst with the Amtex Company, which is located at 4301 Industrial Blvd., Houston, Texas 77007. Although you have met Mr. Cash, you do not know him well.

PLANNING AND WRITING: RÉSUMÉ

Imagine that you are going to apply for a job related to your major field of study. Brainstorm a list of all the reasons you can think of that would make a prospective employer want to hire you. If you have not yet gotten much educational or job experience in this field, pretend that you have and make up some information for the purposes of this assignment. After brainstorming in the following categories, use your list to provide you with information for a one-page résumé to present to the person who will interview you for the job. A sample résumé at the end of this unit presents a suggested format and will give you some idea of the kinds of information to include.*

What kind of position are you interested in?

What personal characteristics or interests qualify you for this field? Are you well organized, good with people, decisive?

What experience do you have that qualifies you for this kind of job? What have you accomplished that would impress your interviewer? Instead of just listing all the jobs you have held, list your accomplishments and the tasks you have been responsible for completing.

What college, university, or technical school degrees do you hold? Did you receive any awards or honors in connection with your post-secondary education? Have you taken additional classes or training that have prepared you for the position you are seeking?

Do you belong to any professional organizations related to the kind of job you are applying for?

*This sample résumé is based on current trends in résumé writing for businesses in the United States. It is not the only form that could be used and may be quite different from the form you should use or the information you should include if you were to seek employment in another country. Naturally, any time you apply for a job, you should find out what format and kinds of information would be most appropriate to use on a résumé in that particular field and culture.

PLANNING AND WRITING: COVER LETTER

Always send out your résumé with an accompanying cover letter that summarizes your strongest points, in an attempt to convince your prospective employer to interview you. As the interview will bring out specific details about your work experience and education, do not go into detail in your letter. Refer to the sample cover letter at the end of this unit, and you will see that it follows a very simple format:

1. If possible, begin by mentioning the name of a contact known to the person to whom you are writing. Indicate the specific position for which you are applying.
2. Summarize your strongest points in one or two sentences.
3. Continue by telling how your qualifications are particularly suited to the needs of the organization to which you are applying. In order to do this effectively, you should get some information about the company's needs and areas of specialization by asking questions of people you know or by looking up the company's annual report, which may be available in a local library or university placement service.
4. End the letter by asking for an interview. Say that you will call to set it up; do not depend on the company to call you.

ANSWERS

Answers to some of the exercises in this part of the book can be found in the answers section between Unit 60 and Appendix I. Other answers are in the Teacher's Manual.

Sample Résumé

ANNA LIA PALUMBO

626 Columbia
Houston TX 77006
(713) 772–3679

Employment Objective: Training, international banking

Qualifications:
Extensive training and experience in crosscultural communications
Openness and sensitivity to other cultures
Three years' experience living, studying and traveling in Japan and Saudi Arabia; competence in Japanese, Arabic, and Spanish
Ability to combine knowledge and creativity in preparing and presenting training programs
Considerable experience in needs assessment, program design, and program implementation
Working knowledge of needs and operational systems of international banking

Experience:
Seven years' experience in crosscultural training and international education: designed training programs to fit the needs of international students preparing to attend United States universities; consulted for numerous businesses, including banks with large international departments, developing crosscultural awareness

for both American and international employees; devised strategies and materials for use in crosscultural training programs; developed a close working relationship with the foremost authorities in crosscultural training; coordinated several local and national conferences on crosscultural concerns; gathered data on the crosscultural experiences of both Americans working abroad and internationals working or studying in the United States; counseled individuals experiencing cultural adjustment difficulties; learned the needs and the operational systems of international banking through consultations for four of the largest banks in Houston.

Education:

B.A., linguistics, University of Houston, 1975
M.A., comparative education, Michigan State University, 1977
Additional training through attending numerous crosscultural seminars, workshops, and conferences since 1977

Professional Affiliations:

American Association of International Educators
Society for Intercultural Education, Training and Research
National Association of Foreign Student Affairs

References:

Available upon request

Sample Cover Letter

626 Columbia
Houston TX 77006
March 19, 1984

Mr. Thomas Graves
Vice President, International Department
First National Bank
200 Commerce Street
Houston TX 77003

Dear Mr. Graves:

Martin Sorrell of your credit department suggested that I write to you about the opening for a training supervisor in your department.

As the enclosed résumé indicates, I have extensive experience devising and implementing crosscultural training programs in the international departments of area banks. I have trained both international employees who are in the process of learning the systems and cultural norms of banking in this country and American employees who deal with international clients and overseas banks. First National interests me particularly because of your large number of international personnel and the volume of international banking that you conduct.

I feel that I have unique qualifications to offer your team, and I would like to call you during the week of March 26–31 to set up an interview at your convenience.

Sincerely,

Anna Lia Palumbo

Anna Lia Palumbo

Unit 42

Applying to a Graduate Program

Writing forms: Business letter; statement of purpose
Writing skills: Using formal and informal English

INTRODUCTION

Calle Travesia Nº 1, 2º 3ª
Barcelona 23, Spain
June 18, 1984

Dr. Philip Cornell
Director of Graduate Studies
Department of Civil Engineering
Southeast Texas State University
Houston TX 77098
United States of America

Dear Dr. Cornell:

I would like to be considered for admission to your master's program in Civil Engineering for the spring semester. Please send me the necessary information and application forms, including special requirements for international students. In addition, I would like to know about housing, cost of living, and financial aid.

Sincerely yours,

Maria dels Angels Pujol

Maria dels Angels Pujol

Every year thousands of letters like the preceding come from abroad to graduate programs at American universities. When the time comes to make decisions, the graduate admissions committee of each department first narrows down the field of applicants, both from the United States and from other countries, to those with the highest educational records and test scores. Beyond this point, they base their decisions in part on each applicant's statement of purpose, which briefly explains why he or she has chosen to pursue graduate studies in this field at this particular time. In this unit you will learn what to say in such a paper, and you will write a statement of purpose of your own.

WARMUP: GUIDELINES TO WRITING A STATEMENT OF PURPOSE

Competition to enter the graduate program of your choice may be intense, particularly if the department is well known and has high standards. You therefore want to do everything possible to make a good impression, to present yourself as the kind of prospective graduate student the program would want to have. Your goal in writing your statement of purpose or intent is to convince the graduate admissions committee (composed of your future professors) that (1) you have made a mature commitment to enter the field professionally, (2) you are well informed about their department, and (3) this degree plays an important part in your future plans. These points are explained as follows:

1. Sound genuinely interested in the field, whatever it is. Graduate programs are not interested in students who are simply "shopping around" for a career they can live with. Even though you may change your mind halfway through the degree program, don't sound undecided when you apply.

Give evidence that you know at least enough about the field to have made a decision to enter it professionally, even if you haven't studied it extensively. The reasons you state should be professional and academic rather than purely personal. Avoid statements like "I don't really know anything about chemical engineering, but I suspect I'd probably like it," or "I want to go into special education because my own child is handicapped and I want to learn how to care for her." Instead, say a little about how or why you became interested in the field: "Although my undergraduate major was not chemical engineering, since graduation I have been employed in a petroleum engineering research laboratory, and observation of the field at first hand has convinced me that I want to enter it professionally." Or, if you do not have direct experience: "Although my undergraduate major was not marine biology, in the past two years I have become so interested in the field that I have read everything I have been able to find on the subject. At this time I am prepared to make a full-time commitment to the field by entering a graduate program."

2. Find out everything you can about the specific programs you are applying to: after all, you want to enter a program that can meet your interests and needs. For example, if you are applying to a political science program and your particular interest is international politics, find out which universities specialize in this area before going to the time and expense of applying. When you write to programs for information, they will send you a list of the graduate faculty and their areas of specialization. These are the professors you would be studying under; find out as much as you can about their research interests, which are the areas of specialization the program offers. Then when you write your statement of purpose, let the committee know that you have informed yourself about their program and that it fits your needs and interests well.

3. Decide on several career options that this degree would prepare you for, and in your statement mention one or two of them as being of great interest to

you. Even if you have no clear idea of what you want to do upon graduation, do not convey this uncertainty to the committee; they would probably give preference to an applicant with clearer goals. (Remember that what you say in your statement of purpose does not obligate you for the rest of your life; you can always change your mind later.)

INSTRUCTIONS:
Following is a list of reasons students may have for wanting to enter graduate programs. Although all of the reasons are sincere, many would not be appropriate to include in a statement of purpose. Cross out the inappropriate reasons and refer to the guidelines they violate; then carefully study the remaining reasons as ones that would strengthen an applicant's standing with a graduate admissions committee.

1. I really don't know anything about geophysics, but I think I would like it.

2. I want to study archaeology because I love being outdoors.

3. I want to go into petroleum engineering because petroleum engineers make a lot of money.

4. I want to go into optometry because I would have a better chance of staying in the United States as an optometrist than I would in some other professions.

5. I want to enter graduate school because I can't find a real job, and my parents will support me if I am a student.

6. I want to attend your university because I am applying to as many universities as I can in hopes that at least one of them will accept me.

7. I want to attend your university because your TOEFL and GRE requirements are low.

8. I want to attend your university because your library is the best in the United States in my major field.

9. I want to attend your university because it is near my apartment.

10. I want to attend your university because my sister studies there and she can give me a ride to school.

11. I want to attend your university because your department has excellent research facilities.

12. I want to attend your university because I have heard that you have a lot of other students from my country.

13. I want to attend your university so that I can study under Professor Loudder, who is world-renowned in my field.

14. I want to attend your university because you have such a beautiful campus.

15. I want to attend your university because the employment opportunities for graduates in my major are better in your city than in other United States cities. I feel that if I study there, I can make important contacts in the business community, which can serve me well after I graduate.

16. I want to attend your university because a degree from you will enable me to find a good job in my field when I graduate.

17. I want to attend your university because I like the city in which it is located.

18. I want to attend your university because you offer a flexible degree plan that will permit me to take courses in a variety of departments in order to receive a broadly-based education.

19. I want to attend your university because my girlfriend lives in the city where it is located, and I want to be near her.

20. I want to attend your university because you offer a specialization in the area of my major that interests me most.

EDITING: USING FORMAL ENGLISH

The following letter is too informal for its purposes. Rewrite it according to the guidelines in Unit 40, making it more appropriately formal in vocabulary, grammar, and sentence structure.

Dear Dr. Cornell:

Thanks for answering so quickly when I wrote you asking for information about being admitted to your master's program. After reading the materials you sent, I have some more questions for you. First, the brochure I got doesn't say what I have to make on the TOEFL. Don't I have to take it, or did you send me the wrong brochure by mistake? I am, as I told you in my first letter, not an American. Second, I have 3 professors who will be writing letters of recommendation for me, but they don't speak English. Should I get the letters translated here, or will you get that done yourself? Finally, you said you need a 250-word statement of purpose. What do you want it to say? Do you want to know my purpose in wanting a master's degree in civil engineering, or why I want to get it at your school, or what I plan to do with it, or what? I'm not clear on this.

Thanks for your trouble. I'm anxious to hear from you.

Your future student,

PLANNING AND WRITING

Imagine that you are applying for admission to a graduate program in your major field of study at an American university. Plan a statement of purpose by brainstorming in the following areas:

1. Make a list of your educational and/or work experience related to this field of study. Include specific courses you have taken, research and study that you may have done on your own, jobs related to the field, and related personal interests or abilities that you can express objectively. If you made high grades or received honors in school, mention them as evidence of your scholastic ability and dedication. If you will be returning to school after an absence of several years, present this as an advantage because of the maturity and experience you have gained. If you have never studied this field and have no job experience related to it, list ways in which you have

learned enough about it to justify your decision to study it at the graduate level.

2. Make a list of your reasons for applying to this particular university. Imagine for the purposes of this exercise that you have obtained information about specific courses, special programs, professors, research facilities, library facilities, and so on. Show the graduate committee that you are well informed about the department.

3. Make a list of about five ways that you could use your graduate degree. What specific jobs might be available to you in private business, teaching, consulting, research, government employ?

When you have completed your lists, cross out all but the strongest reasons and examples to include in a statement of purpose about 250 words in length. Then write it, devoting a paragraph to each of the three areas just mentioned. When you finish, use your checklists to help you make corrections in organization, grammar, and sentence structure. Then revise the paper to make it appropriately formal. Do not turn your paper in until you have thoroughly checked and revised it.

Sample Statement of Purpose

My particular interest in a master's program is fishery biology. There is a great demand in my country for specialists in this field because of our dependence on marine life for food. With this specialty in mind, I majored in biology as an undergraduate and received my B.S. with honors last June. An uncle of mind is a research scientist in our government fisheries laboratory, and over the past several years I have spent a great deal of time familiarizing myself with the facility and the processes of fishery research. In addition to my undergraduate studies, I have read everything available on fishery biology from my university library, from the government laboratory library, and from my professors' personal libraries. I feel that I have exhausted the resources available here in my country and wish to pursue my graduate studies at a university with a better library and more modern laboratory facilities.

Your master's program appeals to me greatly because you have access to the special research laboratories of the National Marine Fisheries Service in Galveston. I am particularly interested in both the extensive aquaria facilities and the ultramodern electron microscopy laboratory. These are the most advanced facilities I have heard of in any country. Another advantage your program offers is the opportunity to work with Professors Summerlin and DuVall, whose research in fishery biology and population biology has appeared in recent issues of the *Journal of Research in Marine Biology*. Indeed, everything I have learned from your office and from fishery specialists here in my country indicates that your program offers a high degree of specialization in my field and the best in facilities.

Upon receiving my degree, I will have the option of entering government employ in the fishery research laboratory here in our capital or of setting up a laboratory of my own. Although the government position offers the advantages of an existing laboratory and stable employment, if I were to open a private research laboratory, I could cut costs by streamlining systems and by avoiding bureaucracy without sacrificing quality. Whichever course I follow, there is no doubt that a degree from Southeast Texas State would open doors and guarantee my future.

❧ Unit 43 ☙

A Controversial Figure

Writing form: Biography
Writing skills: Reading abbreviated English; presenting factual information

INTRODUCTION

Often you are required to write compositions or reports based on dry lists of information from resource books. How can you present such information in a way that is interesting and that shows your intelligence and writing skills? Today's assignment sets you just such a task, providing a list of events from the life of a famous person as the basis for your composition.

One of the most remarkable figures of our century is Indira Gandhi, whose shrewdness and political savoir faire have brought her repeatedly to power in the face of great odds. Here are some facts about her life:

Indira Gandhi

Nov. 19, 1917	born, Allahabad, India
	father: Jawaharlal Nehru, first Prime Minister of India
	education: India and England
1942	married Feroze Gandhi (died 1960)
	two sons: Rajiv (1944) and Sanjay (1946)
1942–43	imprisoned with her husband for political activity
1959	elected president of Congress Party
1964	death of Prime Minister Nehru
	succession of Lal Bahadur Shastri
	appointed Minister of Information and Broadcasting by Shastri
1966	death of Prime Minister Shastri
Jan. 24, 1966	became first woman Prime Minister of India
1972	charged with violating election laws by Raj Narain, her Socialist opponent in 1971 election
June 1975	Narain's suit won; Gandhi's 1971 election declared invalid; Gandhi in danger of losing her seat in Parliament as a result
two weeks later	declared a state of emergency (June 1975–Jan. 1977): imprisoned political opponents

           censored press
           passed laws limiting personal freedoms
           postponed March 1976 parliamentary elections one year
           said state of emergency necessary to restore democracy to country
              in state of anarchy
Aug. 1975 election laws revised by constitutional amendment
           Gandhi's June conviction reversed
     1976 growing influence of her son Sanjay:
              hated by people for his harsh measures in enforcing birth control
                 and slum clearance
              feared as a powerful but negative influence on his mother
              feared as a ruthless political power threatening democracy
           growing unpopularity of both mother and son
Mar. 1977 overwhelmingly defeated in national elections
           succession of Morarji Desai as PM
Mar. 77–Jan. 80 continued to wield great political influence during two short-lived
              opposition governments
Nov. 1978 reelected to Parliament
     1979 accused by investigatory commission of using political influence to
              further Sanjay's business interests
           charged with harassing four government officials
           Sanjay sentenced to two years in prison for destroying a film
Jan. 14, 1980 became Prime Minister again
     1980 death of Sanjay (plane crash)
     1981 rise of older son Rajiv as a political figure with his election to
              Parliament for the Congress Party

Major issues with which Gandhi has had some success:
   strengthening power of central government
   increasing food and industrial production
   controlling population growth (limited success)
   nationalizing banks
   building a nuclear power program
   establishing a space program
   increasing rail transport
   lowering inflation

Major issues still unresolved:
   regional unrest
   sporadic breakdown of law and order
   un- and underemployment
   lack of electricity and drinking water in rural areas

WARMUP I: READING ABBREVIATED ENGLISH

Newspaper headlines, instructions, recipes, and lists of information are often presented in abbreviated English instead of in complete sentences. These shortened, reduced forms can be confusing unless you know how to translate them. Here are some of the rules, with examples from the introduction:

1. Articles, subjects of verbs, and auxiliary verbs (except modals) may be omitted. The verb "to be" may be omitted even if it is the main verb of the sentence.

Example: Nov. 19, 1917   born, Allahabad, India
Complete sentence: Indira Gandhi was born in Allahabad, India, on November 19, 1917.

2. Because auxiliary verbs are usually omitted, the principal verbs that remain may be in either the active or the passive voice. Read the whole item carefully to distinguish the voice of the verb.
Active example: Jan. 24, 1966   became first woman Prime Minister of India
Complete sentence: Gandhi became the first woman Prime Minister of India on January 24, 1966.
Passive example: 1964   appointed Minister of Information and Broadcasting by Shastri
Complete sentence: Gandhi was appointed Minister of Information and Broadcasting by Shastri in 1964.

3. Sentences are often reduced to noun phrases.
Example: 1964   death of Prime Minister Nehru
Complete sentence: Prime Minister Nehru died in 1964.

In the introductory information, wherever a subject is omitted, the subject is Indira Gandhi, with the exception of the verbs *hated* and *feared* for the year 1976, where the subject is Sanjay Gandhi. When writing your composition, convert all abbreviations (Jan., PM) to complete forms (January, Prime Minister).

INSTRUCTIONS:
Convert the following items of information from abbreviated English into complete sentences, using the rules and examples just given.

1. two sons: Rajiv (1944) and Sanjay (1946)

2. Mar. 1977   succession of Morarji Desai as PM

3. June 1975   Narain's suit won; Gandhi's 1971 election declared invalid; Gandhi in danger of losing her seat in Parliament as a result

4. Aug. 1975   election laws revised by constitutional amendment
Gandhi's June conviction reversed

5. Nov. 1978   reelected to Parliament

6. 1979   charged with harassing four government officials

WARMUP II: EXPRESSING RELATIONSHIPS BETWEEN ITEMS OF INFORMATION

Items of information should be presented in a way that shows how they are related to each other. These relationships can be shown through sentence structure, through grammar, or by using expressions such as the following:*

Chronology/Addition	*Contrast*	*Cause and Effect*
and	but	so
as well	although	as a result
in addition	in spite of	because (of)
besides	however	therefore
two years later	nonetheless	lead(ing) to
subsequently	on the contrary	... so ... that ...

INSTRUCTIONS:

Express the following items of information using sentence structure, grammar, or some of the preceding expressions to show their relationships to each other.

Example: 1942   married Feroze Gandhi (died 1960)
two sons: Rajiv (1944) and Sanjay (1946)
In 1942 she married Feroze Gandhi, by whom she had two sons, Rajiv and Sanjay, born in 1944 and 1946 respectively. Her husband died in 1960.

1. 1964   death of Prime Minister Nehru
succession of Lal Bahadur Shastri as Prime Minister
appointed Minister of Information and Broadcasting by Shastri

2. Gandhi in danger of losing her seat in Parliament
declared a state of emergency

3. imprisoned political opponents
censored press
passed laws limiting personal freedoms
postponed March 1976 parliamentary elections one year

4. 1975   declared a state of emergency
1976   growing influence of her son Sanjay
growing unpopularity of both mother and son

*See also Appendix III.

5. 1976   growing unpopularity
   1977   overwhelmingly defeated in national elections

6. 1977   overwhelmingly defeated in national elections
   1978   reelected to Parliament

7. 1978   reelected to Parliament
   1980   became Prime Minister again

PLANNING AND WRITING

Write a biography of Indira Gandhi, using the information in this unit and adding any subsequent information that you think is important. Your teacher may send you to the library to gather additional data. Divide your composition into main periods of Gandhi's life, and use the same principles of paragraphing that you would for any composition. Be sure to write an introduction and a conclusion. Use transitional expressions and a variety of sentence structures, and be careful with verb tenses. When you finish, use your checklists.

You will find a sample composition on Indira Gandhi in the answers section. It is included simply to give you an idea of how to apply the skills studied in this unit; it should not be copied. You will learn more from doing your own work. To avoid being overly influenced by the sample, simply read it over briefly before you start organizing your own composition and do not refer to it again until you have handed your paper in. When your teacher returns your paper to you, compare it with the sample in order to focus on your strengths and weaknesses in presenting factual information.

❧ Unit 44 ❧

A Famous American

Writing form: Biography
Writing skills: Selecting, omitting, summarizing and presenting
  information from research

INTRODUCTION

When hours of library research have provided you with pages and pages of
information for a writing assignment, you are faced with the difficult decisions
of which information to include, how to weigh its relative importance, and how
to express it. Today's assignment will give you guidelines and practice in
making these decisions and an opportunity to use the feedback your teacher
gave you on your composition from Unit 43 in order to write a better paper today.

Your topic is another well-known political leader, although this one had to
struggle in the political arena for many years before finally emerging the victor.
Here are some facts you may not have known about this man:

Ronald Reagan

Feb. 6, 1911	born, Tampico, Illinois
1932	BA, Eureka College, Illinois (economics and sociology)
	radio announcer for station WOO in Davenport, Iowa, and station WHO in Des Moines, Iowa
1937–64	acted in over 50 films
1940	married actress Jane Wyman (divorced 1949) (two children)
1942–45	U.S. Army (made training films)
1947–52 and 1959–60	President of Screen Actors Guild, a labor union
1949	Chairman of Motion Picture Industry Council
1952	married Nancy Davis (two children)
late 1940s, early 1950s	gradually became more conservative politically (had been a liberal Democrat)
1962	joined the Republican Party
1966	defeated Gov. Edmund G. Brown to become Governor of California (conservative Republican)

1966–74   Governor of California
            for cuts in taxes and government spending
            for welfare reform; against welfare cheaters
            against liberal student radicals demonstrating against
            the Vietnam War
1968 & 1976   unsuccessful bids for Republican Presidential nomination
1980   defeated Pres. Jimmy Carter to become 40th President of
         the U.S.A.
         carried 44 states to Carter's 6
         at 69, oldest man to become President

Issues as President:

For	*Against*
capital punishment	government waste & excessive
tax cuts	government spending
balanced federal budget	USSR & communism
reduction in size & influence	detente with USSR
of federal government	SALT II & nuclear disarmament
US military preeminence	gun control
military intervention	busing to achieve school racial
prayer in public school	integration
	abortion
	Equal Rights Amendment
	(defeated 1982)

Crises and Events During Reagan's Administration:

Economic recession or depression during early 1980s
   slump in housing & automobile industries & in related industries such as lumber,
      steel, rubber
   Reagan blamed Carter
   Reagan's economic plan: "supply-side" economics
   Reagan's budget director, David Stockman, expressed lack of faith in supply-side
      economics, leading to crisis in confidence
   1982 saw nation's highest unemployment rate since 1930s Depression
   winter 1982 saw surge in stock market, slowdown of inflation, lowering of interest
      rates, slowdown in unemployment rate
March 30, 1981: Reagan wounded by John Hinckley Jr. in assassination attempt
   1982: Hinckley found not guilty by reason of insanity
Reagan more successful than Carter in winning cooperation from legislature
Cuts in federal assistance to programs such as welfare, arts, federally guaranteed
   student loans
Reagan's goal of a balanced federal budget vs. highest federal deficit in history in his
   proposed budget
Financial crisis because of lack of sufficient funds for Social Security and Medicaid–
   Medicare programs, which assist the elderly & disabled
August 1981: air traffic controllers' strike
   Reagan fired strikers, who were federal employees
Reagan named Sandra Day O'Connor first woman justice on US Supreme Court
Foreign affairs
   tension in Middle Eastern relations
      desire to maintain good relations with both Arab nations & Israel
      Aug. 1981: supported US shooting down of two Libyan jets
      1982: intervened in Israel–Lebanon War

initiated economic sanctions against Poland in response to Polish government's actions again Solidarity trade union

aided El Salvador government against guerillas, believed by Reagan to be supported by USSR

supported Britain against Argentina in Falklands/Malvinas War

engaged in negotiations with USSR concerning the possibility of a bilateral nuclear arms freeze

An early quotation: The United States is "the only island of freedom that is left in the whole world."

An inaugural address quotation (1981): "Government is not the solution to our problem. Government is the problem."

WARMUP I: SELECTING INFORMATION TO USE

When doing research, you will naturally accumulate more information than you can possibly write about. The next step is to look over your notes and discard the details that do not seem important enough to include in your paper.

INSTRUCTIONS:

Go back over the information about Ronald Reagan and cross out details that are not of general interest or that do not seem worth mentioning.

Example: ~~Feb. 6,~~ 1911   born, ~~Tampico,~~ Illinois

WARMUP II: SUMMARIZING INFORMATION

Before you can present your information intelligently, you have to understand it fully. This means that you can look over pages of details and see the underlying categories that tie some of them together, even as you draw conclusions interpreting these groups of details. Because you understand the relative importance of your information, you will also know which groups of details to mention only briefly and which others to present in more detail because of their greater importance. In the following exercise, the information is already grouped for you, but you must make decisions about its relative importance and must interpret it into summary statements.

INSTRUCTIONS:

Read each of the following groups of information carefully. If the information is not very important, reduce it to a brief statement or phrase, omitting most of the details, as in the following example:

Radio announcer for station WOO in Davenport, Iowa, and station WHO in Des Moines, Iowa

Possible sentence: After graduating from college, he worked as a radio announcer before becoming an actor.

In other cases, interpret the details into a summary statement that shows that you understand the implications of the information, as in the following example:

for US military preeminence

for military intervention

against USSR & communism
against detente with USSR
against SALT II & nuclear disarmament
Possible conclusion: Considering his strong stand for United States military
preeminence and against detente with the USSR, it is not surprising that
Reagan opposes the growing nuclear disarmament movement.

The following groups of information require reduction, as in the first example:

1. 1940   married actress Jane Wyman (divorced 1949)
         (two children)
    1952   married Nancy Davis (two children)

2. 1947–52 and 1959–60   President of Screen Actors Guild, a labor union
                   1949   Chairman of Motion Picture Industry Council

3. 1968 & 1976   unsuccessful bids for Republican Presidential nomination
         1980   defeated Pres. Jimmy Carter to become 40th Pres. of U.S.A.
                carried 44 states to Carter's 6
                at 69, oldest man to become President

The following groups of information require interpreting and summarizing, as in the
second example:

4. for capital punishment   against govt. waste & excessive govt.
    for reduction in size &   spending
      influence of fed. govt.   against USSR & communism
    for US military preeminence   against detente & nuclear disarmament
    for military intervention   against gun control
    for prayer in public   against abortion
      schools   against the Equal Rights Amendment

5. Economic recession or depression during the early 1980s. (Refer to the biographical information given, and summarize and interpret the six items on this topic.)

6. Foreign affairs. (Refer to the biographical information given, and summarize and interpret the five entries on this topic.)

7. Write a summary statement that shows how Reagan's positions on issues support his belief that the United States is "the only island of freedom that is left in the whole world."

8. Write a summary statement that shows how Reagan's positions on issues support his belief that "government is not the solution to our problem; government is the problem."

WARMUP III: PRESENTING INFORMATION

The worst way you could present information is simply to list the details, using the same sentence structure over and over, like this:

Ronald Reagan was born in 1911. He graduated from college in 1932. He married Jane Wyman in 1940. . . .

Instead, learn to vary sentence length, structure, and interest by combining ideas. For instance, all this information . . .

late 1940s, early 1950s   gradually became more conservative politically
(had been a liberal Democrat)
1962   joined Republican Party

... can be combined in one well-constructed sentence:

> Although Reagan had always been a liberal Democrat, during the late 1940s and early 1950s he became more conservative politically, eventually joining the Republican Party in 1962.

INSTRUCTIONS:
On a separate sheet of paper, combine each of the following groups of information into one strong sentence. Concentrate on varying your sentence structure.

1. for tax cuts; for balanced federal budget; against government waste and excessive government spending

2. for reduction in size and influence of federal government; against government waste and excessive government spending

3. Reagan's economic plan: "supply-side" economics; Reagan's budget director, David Stockman, expressed lack of faith in supply-side economics, leading to crisis in confidence

4. for tax cuts; for balanced federal budget; against government waste and excessive government spending; made cuts in federal assistance to programs such as welfare, arts, federally guaranteed student loans

5. for military intervention; against USSR and communism; aided El Salvador government against guerillas, believed by Reagan to be supported by USSR

PLANNING AND WRITING

Plan a biography of Ronald Reagan. First look at the information given and decide how to organize it into paragraphs: that is, divide Reagan's life into three stages. When you begin to write, you may decide to further divide the presidency into two paragraphs.

Second, decide which information to include, which to leave out, which to summarize, and which to include in more detail. Make notes. Write an outline. Include additional information from your own research if you wish.

Only after you have done all this are you ready to write. At this stage, concentrate on varying your sentence structure and combining ideas in a way that makes your paper interesting and convinces your reader that you are an intelligent and sophisticated writer. Summarize the information given into a biography to be written in forty minutes. Then give yourself five more minutes to check your paper before handing it in.

❧ Unit 45 ❧

Taking Lecture Notes

INTRODUCTION

Although no one but you will ever read them, the notes you take from your professors' lectures are one of the most important kinds of writing you will do in your college or university career. Do not assume that you will be tested only on the information in your textbooks; your professor would not spend time lecturing if he or she did not consider this additional information crucial to the course. You therefore want your class notes to be readable, well organized, and informative enough that you can prepare yourself well for your examinations by studying them as a supplement to your texts.

If you are planning to study at an American college or university, you will find that time is your greatest enemy in the lecture hall. It will take you longer than a native speaker of English to understand the professor and to write down what he or she says. Because time is such a problem, you should do everything possible to streamline the process of notetaking. In today's unit you will learn some guidelines that will aid you in taking notes quickly and clearly, and then you will apply them in taking notes from a lecture your teacher will give.

WARMUP: GUIDELINES TO TAKING LECTURE NOTES

The first stage in taking lecture notes is to prepare yourself for the lecture by reading the section of your text that deals with the topic. Learn the definitions and pronunciation of key vocabulary items. The better you know what to expect, the more easily you will be able to take notes during the lecture itself.

The second stage is taking the actual notes during the lecture. If the professor closely follows the information in your text, you may want to make notations in the margins of the book, but generally more information will be given than you will have room to write there. You should write most of your notes in a notebook, keeping all the notes for each course separate.

What exactly should you write down during the lecture, and what can you leave out? Always begin by writing the date of the lecture. Then as the professor speaks, because time is working against you, do not attempt to write down everything he or she says. Omit information that you already understand fully, stories that digress from the topic, or information that seems unimportant. Unfortunately, there is no guideline that can tell you which information is important and which is not: use your own judgment, and when in doubt, write. Make a point of copying everything the professor writes on the chalkboard.

As he or she speaks, your professor will give you verbal cues that will help you know what to expect, how the material has been organized, and how the items are related to each other. Many of these cues will be the same ones you have studied in this book for use in your compositions. The professor may introduce the topic using one of the methods suggested in Units 6 and 25. When expressing relationships of addition/process, contrast, and cause and effect, he or she may use any of the methods given in Appendix III. Learn to recognize these verbal cues so that you will understand not only the items of information, but also the larger context of the whole lecture in which they appear.

You must also keep in mind what the professor has already said so that you will be able to understand references to previously given information. For example, he or she may say:

"two years later"	(than what?)
"the former/the latter"	(what came first? what last?)
"he returned to his birthplace"	(where was that?)
"Callahan's theory was a great improvement"	(over what?)
"Unfortunately, the two researchers never collaborated"	(who were they?)

In addition to knowing what to write down, you must consider how to write it. Obviously you are not going to have time to write complete sentences. You should reduce the information you hear to the briefest notation possible; for example, if your professor says, "Schrackle devoted the rest of his career to attempting to prove a theory that we know today was erroneous," you should write simply, "Schrackle wrong." Do not even write out words in full if you can abbreviate them. Many common words have "standard" abbreviations or symbols that students use in taking notes:

imp.; maj.; prim.; max.; min.	important; major; primary; maximum; minimum
>; <	more than, leads to; less than, results from
=; $\cong$; $\neq$	is, are, equals; is approximately; is not, does not equal
c.	approximately
e.g.	for example
i.e.	that is (used before an explanation of something just mentioned)
w, $\bar{c}$; w/o	with (the second form is used in medical fields); without
$\therefore$	therefore, as a result
re	concerning, with reference to
&, +	and

Naturally, you will devise other abbreviations for use in the specific lectures you attend. In a lecture on Albert Einstein and the theory of relativity, you might refer to Einstein as "A.E." and to the theory of relativity as "T.R." It doesn't matter what or how you abbreviate as long as you can understand your notes when you reread them a day, a week, or even a whole term later.

Another form of abbreviated writing is shorthand, which secretaries use when taking dictation. If you know some form of shorthand, by all means use it. If not, you may want to devise symbols of your own to represent often-repeated words and parts of words, such as the following:

to
for
from
in
at
before
of
off
a, an
the
he
she
it
that
there is
as
but
so
because
if
-tion
-ment
-ing
-ed
be-

Sometimes students speed up their notetaking by omitting the vowels in words; "Smtms stds spd up thr nttkg by omttg vwls n wrds."

Besides taking down the information from the lecture, mark your notes and text so that when you study them for an examination, your eye will be drawn to the most important information on the pages. If the lecture follows information in your textbook, keep it open and underline, highlight, circle, and make marginal notes to yourself in it. Don't be afraid to write in it; it's not a holy book. Students who don't underline because they want to sell the book back at the end of the term will find it hard to study efficiently for exams. Make the same kinds of notations in the margins of your notebooks. If you need to check data, to look something up, to refer to a page in the textbook, or to ask for an explanation, write these reminders to yourself in the margins as you take notes.

As you write your notes, outline if at all possible, or at least indent supporting information under major points. Indentation saves you study time by enabling you to see at a glance the relationships between ideas. Compare the two following examples and notice how much clearer example B is.

Example A	*Example B*
problems of nuclear waste disposal	problems of nuclear waste disposal
packaging materials	packaging materials
glass	glass
metal	metal
ceramic	ceramic
storage locations	storage locations
ground level	ground level
sea bed	sea bed
outer space	outer space
underground	underground

The third stage of this process is to reread your notes as soon as possible after the lecture is over, adding information that you may not have had time to write down, while you can still remember it. This review will also help to fix the lecture in your memory. Ideally, you should try to outline your notes, even if this means rewriting them. Outlining (see Units 7, 13, 14, 23, 26, 47) helps you distinguish major points from supporting points and enables you to study more efficiently. If you are unsure of the quality of your notes, compare them with another student's after the lecture. Chances are that both of you will benefit.

WRITING

At this time your teacher will give you a practice lecture. Take notes, using as many of the preceding guidelines as you can. At the end of the lecture, go back over your notes and supplement them while the material is still fresh in your memory. Then compare them with another student's in order to check your information and supplement it further. Your teacher will then review the guidelines with you, asking how well you were able to apply them. Listen carefully to what your classmates have to say during this discussion; you can learn a great deal from the methods they used.

❦ Unit 46 ❦

Taking Tests

INTRODUCTION

For many students, examinations are the most important but the worst aspect of their university education. They dread them, they worry about them, they stay up all night studying for them, and sometimes they are so tired and nervous that they fail them. But consider the purposes that examinations serve: first, they force students to study the course material; second, they offer them an opportunity to demonstrate to their professors how much they have learned. Neither of these functions is particularly intimidating, and examinations lose much of their aura of fear and dread when they are considered in such a light. And since they are inevitable, why not try to think of them as positively as possible, so that they will lose their power to destroy your peace of mind? In this unit you will learn some positive guidelines to assist you in preparing for and taking examinations, and you will practice applying these guidelines as you take a test on the lecture you heard in Unit 45.

WARMUP: GUIDELINES TO PREPARING FOR AND TAKING EXAMINATIONS

Before the Examination

You cannot do well on an examination unless you are well prepared, and the best way to prepare is to study all along instead of waiting until the night before the test. If you don't know the material by then, it's too late to learn all of it. Study everything: your textbooks, handouts that the professor has given you, your class notes (including everything that the professor has written on the chalkboard), your homework papers, other tests on the same material, information from library assignments. If there is something you don't understand, make every attempt to get the help you need, either from another student or from your professor, if he or she has extra time to give you.

About a week before the test, ask your professor for some information about it. What percentage of your course grade will this test make up? What form will it take? The way you study will depend on whether the questions will be essay, short answer, fill in the blank, matching, multiple choice, true–false, or some other form. What aids, if any (texts, notes, dictionaries), can you use? What supplies will you need to bring with you: does the professor require pen rather than pencil; must you use a certain kind of paper?

One useful method of studying for a test is trying to anticipate the questions that the professor may ask and giving yourself a practice exam. It is especially important to test yourself in areas of the material in which you feel weak. Try explaining parts of the material out loud to give yourself practice in expressing it.

Budget your time about a week in advance so that you can study for a given period each day instead of staying up late the night before the test. That night you should try to get plenty of sleep, and you should eat a light meal shortly before taking the test so that you will feel rested yet energetic.

During the Examination

Bring to the test whatever supplies you are required to have. Your professor may not allow you to borrow dictionaries or erasers during the exam.

Before you begin writing, look over the whole test and plan your time carefully. Note the values of the various answers, and devote the most time to those that carry the most credit. If you do not know the answer to a question, don't waste time trying to think of it; answer the other questions first.

Don't copy the questions unless your professor asks you to or unless that is the custom in the country where you are studying. (It is not the custom at American universities.) But be sure to number your answers correctly.

Read the directions carefully, and then follow them. If you don't, you will lose points, no matter how well you know the material. The same thing is true of the questions: *Be sure that you answer the question that is asked.* If you give information that is related but that does not answer the specific question, you may lose the total number of points for that question.

In an essay examination (where your answers take paragraph or composition form), your organization is almost as important as your information. Be sure to outline your answer briefly before you begin and to express yourself as clearly as possible. The more easily the professor can follow your answer, the better your grade will be.

Write clearly. If the professor cannot read your handwriting, you will lose points for failing to communicate.

If you are studying at an American college or university, you will be expected to follow the honor code described in Unit 35. Your professor may not even be in the classroom when you take the test, but you will be on your honor not to give or receive information and to report any student who does. Naturally, any other student may report you too if you violate this code. If this system makes you uncomfortable, cover your paper so that other students cannot see your answers (thus you cannot be accused of giving information) and simply don't look around the room during the test (thus you will not see and cannot be expected to turn in students who may cheat.)

Write your name at the top of each page of the test. If you finish early, use the remaining time to check your answers before turning your paper in.

After the Examination

When your test is returned to you, read it carefully to find out what your strengths and weaknesses were. If you are going to be tested on the same material on a later exam, you may discover that some areas need more of your attention.

WRITING

Today your writing assignment will be to take an open-book test on your notes on the lecture from Unit 45. You may use your notes, this book, and your dictionary. Follow the guidelines just given. You will have one hour to complete the test. You will need several clean sheets of notebook paper, and your teacher will tell you whether to write in pencil or in ink.

OPEN-BOOK TEST FOR "ROBOTICS" LECTURE

True/False: Circle the correct letter, T or F. (2½ points each)

1. T F   The statistics on the number of robots in the world today are uncertain.

2. T F   Blue-collar jobs may be threatened by the increasing use of robots, but white-collar jobs are not.

Multiple Choice: Circle the letter of the correct answer. (2½ points each)

3. Which of the following countries is *not* one of the world's leading users of robots?
   a. Sweden
   b. France
   c. West Germany
   d. Britain

4. For which of the following jobs are robots currently used?
   a. Electronics assembly
   b. Research
   c. Maintenance
   d. Supervision

Fill in the Blanks: Supply the correct answer for each blank. (2 points each)

5. The word *robot* was coined by _____ , a playwright from _____ , and was first used in a play he wrote in the year _____ .

Short Answer: Answer each question with a complete sentence.

6. How was a modern industrial robot defined in the lecture? (5 points)

7. Of what two basic parts does a modern industrial robot consist? (2 points each)

Essay Questions: Write the answers on notebook paper. Use complete sentences and paragraph form. Your answers will be graded on the completeness and accuracy of your information, on your organization and paragraph form, and on your English grammar and sentence structure.

8. Describe how a robot is "taught" a task. (10 points)

9. Explain why American blue-collar workers feel threatened by robots (include projected statistics) and why Japanese blue-collar workers do not. (15 points)

10. Discuss the jobs that robot perform: the kinds of jobs, the specific tasks, and the industries in which these jobs occur. (20 points)

11. Discuss the advantages to manufacturers of using robots instead of human workers. (30 points)

❧ Unit 47 ❧

Summarizing

Writing skills: Finding or inferring main ideas; distinguishing main points from supporting detail; summarizing a long passage

INTRODUCTION

Summarizing is a skill used in almost every major field of study because it shows that you understand and can clearly express the essence of a lecture or reading passage. In order to summarize effectively, you must be able to

1. Understand the lecture or passage fully.
2. Know the main points from the minor points or supporting detail.
3. Express the central idea(s) in good, clear English.

The trick of summarizing is to say neither too much nor too little. You must be sure you cover the main points adequately, yet remember that a summary is by its nature considerably shorter than the original statement or passage.

WARMUP: FINDING OR INFERRING MAIN IDEAS

The essence of a speech, an article, or even a book can generally be summed up in a few sentences. The rest of the material consists of detail, explanation, examples, reasons. Your success at the university is going to depend heavily on your ability to recognize and restate these main ideas in compositions, in research papers, and on examinations. If you are lucky, the author will state the main idea clearly; if not, it will take more thought on your part to figure it out.

INSTRUCTIONS:
In the following paragraph from a paper on ownership of handguns by private citizens, underline the sentence that expresses the main idea.

Ownership of handguns by private citizens is an issue on which the American public is sharply divided. Opponents of gun control argue that if handguns could not be legally owned, only criminals would have them, leaving honest people defenseless. But although it is true that the majority of murders in the United States are committed with handguns, statistics also show that most victims are killed not by strangers, but by people they know—"friends," family members,

217

spouses—who reach for the household handgun in a moment of rage or fear. Surely the majority of these murders would never occur were a gun not at hand, for people are much less likely to stab or strangle than to shoot, and the former recourses are less likely to be fatal anyway. Obviously, if handguns were not legally available to private citizens, American murder statistics would be drastically reduced.

There is no topic sentence in the next paragraph, which comes from a paper entitled "Is Progress Possible for Mankind?" You will have to "read between the lines" to determine the author's point.

INSTRUCTIONS

1. After reading the following paragraph carefully, express the main idea in a sentence of your own.
2. Then look at the four sentences that follow and decide which one best expresses the main idea of the paragraph. Do not look at these suggested answers before writing your own. Your expression of the main idea can be rather different, yet still be correct.

This "progress" we congratulate ourselves on so heartily bears closer scrutiny. At the dawn of humanity, our forebears were little more than clever apes. They lived mean, uncertain lives, made war on their neighbors, and generally died as a result of violence, disease, or malnutrition. Suspicion and selfishness ruled the day. But of course they did not have the benefits of religion and philosophy, higher learning, or technology. In contrast, how fortunate we are to live in an age in which human tolerance and mutual understanding prevail, permitting us to rear our children in a world to which the marvels of technology have brought peace, plenty, and health to all mankind!

Your sentence:

Which of the following sentences best expresses the main idea of the preceding paragraph?

1. Let us scrutinize the progress of mankind more closely.
2. Man's progress has been in the areas of religion and philosophy, higher education, and technology.
3. Man has not made any real progress because his basic nature has not changed.
4. Religion, philosophy, higher education, and technology have brought peace and plenty to all mankind.

INSTRUCTIONS:
Given the following information in outline form, complete the outline by writing a sentence that expresses the main idea at the top, after Roman numeral one.

I.

    A. Rising cost of petroleum
    B. U.S. dependence on foreign petroleum
    C. Dwindling supplies of world petroleum

READING AND WRITING: SUMMARIZING A LONGER PASSAGE

INSTRUCTIONS:

Read the following passage carefully as many times as it takes to understand it fully. It has not been simplified for international students. Your dictionary will help, but it probably will not include some of the idioms and grammatical constructions. This is at least the level of difficulty you can expect in American university textbooks.

After you feel you understand the text as well as possible, make a list of the main points and of whatever minor points support them. Standard outline form uses the following system of numerals and letters:

   I. Main point
      A. Support for main point
      B. Support for main point
         1. Support for B
            a. Support for 1
            b. Support for 1
         2. Support for B
      C. Support for main point, and so on

Our political response to the problems that we face has been feeble almost beyond credence. During virtually all of 1977 and 1978 we, and the world, were exposed to the unedifying spectacle of a Congress, paralyzed and unable to devise even a minimal energy policy which, at best, is only a beginning. The near collapse of the dollar on money markets abroad during that time reflected not only the succession of massive national deficits but also indicated the lack of confidence there that Congress would ever pull itself together to generate such a policy. Our representatives as a group have certainly not distinguished themselves in this task.

Why, a reasonable person might ask, has the political response been so inept and so inadequate? Our legislators can certainly make their own excuses, but three reasons seem to stand out. In the first place, although most of our representatives would concede that there is an energy problem, few appear to have realized the awful logic of its depth and inevitability. Few legislators have time to read and thoughtfully digest for themselves the rather technical reports and other writings that have given a warning. There are many matters pressing for a Congressman's attention, many hot issues of the day, many constituents to please. Immediate problems that can be solved quickly will receive attention first. The energy problem is a long problem, a hard and complex one, and few Congressmen have yet much appreciation of it.

Secondly, those members of Congress involved actively in the debate are subject to great lobbying by special interest groups, each with its own point of view and its own advantage to press for. Energy represents very big money, and big money has big lobbying power. . . . even a small contribution to our overall energy needs represents very large amounts of money indeed. The gas-producing companies naturally want to press for a price de-regulation schedule that is to their greatest advantage; they owe it to their stockholders to maximize profits. Utility lobbyists press for and environmental lobbyists oppose the construction of new nuclear power plants. The large oil companies have their lobbyists, as do the small ones, high technology firms lobby for a place in OTEC or the development of photovoltaics. Lobbying is a fact of political life in the United States (and probably everywhere). Is there any wonder that Congress, surrounded by great pressures from all directions, was unable to move in any?

The third reason is intrinsic to the American political system. There is, in effect, an election every two years, off-year elections alternating with full Presidential ones. Any member of the House of Representatives, once elected, must immediately start electioneering for the next time. He must help in the quick solution of relatively easy problems, he must take stands on popular issues so that there will be something to show before he again faces the voters. The energy problem is not a two-year problem nor a four-year one; it will certainly not be solved before the next election. Even with massive and successful effort, it will be twenty years before new energy sources are contributing a significant fraction of our national energy supply. Solid achievements are likely to be slow in coming, but the decisions must be made quickly so that progress is possible. A politically monolithic country, whose leaders face only pro-forma elections, can embark on a series of five-year plans which may or may not be successful, but they are certainly easier to develop. We are not about to change our political system to achieve this; the only real alternative is continued public awareness of the problem, translated into consistent pressure that it be faced in all its aspects—political, economic, societal, and technical. There is no single solution, no magic panacea. Progress will come through a net of intertwining new energy sources of different kinds to complement one another and to satisfy the diversity of our needs, but, as yet, little has been accomplished. There is so far to go and we have hardly begun the journey.

[Owen Phillips, *The Last Chance Energy Book* (Baltimore, MD: Johns Hopkins University Press, 1979), pp. 129–31.] Reprinted by permission.

❧ Unit 48 ❧

Paraphrasing

**Writing skills: Paraphrasing; summarizing; quoting;
    avoiding plagiarism**

INTRODUCTION

Paraphrasing is the skill of expressing someone else's ideas in words of your
own. As such, it is essential to your success in writing for university coursework:
you will paraphrase every time you write a report, a research paper, a thesis, a
dissertation, or any paper based in part on other people's writings. Your ability
to paraphrase well depends strongly on your ability (1) to summarize and (2) to
express the same information in a variety of ways. Also related are your ability
to use quotations effectively without overusing them, and your understanding
of what constitutes plagiarism and how to avoid plagiarizing. In this unit you
will learn guidelines for all these skills and will practice applying them.

WARMUP I: PARAPHRASING

In a sense, a research paper is a composition of your own in which you include
some information from published sources and the opinions of some specialists on
matters related to your topic. In other words, a research paper (or a report, a
thesis, a dissertation) is basically your own organization and wording, not just a
collection of quotations from experts. You have to be able to paraphrase well in
order to write such a paper, because putting other people's ideas into your own
words tells your professor how well you understand the material. (At the same
time, it tells how proficient you are in English.)

One of the most common weaknesses of research papers is that students quote
too much and don't paraphrase enough. Although occasional quoting is acceptable, there are specific guidelines to follow in deciding when and how to quote
(see Warmup II). For the purposes of this exercise, do not quote at all: reexpress
everything in words of your own.

The principles of paraphrasing might best be presented through an example.
Suppose that you are doing research for a term paper on alternative energy

221

sources, and you decide to include the idea expressed in the following quotation by the late Senator Henry M. Jackson:

> A major factor contributing to our present energy crisis is that the necessary research and development efforts which could have provided us with the technological options and capabilities we now need so desperately were not undertaken in the past. (Hammond et al., 1973, p. 47)

INSTRUCTIONS:
Use the following methods in order to paraphrase Senator Jackson's statement:

Method 1.
A. Read the passage carefully, and then without looking back to it at all, attempt to express it in a sentence of your own. Write it here:

B. Now compare what you have written with the original sentence. Did you (1) capture the essential meaning of the original (2) without repeating the vocabulary or sentence structure? If so, this may be the best technique for you. If not, try the following approach.

Method 2.
A. Take some of the key vocabulary from the original statement and write down synonyms and related words. (A thesaurus and a dictionary can help you.)

major: _____   factor: _____   present: _____

provided: _____   options: _____

B. Now rewrite the original sentence, changing its structure somewhat and using the words you have just written down in place of the original vocabulary. Write it here:

You might have said something like this: "Senator Henry Jackson believes that one of the main reasons for the current energy crisis is that in the past, no one began the sorts of studies and experiments that could have given us the energy alternatives we need so much now."

Notice that not every word and phrase has been changed. *Energy crisis* was kept because it has become almost a technical phrase for which there is no adequate equivalent; it is not a term coined by Senator Jackson. It is acceptable to retain such words and phrases in your research paper without putting them in quotation marks.

INSTRUCTIONS:
Following the preceding methods, paraphrase the following sentences.

1. Fossil fuel resources in the United States are running out faster than nuclear fuels can replace them, and the growing reliance on nuclear fuels could be dangerous and environmentally damaging. (Hammond et al., 1973, p. 47)

2. For the present, . . . the U.S. energy industry is firmly structured around petroleum, and it is likely to remain that way for some time. (Hammond et al., 1973, p. 3)

3. Natural gas is one of our most precious energy resources. Not only is it the cheapest and most versatile fossil fuel available but, perhaps most important, it is also the least polluting. (Hammond et al., 1973, p. 11)

4. . . . opposition to nuclear power plants on environmental grounds has led to bitter disputes over their siting and delays in their construction. (Hammond et al., 1973, p. 32)

5. The remaining problems require concerted effort as well as substantial sums of money for exploration and technology development. The prospects, however, seem well worth the price. (Hammond et al., 1973, p. 60)

WARMUP II: USING DIRECT QUOTATIONS

When you are writing a research paper, you may feel that because you are neither an expert on the topic nor a professional writer, your paper should present the exact words of authorities who are both. However, you should resist this temptation. Although such respect for authority is admirable, a professor will not be impressed by a paper that is essentially a collection of quotations. Professors at American universities want to know not just that you have located important information, but also that you have thought about it, understood it, and used it as the basis for some coherent presentation of your own devising. The paper should be your work; you are the author. Reference to published works should be made only in order to support your ideas, to show the reader that facts and the opinions of authorities verify the conclusions you have drawn in the paper. Such a paper is evidence to the professor that you have really learned something from doing the research.

In keeping with this approach to writing research papers, you should paraphrase wherever possible. In fact, the only time when quoting directly from an author's work is justifiable is when *both* the following conditions are fulfilled:

1. When the author is such an authority or important personage that the reader would be impressed at knowing her or his exact words.
2. When there is really some reason why the exact wording is important.

For example, observe when and how Daniel Ford uses quotations in the following excerpts from his book *The Cult of the Atom: The Secret Papers of the Atomic Energy Commission* (1982):

> Although Congress and the Administration wanted, as President Truman said, to "make a blessing" of atomic energy, the Cold War, as well as bureaucratic, technical and economic obstacles, stood in the way. (p. 31)

> In response to the persistent questioning of plant safety, Schlesinger [a senior Atomic Energy Commission official] argued that the chance of a catastrophic accident was "virtually zero." (p. 135)

> In the article he stated his belief, supported by reference to industry reports, that the emergency cooling systems installed on American nuclear plants were adequate to prevent meltdown accidents. The risk of major accidents was "very small" and "insignificant," he said. (pp. 140–41)

Throughout the book, Ford uses his own words, not direct quotations, when giving *facts* to the reader. Of course, he drew these facts from his research, but there is no reason to quote them directly. He quotes only when it is important that the reader know the exact words that reveal key persons' *attitudes, opinions,* or *interpretations* of facts. Of course Ford could have paraphrased these quotations too—anything can be paraphrased—but in certain cases it was important to give the reader these people's exact phrasing.

In this exercise you will apply the guidelines just enumerated when paraphrasing or quoting from the following passages.

INSTRUCTIONS:

On a separate piece of paper, paraphrase most of each of the following passages, retaining only the underlined phrases as direct quotations. Follow Ford's examples of quotation mark and punctuation form.

1. [Edward Teller, physicist, head of the Atomic Energy Commission's Reactor Safeguard Committee, to the Joint Committee on Atomic Energy in 1953:] . . . no legislation will be able to stop future accidents and avoid completely occasional loss of life. It is my opinion that the unavoidable danger which will remain after all reasonable controls have been employed must not stand in the way of rapid development of nuclear power. (Quoted in Ford, 1982, p. 43)

2. To the extent that we relearn the forging of consensus, energy policy too will benefit. Without it, energy policymaking will continue as the major battleground for opposing philosophies, lifestyles, and perceptions of the national destiny. That perhaps is the hard core of the energy problem. (Landsberg, 1981, p. 71)

3. Coal and nuclear power face political barriers. They inflict penalties or side effects paid for not directly by utility customers, but by the general public: air pollution caused by burning coal, unsightly damage caused by strip mining, fear of a nuclear accident, and the dislike of passing nuclear wastes along to future generations.

   Controversies about these side effects must be solved politically. This inevitably means a slower solution than if the issues could be decided in the marketplace.

   Still, some increases in coal and nuclear output will occur, perhaps enough to offset probable decreases in oil and gas output. The likely result: zero growth in energy supply for at least a decade. (Stobaugh, 1981, p. 72)

4. Though political oppositions will be formidable, we should let oil prices rise to world levels, to reflect the desirability of reducing oil imports. We should decontrol the price of all natural gas and encourage electricity pricing that reflects the cost of building new power plants. Meanwhile, the government should give financial incentives to investments that improve energy efficiency. (Stobaugh, 1981, p. 72)

5. As we have seen, the basic reason for the energy crisis is that nearly all the energy now used in the United States (and in the world) comes from nonrenewable sources. As a nonrenewable source is depleted, it becomes progressively more costly to produce, so that continued reliance on it means an unending escalation in price. (Commoner, 1979, p. 49)

WRITING: PARAPHRASING AND SUMMARIZING

When writing a term paper, in most cases you will want to include only the main ideas of even rather long reading passages from your research. You will therefore need to use your summarizing as well as your paraphrasing skills.

INSTRUCTIONS:

Following the guidelines from Unit 47 and from Warmup I of this unit, write a paraphrased summary of each of the following passages.

1. American attitudes toward energy were not always so cavalier. When wood was a primary fuel and had to be cut by hand, it was used sparingly; in the early years of this century, turning off electric lights was a common habit. Nor was energy conservation just a matter of personal values— energy was expensive. But between World War II and 1971, energy prices dropped steadily and there were no major shortages. What might have been seen as a warning sign—the declining overall efficiency of energy use in the United States since 1967—was largely ignored. Now both higher prices and temporary shortages seem inevitable. (Hammond et al., 1973, p. 127)

2. Not long ago, proposals for using the sun's energy were apt to be received with considerable skepticism. Within a few agencies of the federal government and at an increasing number of university and industrial laboratories, that is no longer the case. Indeed, perhaps the most impressive testimony to the prospects for this type of energy is the score of prestigious scientists and engineers who have begun working on methods for converting the sun's radiation into forms more useful to man—heat, electricity, or chemical fuels. (Hammond et al., 1973, p. 61)

3. Coping with such [energy-related] problems [in the future] involves four basic tasks:
    • Adjusting to high and rising energy prices.
    • Moving to a different mix of energy sources, in which oil, and after a while gas, will decline in importance. Coal and, if we are lucky, nuclear energy will rise, and in the longer run nondepletable sources will come to play an ever increasing role.
    • Accomplishing the above tasks with the least damage to the economy, the environment, and world peace.
    • Adopting measures that will enable us to withstand the inevitable shocks and new stresses that lie ahead. (Landsberg, 1981, p. 71)

4. The facts are these: that, despite our dependence on imports, there is enough oil and natural gas under the ground in the United States to meet our needs for years to come; that the problem with relying on these fuels is that they become more and more costly as they are depleted—and that their rising price has become a major cause of inflation; that the solution to the energy crisis is not a larger military budget or a war in the Middle East, but a transition to a source that is plentiful, renewable, and stable in price—solar energy; that the transition to solar energy can begin at once; that we could, for example, easily make up for any shortage of fuel from Iran by producing a solar fuel—alcohol made from our own grain crops—a measure that could help the farmers' income, control gasoline prices, and keep inflation in check; that a solar transition, begun now, would end the need for new nuclear power plants and gradually phase out the existing ones; and that the solar transition would solve not only the energy crisis, but the economic crisis as well, for it would improve the efficiency of production, stimulate the economy, and reveal as counterfeit the notion

that the United States, the richest country in human history, must enter an age of austerity. (Commoner, 1979, p. vii)

5.   The pencil-thin fuel rods used in United States nuclear plants are twelve feet long and are stacked upright inside the reactor. The fuel rods consist of hollow tubes made of Zircaloy—an alloy of zirconium—which are filled with pellets of uranium dioxide fuel. . . . There are thirty to forty thousand Zircaloy fuel rods in a large nuclear reactor, and they are packed together tightly to form the reactor's "core"—which is typically only twelve to fifteen feet in diameter.

During normal operation, a continuous river of cooling water flows upward through the narrow channels between the fuel rods. The flowing water keeps the fuel rods at a normal temperature of about 600 degrees Fahrenheit. During an accident in which the normal cooling water is lost as a result of a major pipe rupture, emergency cooling water is supposed to be injected into the reactor. It would also have to flow through the tiny channels in between the fuel rods.

Since it would take several minutes, even under the most favorable circumstances, before the normal cooling water could be replaced, the temperature of the fuel rods inside the reactor would increase temporarily before they were doused with emergency cooling water. The fuel-rod temperatures might increase from 600 degrees to more than 2,000 degrees within the first few minutes of a serious loss-of-coolant accident.

This was worrisome to safety analysts for several reasons, and one particular concern was that the fuel rods, as they heated up, might begin to swell. The rods were spaced together so closely that if they expanded substantially, they might block the channels through which emergency cooling water was supposed to flow. "Flow blockage" caused by swollen fuel rods could delay the arrival of emergency cooling water in parts of the core, allowing the fuel-rod temperatures to increase. If the blockage was bad enough, it might possibly allow some of the fuel to begin to melt. (Ford, 1982, pp. 95–96)*

AVOIDING PLAGIARISM

Plagiarism is the act of using another person's ideas or wording without giving that person credit. In a research paper, plagiarism takes place if you do not inform the reader that certain information or ideas were obtained from a particular source or sources and were not your original ideas. But even if you tell the source of the information, if you directly quote a paragraph, a sentence, or even a phrase without also telling the reader that this exact wording is not your own, you are guilty of plagiarizing. Plagiarism is considered a form of literary stealing and is such a serious offense that at American colleges and universities, a student found guilty of it can fail the research paper or even the whole course. Sometimes international students plagiarize unintentionally because they do not understand the strictness of the requirements for avoiding plagiarism, but professors do not generally make allowances for accidental or unintentional plagiarism; all students are expected to know the rules for giving credit where credit is due.

In order to avoid plagiarizing, follow these simple guidelines:

1. In your paper, identify the source of every idea or piece of information that did not come out of your own head. (In Unit 54 you will learn the correct forms of giving credit and citing sources.) Even when you have paraphrased everything into your own words, you still have to cite your sources.

2. Just telling the source is not enough if you actually use any of the author's original wording. If you directly quote a paragraph, a sentence, or even a phrase, you must also indicate to your reader that these are not your original words by enclosing them in quotation marks or (if the quoted passage is longer than three typewritten lines) by indenting the passage.

INSTRUCTIONS:

Here is a passage quoted directly from Daniel Ford's book *The Cult of the Atom*. Following the passage are examples of how five students used it in their research papers. All of the examples but one violate the plagiarism guidelines. Identify the one that does not, and identify the specific violations in the other four.

The nuclear power program in the United States, which has risked both public safety and billions of dollars over the last three decades, is an example of a government-sponsored enterprise that obeys the laws of inertia. The Atomic Energy Commission was asked by Congress to promote the use of nuclear energy for peaceful purposes. It was a powerful, mission-oriented bureaucracy, and it set out to do its assigned task with a single-minded fervor. There had been no debate in Congress about the desirability of a large nuclear-power program—its virtues were unquestioned—and there was none within the A.E.C. . . .

The A.E.C. and the N[uclear] R[egulatory] C[ommission], which was made from it, were able to ignore what they did not wish to believe and were inclined to cover up everything discreditable. . . . The agencies disregarded the warning signs—the numerous reports of trouble at the operating plants—as well as the advice from Hanauer [a nuclear safety expert] and other experts who questioned the official safety assurances. . . . The problems did not go away, of course, merely because they were ignored and have accumulated, uncorrected, in the plants now operating around the country. In many cases it was difficult to fix them even if anybody wanted to, since many of the most serious problems involve basic design mistakes. Other problems, which could have been corrected—and still could be—remain uncorrected because the cost of fixing them is more than the economically depressed nuclear industry thinks it can afford. (pp. 236–37)*

Student's Example 1

In the interests of building up the nuclear power industry, the U.S. government's Atomic Energy Commission and its successor, the Nuclear Regulatory Commission, have neglected or in some cases even refused to require that industry to meet acceptable safety standards. Unsafe conditions have prevailed in part because of basic design mistakes and in part because of the great expense that meeting safety standards would entail.

Student's Example 2

In the interests of promoting the nuclear power industry, the U.S.-government-sponsored Atomic Energy Commission and its successor, the Nuclear Regulatory

Commission, have ignored or in some cases even covered up violations of safety standards. Unsafe conditions have prevailed in part because of basic design mistakes and in part because the cost of fixing them is more than the economically depressed nuclear industry thinks it can afford. (Ford, 1982, pp. 236–37)

Student's Example 3

In the interests of promoting the nuclear power industry, the U.S.-government-sponsored Atomic Energy Commission and its successor, the Nuclear Regulatory Commission, have ignored or in some cases even covered up violations of safety standards. Unsafe conditions have prevailed in part because of basic design mistakes and in part "because the cost of fixing them is more than the economically depressed nuclear industry thinks it can afford." (Ford, 1982, pp. 236–37)

Student's Example 4

In the interests of building up the nuclear power industry, the U.S. government's Atomic Energy Commission and its successor, the Nuclear Regulatory Commission, have neglected or in some cases even refused to require that industry to meet acceptable safety standards. Unsafe conditions have prevailed in part because of "basic design mistakes" (Ford, 1982, p. 237) and in part because of the great expense that meeting safety standards would entail.

Student's Example 5

In the interests of building up the nuclear power industry, the U.S. government's Atomic Energy Commission and its successor, the Nuclear Regulatory Commission, have neglected or in some cases even refused to require that industry to meet acceptable safety standards. Unsafe conditions have prevailed in part because of "basic design mistakes" and in part because of the great expense that meeting safety standards would entail. (Ford, 1982, pp. 236–37)

SOURCES CITED IN UNIT 48

Commoner, Barry [professor of environmental science, Washington University, St. Louis, Missouri; chairman of the executive committee, Center for the Biology of Natural Systems; chairman of the board of directors of the Scientists' Institute for Public Information]. *The Politics of Energy*. New York: Alfred A. Knopf, 1979.

Ford, Daniel [Economist, author, specialist on nuclear policy concerns; former executive director, Union of Concerned Scientists]. *The Cult of the Atom: The Secret Papers of the Atomic Energy Commission*. New York: Simon and Schuster, 1982.

Hammond, Allen L., et al. *Energy and the Future*. Washington, D.C.: American Association for the Advancement of Science, 1973.

Landsberg, Hans H. [Center for Energy Policy Research, Resources for the Future]. Quoted in "What Six Experts Say." *National Geographic Special Report on Energy*. Washington, D.C.: National Geographic Society, 1981, pp. 70–73.

Stobaugh, Robert B. [Harvard Graduate School of Business Administration]. Quoted in "What Six Experts Say." *National Geographic Special Report on Energy*. Washington, D.C.: National Geographic Society, 1981, pp. 70–73.

❦ Unit 49 ❦

Synthesizing

Writing skill: Synthesizing information from a variety of sources

INTRODUCTION

When you finish doing the research for a term paper, thesis, or dissertation, you will have accumulated information from a variety of sources. One of the tasks in writing the paper will be to *synthesize,* or combine, related information from various sources into sentences and paragraphs of your own. For example, in one paragraph you may want to include information taken from two or three sources. Instead of simply listing it, you will want to combine it into coherent, well-constructed sentences that show how the different items or ideas are related to each other. In order to synthesize information well, you must be able to summarize and paraphrase effectively, as well as to combine ideas in ways that show their relationship to each other.

WRITING: SYNTHESIZING INFORMATION FROM A VARIETY OF SOURCES

There are three basic steps to synthesizing information from research.

1. Make sure you understand the passages whose information you want to synthesize.
2. Summarize each passage in your own words, following the guidelines for summarizing and paraphrasing in Units 47 and 48.
3. Determine the relationship between the passages. Is it one of contrast? Cause and effect? Agreement? Addition? General statement and example? Write a brief summary that includes the pertinent information from the two or three sources you are using, showing the reader clearly what this relationship is.*

*For ways to express addition, contrast, and cause and effect, see Appendix III.

Example 1

Geography Professor Johannes Philippi says that the cause of the energy crisis is that the United States has wasted too much of the world's energy supplies since World War II.

Economics Professor Yow-Ning Chang says that it is immaterial whose fault it has been: the ultimate cause is that the whole world has been relying on depletable energy supplies instead of developing renewable ones, so a crisis was inevitable.

Synthesis: Whereas Philippi (1982) blames the current crisis on the United States having squandered world energy supplies, Chang (1983) sees a crisis as having been inevitable in light of world dependence on nonrenewable sources.

Example 2

Environmentalist Julio Sanchez says that one of the worst drawbacks to dependence on coal as an energy source is air pollution.

Agronomist Maulin Desai says that strip mining for coal destroys thousands of square kilometers of potential farmland.

Synthesis: Two disadvantages to dependence on coal as an energy source are air pollution (Sanchez, 1979) and destruction of arable land through strip mining (Desai, 1981).

Example 3

Ernest Bellinetti, director of the Institute for Energy Solutions, says that the United States' dependence on imported oil could be cut in half over the next ten years if the federal government would subsidize the development of solar power.

Energy researcher Sunday Olanaran reports on the success of a California experiment in which solar power was used to provide for all the energy needs of a twenty-unit apartment building over a nine-month period.

Synthesis: Ernest Bellinetti, director of the Institute for Energy Solutions, contends that federal subsidy of solar power development would halve United States dependence on foreign oil over a ten-year period (1982). A California experiment lends credence to his belief: solar power was used to provide for all the energy needs of a twenty-unit apartment building over a nine-month period (Olanaran, 1983).

INSTRUCTIONS:
Following the guidelines and examples just given, synthesize each of the following groups of quotations into a brief, well-constructed paragraph in your own words. If you choose to quote, limit yourself to not more than one phrase per synthesis, and follow the format for using quotation marks from the examples in Unit 48. Follow the preceding examples for the format for citing sources; remember that you will be guilty of plagiarizing if you use information from outside sources without giving credit to the author.

GROUP 1

A. Coal burning is a major culprit in pumping carbon dioxide into the atmosphere, which, some experts maintain, is creating a greenhouse effect. They fear a planetary warming that will change weather and agriculture patterns and melt polar ice caps enough to raise the ocean levels. The federal government has launched a five-year study to define the threat. (Canby and Blair, 1981, p. 86)

B. Burning coal (or any fuel containing carbon) may cause permanent changes in the world's climate. These fuels, when burned, release into the atmosphere a gas, carbon dioxide, that is not normally considered an air pollutant. But carbon dioxide in the air acts like a "one-way mirror"; it lets the sun's rays reach the earth's surface but won't let the heat escape from the earth into outer space. This process is called the "greenhouse effect," because it is similar to the way glass traps heat inside a greenhouse. If, over long periods of time, large amounts of carbon dioxide accumulate in the atmosphere, global temperatures may increase by a few degrees. This increase might melt snow and ice in the polar areas, thereby raising the level of the oceans to flood coastal areas, where many people now live. A rise in temperature could bring rain to the Sahara or turn U.S. corn-growing areas into dry prairies. There is no immediate danger from the buildup of carbon dioxide in the atmosphere. Nonetheless, considering the vast amounts that might be added in the future from the burning of fossil fuels, especially coal, we must gain a better understanding of how possible changes in the atmosphere may upset the earth's climate. (Kiefer, 1979, pp. 50–51)

GROUP 2

A. In summary, the immediate course for national survival in this unwanted revolution can only rest on conservation, both individual and national, and on a rapid development of alternative fuels based on coal. . . .

Conservation and coal conversion—there seem to be no immediate workable alternatives. The one is being forced upon us by the relentless increases in the prices of oil that lie ahead. The other can be done, it *has* been done, but will it be done again on the massive scale that is needed if our society is not to choke of economic strangulation? (Phillips, 1979, pp. 100–101)

B. We have stated that there were illusions in the past about how long coal would last. Many countries have large amounts under the ground, in terms of tons, but the point is that the expansion rate of the economies, and the need to replace oil with coal, will use up the coal about 10–20 times faster than had initially been expected. A lot of calculations have been done on this. It turns out that the time when coal will be exhausted with the assumption of *prosperity* (and not depression) in the Western world will be around 2030–2050 . . . . (McGown and Bockris, 1980, p. 50)

GROUP 3

A. Unlike the burning of fossil fuels, burning of dried plant material should not increase the carbon dioxide content of the air because it is only returning carbon dioxide that was taken from the air a relatively short time earlier during the growth of the plant. A significant factor that limits the growth of plant life and must be considered in land-based biomass systems, however, is lack of adequate water supplies. (*Energy: Fuel of Life,* 1979, p. 225)

B. At present the extent to which such [biomass] sources can replace conventional fuels is not known, but the possibilities appear to be large. Another uncertainty is cost, but, as with all other new developments, initial costs are usually not indicative of final costs; after a product is more widely used, mass production of equipment and supplies becomes possible. (*Energy: Fuel of Life,* 1979, p. 227)

C. Plants, or biomass, are as easy to burn as coal but produce relatively little pollution. Biomass contains almost no sulfur and leaves no ash. However, it often contains dirt, stones, and water, which do not burn. Biomass is awkward and expensive to handle, but like coal, it can be converted to gases and liquids that are easier to handle. (Kiefer, 1979, p. 110)

D. There are a number of drawbacks to producing energy from biomass. A large amount of land is required, land on which food could be grown. ... Large amounts of fertilizer and water also would be needed, and it might be that more energy is consumed in the process than is produced. (Kiefer, 1979, p. 114)

GROUP 4

A. Though political oppositions will be formidable, we should let oil prices rise to world levels, to reflect the desirability of reducing oil imports. We should decontrol the price of all natural gas and encourage electricity pricing that reflects the cost of building new power plants. Meanwhile, the government should give financial incentives to investments that improve energy efficiency. (Stobaugh, 1981, p. 72)

B. We have ample sources of oil, natural gas, coal, uranium, and geothermal energy available within our borders, more of each than has been produced so far in the history of our nation. These energy sources will be able to carry us not only until synthetic oil and gas are available in large quantities from oil shale and coal, but also until solar power and other nontraditional energy forms are developed. (Hartley, 1981, p. 72)

C. If we are to win back control over our energy future, however, the nation must accept a program of regulatory consistency and balanced environmental law, put greater reliance on free-market forces for pricing of energy, provide access to public lands for energy exploration while preserving the great wilderness areas, promote use of coal and nuclear power without sacrificing health and safety considerations, and continue a vigorous stress on energy efficiency. Higher prices, more efficient energy-consuming machines, and greater dedication to the total conservation ethic have resulted, incidentally, in a 20 percent drop in oil imports in 1980 from the previous year. (Hartley, 1981, p. 72)

D. Decontrol is a cruel policy. It is a policy that imposes disproportionate sacrifices upon those who can least afford them; it fuels the inflation that is steadily eroding the economic gains that the working men and women of this nation have made in recent years; it surrenders the last vestiges of independence that this country has from the pricing decisions of the OPEC cartel. (Metzenbaum, 1979, p. 18)

E. The oil companies do not need more incentives to produce in this country—they already have the most generous incentives in the world. Yet, in spite of those incentives, production in the Lower 48 States continues to fall. The oil companies say that they need high profits to restore domestic production. They say that they need money to bring on line new sources like shale oil and tar sands and heavy oils. However, the record shows that, too often, the industry does not use its profits to increase energy production. The record shows that, time and again, the major oil companies use their earnings to expand in areas that are wholly unrelated to gas and oil. (Metzenbaum, 1979, p. 18)

F. Decontrol is a dead end. It has *not* worked to increase the supply of natural gas, and it will not work for crude oil either. It will strengthen OPEC, it will massively boost inflation, but it will do nothing—absolutely nothing—to lessen this country's dependence on foreign oil.

Decontrol will do nothing—absolutely nothing—to restore stability to our economy. It will do nothing to rally the American people behind a fair and balanced national energy policy. Deconutrol is a policy that abandons even the hope that our government can determine the energy future of this nation. (Metzenbaum, 1979, p. 19)

SOURCES CITED IN UNIT 49

Canby, Thomas Y., and Jonathan Blair. "Synfuels: Fill 'er Up! With What?" *National Geographic Special Report on Energy*. Washington, D.C.: National Geographic Society, 1981, pp. 74–95.

Energy: The Fuel of Life. Prepared by the Editors of Encyclopaedia Brittanica. New York: Bantam/Brittanica, 1979.

Hartley, Fred L. [chairman and president, Union Oil Company; president, American Petroleum Institute]. Quoted in "What Six Experts Say." *National Geographic Special Report on Energy*. Washington, D.C.: National Geographic Society, 1981, pp. 70–73.

Kiefer, Irene. *Energy for America*. New York: Atheneum, 1979.

McGown, Linda Baine, and John O'M. Bockris. *How to Obtain Abundant Clean Energy*. New York: Plenum Press, 1980.

Metzenbaum, [Senator] Howard M. [Democrat, Ohio]. "The Case Against Oil Price Decontrol." *USA Today* 108 (September 1979): 18–19. Copyright © 1979 by the Society for the Advancement of Education.

Phillips, Owen. *The Last Chance Energy Book*. Baltimore, MD: Johns Hopkins University Press, 1979.

Stobaugh, Robert B. [Harvard Graduate School of Business Administration]. Quoted in "What Six Experts Say." *National Geographic Special Report on Energy*. Washington, D.C.: National Geographic Society, 1981, pp.70–73.

❧ Unit 50 ❧

Revising V

Writing forms: Review of forms used in previous units
Writing skills: Revising; rewriting

INTRODUCTION

This unit offers you the opportunity to reread your previous compositions, generalize about your strengths and weaknesses, and do what any good writer must do: revise and rewrite, as was first practiced in Unit 11.

PLANNING AND WRITING

Reread the compositions that you have not previously reread or revised. You should have corrected them by now and they should be in your folder. Review the notebook or the sheets (suggested in the introduction to this textbook and in the tip in Unit 6), and bring your comments up to date. You should be able to tell from the pattern of mistakes how much progress you have been making.

Choose one of your previous compositions that you feel needs to be rewritten and look it over carefully, taking notes on improvements that you feel you can make. Read the checklist for additional suggestions.

When you are satisfied that you have carefully thought about the content, theme, and organization, make a simple outline before you begin to write. Then write the composition, reuse the checklist, and make any final changes. Turn in your outline, folder, and rewritten paper.

❧ Unit 51 ❧

Understanding the Term Paper: Choosing Topics, Finding Sources, and Using the Library

Writing form: Research or term paper
Writing skills: Determining the appropriateness of topics; selecting a topic; evaluating sources; using the library effectively

INTRODUCTION

In a wide variety of academic fields, at the thesis level in master's and Ph.D. programs, and in research work in general, the term or research paper is a standard form. If you are properly prepared, you will be able not only to benefit from writing such a paper and earn a good grade, but you will also find it an enjoyable and stimulating experience.

Professors often assign term papers to allow you to learn how to narrow a topic, how to find sources, how to use the library facilities, and how to gain maturity in developing the topic. The instructor, therefore, will not give you a specific topic, list all the sources you should use, tell you how to use the library, or tell you in advance how to treat the subject. These are matters that you will normally be expected to handle by yourself.

The following eight units are designed to give you all the basic information and guidance that you will need in order to succeed in writing a term paper. The first four units offer a general introduction; the next four guide you through the actual process as you write a paper. You will need to be familiar with a good library, and if you are not, you should make arrangements to visit one or take a guided tour.

TIP

As soon as you find out about an important writing assignment, begin looking into the topic and writing down ideas. The longer the period in which you collect information and plan your presentation, the better the paper will be.

236

WARMUP I: DETERMINING THE APPROPRIATENESS OF TOPICS

An overview of the process of writing a term paper might look like this:

1. The professor gives a general area on which you are to write; tells when the paper is due; and offers rough criteria on how long it is to be, whether it must be typed, and so on.
2. You use various methods of narrowing the topic and finding sources. Unless this is a major paper (such as a master's thesis), you will not have more than a few weeks to complete it, and you will be busy in other courses, so you will have to plan your time and your energy carefully.
3. You will spend about half of your time reading your sources and taking notes.
4. You will plan an original way of dealing with all the information and will write a draft, carefully noting from which sources you obtained your ideas.
5. You will revise your draft and complete the bibliography, title page, abstract (if required), and other parts of the paper. Then you will type it neatly on standard-sized paper (8½ by 11 inches in the United States).
6. You will turn it in on time, keep a copy for yourself, wait for the professor to read and grade it, and then eagerly look for the grade and comments when you get it back. You also will probably keep it for a long time.

In the following exercises you will be asked questions that will help you review principles that you probably have already studied. You should ask your teacher for an explanation if the answers are not clear to you.

INSTRUCTIONS:
The kind of paper you write will depend on your field, your level, and the type of course you are taking. Sort the following topics into the three categories and be prepared to explain your choices.

Categories:

A. Popular topics, generally appropriate for basic "general education" or undergraduate courses.
B. Specialized topics, but at the introductory level, appropriate for undergraduate or introductory graduate-level courses.
C. Narrowly specialized topics appropriate for advanced graduate courses.

1. ____ Better sources of energy.

2. ____ The use of vacuum technology in the production of crystals.

3. ____ The political impacts of population-control programs in developing nations.

4. ____ How to have good health.

5. ____ The influence of job-related stress on mental health.

6. ____ The presence and effects of heavy metal traces on protein synthesis in fish.

7. _____ Photochemical reactions and the breakdown of sulfur dioxide emissions.

8. _____ How to have world peace and understanding.

9. _____ Meditation: its neurochemical correlates.

10. _____ Family structure in Japan.

11. _____ Racial prejudice in United States cities.

12. _____ The effects of the use of primary colors on the interpersonal behavior of children.

13. _____ The role of electric cars in modern public transportation systems in large cities.

14. _____ The use of television in education.

15. _____ Is art more important than science in modern life?

16. _____ Mothers who work: effects on how early their infants learn to talk.

17. _____ How industrialization affects society.

18. _____ The use of aluminum in modern office buildings.

19. _____ Science in modern life.

20. _____ Cognitive processes in advanced writing.

WARMUP II: FACTORS IN SELECTING A TOPIC

INSTRUCTIONS:
Decide how important each of the factors listed here is in selecting a topic. Be prepared to explain your choice. Use this scale:

A. Very important
B. Important
C. Not very important

1. _____ The opinion of the teacher who will read and grade the paper.

2. _____ The opinion of your classmates who will not read the paper.

3. _____ Whether or not there is sufficient information about the topic in the library system.

4. _____ Whether the topic is appropriate to the level and subject of the course.

5. _____ How convenient it will be to find the sources in the library.

6. _____ Whether you will need to use charts and graphs in the paper.

7. _____ Whether there is enough time to collect the essential information before the paper is due.

8. _____ How related the topic is to the other reading assignments you have in other courses.

9. _____ How comfortable the chairs are in the library.

10. _____ Whether your friends will meet with you when you go to the library.

11. _____ Whether the topic is of personal interest to you.

12. _____ Whether you can find a copy of a similar paper written by one of your friends.

13. _____ Whether many other students are writing on the same topic and using the same books.

WARMUP III: THE VALUE OF DIFFERENT SOURCES FOR FINDING INFORMATION

To write a relevant, up-to-date, informative, and accurate paper you need to find relevant, up-to-date, informative, and accurate sources. The following exercise will help you focus on the issues.

INSTRUCTIONS:
Imagine that you are going to write a specialized paper in your major field. Listed here are eighteen possible ways of getting the type of specific information that you would want to use in your paper. Rate each for its direct significance in helping you plan the content, and be prepared to explain your choices. Use this scale:

A. Most useful
B. Somewhat useful
C. Of little use

1. _____ A newspaper article with general information on the subject.

2. _____ The reference librarian in the library.

3. _____ A general index, such as *Readers' Guide to Periodical Literature*.

4. _____ A subject-specific index in your special field.

5. _____ *Dissertation Abstracts* (abstracts of doctoral dissertations).

6. _____ A modern general encyclopedia.

7. _____ The bibliography of a recent journal article on the same topic.

8. _____ The typist who will type your paper.

9. _____ A popular magazine article.

10. _____ A computer search of a large bank of articles (as provided in some modern libraries).

11. _____ A suggested reading list provided by the professor on the topic.

12. _____ A recent article on the subject by your professor.

13. _____ The library card catalogue.

14. _____ A book review of a book on the subject.

15. _____ A recent annotated bibliography in the area. (*Annotated* means that there is a brief review or evaluation of each entry.)

16. _____ A classmate who is planning to write on the same topic.

17. _____ A private agency or company that offers to sell you a good, finished paper on your topic.

18. _____ The teacher in this writing class.

EDITING

The mistakes in this exercise occur in the areas of sentence length, completeness, and complexity; they are not marked. There are no grammatical mistakes as such.

There are four main libraries on campus. There is the main library. There is the science library. There is the art library. And also there is the business library. The main library is at the center of the campus. The science library is near the auditorium. However, the main catalogue is at the main library.

Books are arranged in the catalogue. They are arranged by subject. They are arranged by title. For example, you may know the title or author of the book. You can look in the title catalogue. You may want to find books on a certain subject. You can look in the subject catalogue. There are many cards in the catalogue. Each card contains information. The information is important in finding a book. The information is important in helping you decide about the book. For example, do you want to look at it?

The computer searches of a large literature base are another feature of the library. Computers may also be used in locating a book. They also help in telling you if the book is checked out. They can tell you when it will be back, too.

To use a computer search to locate books or articles in a large literature base, you must do several things. You must fill out a form. You must select key words. The words are related to the main concepts of your topic. You must pay a small fee. The fee depends on the field. It also depends on the size of your list.

PLANNING AND WRITING

The writing assignment for this unit is to answer the following questions about your library system. You may simply give a list of answers, or if you wish to do a little extra work and end up with an attractive composition, tie your answers together into well-organized paragraphs.

You will need to be familiar with your library or go directly to the library to get the information. Take the library tour if there is one.

1. Where is the main library located?
2. Are there other libraries connected with this library or in the same general area that are of use or interest to you? Which ones?
3. What are the requirements regarding the use of the library? Do you need a card to use it? Can *you* check out books?
4. Where can you go in your library to get general help or information?
5. In general, what are the main parts or functions of your library?
6. Which types of books are in the reference section of your library?
7. Where is the general catalogue of your library located? How do you use it?
8. Which numbering system does your library use? If you do not know the name, give an example of a call number and tell to which subject area it refers.
9. In general terms, where are books in different subject areas located?
10. Is there a microfilm room? If so, which types of machines are there, and how are they used?
11. Does the library have copy machines? Which types? How much do they cost to use?

12. Which types of computer searches are available in the library?
13. If a book you are looking for is not on the shelf where you expected to find it, where might you check to find out where it might be? If you need it and still cannot find it, how do you proceed?
14. Is there a reserved reading area where books can be used only for a few hours or overnight? Which types of books are kept there?
15. Are there special collections in your library?
16. List one or two indexes in the reference section that you might use to find journal articles in your special area. Also list an index that you would use to find articles from popular magazines.
17. Where do you find a list of all the magazines and journals the library has?
18. What would you do if you wanted to use a book checked out by another person?
19. What is the periodical reading room?
20. Which part of the library is the most interesting and enjoyable for you? Which is the least pleasant (if any)?

The answers to the warmup and editing exercises are listed in the answers section after Unit 60. The answers to the planning and writing exercise are not provided, but you should continue working until you are confident you have answered at least 17 of the questions accurately. Do not consult the answers section in any of the following units until *after* you have finished each exercise.

❧ Unit 52 ❧

Understanding the Term Paper: Taking Notes on What You Read

Writing form: Term paper
Writing skills: Summarizing; taking notes

INTRODUCTION

Writing a term paper requires that you read a sufficient amount of relevant, useful, and up-to-date material to support your point of view. By choosing an appropriate topic, using available bibliographies, and searching through the professional indexes and the card catalogue, you should be able to find useful sources. Finding them and even reading them, however, will be insufficient. You will have to make a systematic record of what you found and exactly where you found it.

This unit will introduce the topic of solar energy as the basis for the explanations and exercises. At the level it is presented here, the topic would be suitable for an introductory university course.

To complete the writing assignment at the end of this unit, you will need a newspaper or magazine that has articles that you would find interesting. You will also need the skills of summarizing and paraphrasing that were studied in Units 47 and 48.

TIP

When you discover information and write it down, both the ideas and the words are considered yours. If other writers use them without recognizing you, they are literally stealing from you. To use the technical term, they are plagiarizing. Furthermore, if you had your materials copyrighted (legally certified as yours), and someone made copies of your work in a way that prevented you from getting the expected pay for your material, that person would be violating copyright laws and could be sued. Naturally, you might write material (such as the sample compositions in this book) that you intended to have others imitate. The law also allows certain types of copying.

Strongly resist the temptation to plagiarize. Don't use others' phrases or ideas without directly giving the person credit. If you intend to make copies of published materials for more than your own use, be sure you do not violate copyright laws in doing so. Stealing, of this or any other kind, could jeopardize your academic career.

WARMUP I: SUMMARIZING (A REVIEW)

In collecting information for writing a term paper, you will largely be taking down specific details, usually in the form of short, concise notes. These will be in your own words, and each note will contain only one major idea.

On other, much less common occasions, you will be writing down the exact words that you read. Since general practice suggests that no more than about five percent of your finished paper should be quotations, you should write down only key definitions or unusual or striking statements. Be sure you record the exact page number on which the quotation appears. Copying large amounts may save time in the short run, but in the long run you will still have to think about the material, and in addition you will have a greater temptation to plagiarize than if you put the ideas into your own words in the first place.

On still other occasions, you will find material that is somewhat general or that presents an overall picture of the material, and you will want to write a summary.

INSTRUCTIONS:
Take about 15 minutes to write a summary of the first four paragraphs of the sample reading selection at the end of this unit. Note the source and correct bibliogaphical reference. Use these guidelines:

1. Include all the major ideas.
2. Keep it as short as possible (no more than one quarter of the original).
3. Avoid making any of the subordinate ideas more prominent than the major ones.

After you have completely finished your own summary, look at the suggested summary in the answers section. If you feel yours can be further improved, take a few additional minutes before proceeding with Warmup II.

WARMUP II: TAKING NOTES

As just mentioned, you normally do not summarize everything you read. Rather, you take concise notes. In fact, you do not even take notes of everything you read for at least three reasons:

1. You may read the same information in several places, and taking complete notes from each source is obviously a waste of time.
2. Much of what you read may be common knowledge, that is, information that a reasonably well-informed reader could be expected to know. You will not have to refer to the source in using such knowledge, so spending time writing notes is unnecessary.
3. In writing a term paper, you are not simply reporting on everything you have read, but rather putting together a well-organized and focused

treatment of the subject. Taking notes of material that you clearly do not intend to use is pointless.

Look then for information, ideas, and details that you feel will directly contribute to your topic and write down, in as brief and accurate a form as possible, only that information that you think you will need. Naturally, you cannot know exactly, in advance, what you are going to say in the term paper, so you will collect more information than is necessary. However, avoid the temptation to record everything, to copy (or photocopy) every graph and table, and to laboriously follow through every argument and discussion. Especially avoid the temptation to copy down the exact words (or a slightly modified version of the exact words) in your notes. Quote your sources only if the material is a carefully worded definition or if it is remarkable or unique in some obvious way.

A popular and efficient way to take notes is as follows:

1. Use note cards of sturdy paper, rather than large sheets of paper. These cards are easy to handle and organize, do not tear with use, and are large enough for most notes. The two standard sizes in the United States are 3 × 5 inches and 4 × 6 inches. You can also buy plastic or metal containers designed especially for storing and filing these cards.
2. Use one card just to record the *exact* bibliographical reference of the source, including author's full name; name of article, journal, or book; date; and number of pages. Later units will cover this reference form in complete detail. You should also record the library call number.
3. Use one note card to record one idea or detail. That is, do not write several different major ideas on one card, and if possible, avoid spreading one major idea out over several different cards. Use the back, or staple two cards together if necessary. Later on you will want to sort your ideas, and if two different ideas are on one card, you will find sorting impossible.
4. On each card record both the page number and the source of the information. If you use a code (such as a series of letters or numbers or the author's initials, as will be illustrated in the next units), you can quickly and efficiently refer back to the first note card (the one with the bibliographical reference). Remember that if you have information but do not know where you found it, you really cannot use it.
5. If you use the author's words (other than the technical terms that are appropriate to the field), you must use quotation marks ("...") and give an exact page number. If you neglect to put such marks in your notes, you are making it easy for yourself to plagiarize.

INSTRUCTIONS:

Imagine that you are preparing to write an introductory term paper on the topic of solar energy and are reading the report quoted in the sample reading selection at the end of this unit. Use the four "note cards" given here. Each one guides you by listing the type of information you should record. When you are completely finished, check the answers section, and if your notes do not fit the model, continue working for an additional five minutes. The first card (the one with the bibliographical reference and a few general comments) has been completed for you. Be sure your notes are in your own words, or if not, that you use quotation marks.

Card 1 (as it should be):

> Weaver, Kenneth. "Our Energy Predicament." In *Energy, A Special Report*. Washington, D.C.: National Geographic Society, 1981.

> Comments: A special report by the National Geographic Society that appeared as a special issue in February 1981. Written in a popular style, with many colored graphs and pictures. Many articles by different authors. This article appears on pages 2–23.

Card 2 (Write your notes here on the general history of the use of resources, especially on the role of the twentieth century):

Card 3 (Write your notes here on gas reserves):

Card 4 (Write your notes here on the reserves in the U.S.A., the Soviet Union, the North Sea fields, and Arabic countries):

Card 5 (Write your notes here on the role of coal, listing its advantages and disadvantages):

EDITING

The mistakes are in accuracy, plagiarism, redundancy, and completeness of this so-called summary of the sample reading selection at the end of the unit. Referring to the sample reading selection and to the information in the preceding warmup exercises, rewrite this summary so that it is free from these serious errors.

I think that my children will look back over the long sweep of history and note with awe that people living in the twentieth century used up most of the world's supply of nuclear fuels, which were developed underground billions of years ago. Earl T. Hayes, former chief scientist at the U.S. Bureau of Mines in Washington, D.C., U.S.A., says that we are finding only about half as much new coal as we are using, and that it will be used up in ten years if unconventional sources should not come through. Likewise, oil reserves will be very low in Arabic countries by the year 2000, and North Sea and Russian sources will decline completely in the 1980s. Of coal there are reserves so immense that they are not in danger of exhaustion for some time, but transporting coal is unpopular politically and causes pollution.

PLANNING AND WRITING

Use a newspaper or magazine that has relatively short articles, and pick two or three that you think might be interesting. Write a short summary for one article, using the principles in Warmup I.

Write a series of notes for another article. Be sure to put the bibliographical reference on the first card and only one major idea or set of data on each subsequent card. You will study bibliographical forms later. For today, follow this basic formula:

Last name, first name. "Name of Article." *Name of Newspaper or Magazine* Volume (Month Year): page–page.

For example:

Wilhelm, John. "Solar Energy, the Ultimate Powerhouse." *National Geographic* 149 (March 1976): 380–97.

Sources of Energy

The bounty of hydrocarbon fuels—coal, oil, and gas, which biology and geology conspired to trap underground millions of years ago—is limited, and is not being replaced. Once a barrel of oil is burned, it is gone forever.

Over the long sweep of history, human beings will look back and note with awe (and chagrin) that their ancestors stripped the planet of most of this exhaustible endowment within the span of a few hundred years. Twentiety-century people alone will have used up the bulk of it.

Many analysts believe that, despite the current frenzied search for new deposits, the dwindling of our proved reserves of oil and gas can only be slowed, not halted.

If unconventional sources should not come through, gas reserves would be gone in another ten years at recent rates of use, without any further additions. And the new finds of the past decade have averaged only about half of what we consumed.

The oil situation seems no less gloomy to many experts. As Earl T. Hayes, former chief scientist at the U.S. Bureau of Mines, pointed out: "There is no longer much argument with the conclusion that U.S. resources of conventional oil will be seriously depleted by the year 2000." . . .

Moreover, government reports indicate, the situation abroad is not much different. Oil production in the Soviet Union, largest producer in the world, is expected to peak in the early 1980s. And the rich North Sea fields will probably begin to decline by 1984.

Arabia's wealthy oil sheikhs recognize that even their vast pools could be played out within a few decades.

Coal is the one fossil fuel whose reserves are so immense that they are not in danger of exhaustion within the near future. But rapid expansion of facilities for coal transport is difficult. Moreover, the burning of coal poses special problems of serious pollution that may sharply limit its usefulness within a few years.

[Kenneth Weaver, "Our Energy Predicament," in *Energy, A Special Report* (Washington, D.C.: National Geographic Society, 1981), pp. 16–18.]

❧ Unit 53 ❧

Understanding the Term Paper: Using Notes to Write a Paper

Writing form: Term paper
Writing skills: Reviewing note cards; arranging them for an outline

INTRODUCTION

In the process of writing a term paper, after choosing a topic, finding sources, and taking notes, you are ready to start planning and writing. If you take notes as suggested in Unit 52, you will have a large number of separate ideas, each on a different card. After reading through your cards a few times, you will begin to see ideas that fit together, and by arranging your cards by the ideas they contain (instead of by which book or article they were in), you will almost naturally begin to form an outline for your paper.

In this unit you will practice this procedure by sorting through and arranging a set of notes on the topic of solar energy. Later on, of course, you will need to use your own set of notes on a topic that is of direct relevance to you.

TIP

Plan your time wisely, especially in longer writing projects. Allocate sufficient amounts of time to each of these stages: finding, recording, analyzing, synthesizing, writing a first draft, revising, and writing the final draft. If you spend too much time on the initial stages you may find yourself too rushed at the end to put together a high-quality, attractive term paper.

WARMUP I: REVIEWING NOTE CARDS

Deciding what you are going to say and how you are going to say it, even after you have read extensively and taken careful notes, is by no means an easy task. Plan to spend several hours at least, and spread the work out over several days if possible.

Perhaps the best method of developing an organizational outline is to follow these steps:

1. Read through all your note cards. By doing so, you will effectively review all the important ideas and have them fresh in your mind.
2. Read through the cards again, this time sorting them into several piles. In other words, put cards together that have similar or related information.
3. Read through each separate pile, resorting any cards that are out of place, noting which cards contain more introductory material and which ones have more advanced material. Determine if there are informational gaps that you will have to do more reading and notetaking to fill.
4. Unless you are completely satisfied with the arrangement and organization that has resulted from following the three preceding steps, leave your cards for several hours or days, come back to them with a fresh perspective, and repeat the steps. If the same organization reappears, you can feel satisfied that it is the most natural and appropriate one.

INSTRUCTIONS:

Imagining that each of the following entries is a separate card containing notes you have taken on the subject of solar energy, do step 1 as just enumerated (that is, read the card to get an overview of your information). You will do steps 2 and 3 in the next warmup. To help guide you in reading the notes, decide which of the following four topics you might be able to write effectively about using these notes:

1. The methods of building a solar house.
2. The reasons and possibilities for using solar energy.
3. The disadvantages of nuclear energy.
4. Indirect means of using solar energy.

Imagine that the following are cards that *you* have written while reading on the topic of solar energy. The words that appear are, therefore, *your own* words, not quotations. The sources, as suggested in Unit 52, also appear on cards (such as card 1) with the full bibliographical reference (which will be discussed in Unit 54). The letters and numbers at the beginning of each card are a code that refers back to the source.

Card 1

Wilhelm, John. "Solar Energy, the Ultimate Powerhouse." *National Geographic* 149 (March 1976): 380–97.

A nicely illustrated and informative article of popular and general interest.

Code: JW *NG* 76

Card 2

JW *NG* 76: 381, 385 (This means that the information on this card is taken from the source on card 1, pages 381, 385.)

Almost all the energy ever used by mankind has been from the sun. Wood, coal, oil, gas, and so on were formed from plants that grew because of the sun. Even the wind is caused by the sun.

Card 3

JW *NG* 76: 385

We will use up as much stored energy in the next 25 years as has been used in all of previous history. Obviously, we will eventually use it all up, but the sun will still be shining.

Card 4

JW *NG* 76: 385

Tremendous energy comes from the sun. For example, what falls on the Arabian Peninsula in one year is two times the amount of energy in all the oil in reserves in the world. The sun falling on Connecticut has as much energy as is used in the entire U.S.A.

Card 5

JW *NG* 76: 385

By 2000 AD solar energy will probably be a $25-billion-a-year industry.

Card 6

JW *NG* 76: 388–89

Houses can presently be designed to use solar energy for heating *and* cooling and to provide hot water. The systems cost about $10,000. Other methods are presently cheaper. Also, there are so many different house builders that it will be a long time before they can be trained properly to install such systems. Also, zoning laws regarding the types of buildings that are permitted need to be modified. Also the designs of the systems often have weaknesses.

Card 7

JW *NG* 76: 389–95

Other ways of using solar energy include (1) growing fast-growing trees, grasses, seaweed, or using actual photosynthesis for energy; (2) using differences in ocean water temperature (caused by the sun) to run low-pressure ammonia turbines to make electricity; (3) using solar cells to convert sunlight directly into electricity.

Card 8

JW *NG* 76: 397

One way to collect electricity directly from the sun would be to have huge satellites (like "gigantic butterflies" p. 397) in synchronous orbit thousands of miles above the earth that would beam down enormous quantities of electricity (via microwaves). Each satellite could produce up to 5,000 megawatts.

Card 9

Halacy, Daniel. *The Coming Age of Solar Energy.* New York: Harper & Row, 1973.

A comprehensive treatment of solar energy, with a lot of reasons for not relying on present sources of energy. Interesting and easy to read.

Code: DH *CASE* 73

Card 10

DH *CASE* 73: 9

U.S. consumption of energy in 1970: 95.9% fossil fuel; per capita equivalent of 2,700 gallons of gasoline; daily consumption 15 million barrels (or about 62,000 railroad tank cars); 35% of all the energy consumed in the world.

Card 11

DH *CASE* 73: 11–14

Nuclear energy is dangerous, not unlimited, produces a lot of waste heat, and has dangerous waste products.

Card 12

DH *CASE* 73: 15–16

Use of fossil fuels is raising the temperature of the environment, increasing (in 100 years) the carbon dioxide concentration from 290 parts per million to 400 (in 2000 AD), about a 30% increase.

Card 13

DH *CASE* 73: 32–33

Other sources and disadvantages: *wood* could require all available farm land to produce 10% of energy needs; *wind* could produce millions of megawatts (many times U.S. needs), but would require 3,000,000 windmills for U.S. needs; *hydropower* is already well developed except in countries that lack financial resources to develop it; *geothermal* and *tidal* power have relatively small potential.

Card 14

DH *CASE* 73: 33

Solar power seems to be the only safe and reasonable solution, but it will take up to fifty years to develop it. So we must begin now.

Card 15

Brinkworth, B.J. *Solar Energy for Man.* New York: John Wiley & Sons, 1972.

The first section has a lot of general scientific information on the limitations of other types of energy.

Code: BB *SEM* 72

Card 16

BB *SEM* 72: 16

Photosynthesis (use by plants of sunlight) on land produces many times the energy needed by mankind (more than a hundred million million kilowatt hours of energy per year), but obviously, only a small part of that can be used.

Card 17

BB *SEM* 72: 17

Hydroelectric power is significant in Switzerland and Scandinavia (more than ½ of their needs). Parts of Africa and South America have great potential. But hydroelectric power can only supply a *portion* of total needs.

Card 18

BB *SEM* 72: 17

We can calculate the total energy of the tides (by estimating how much they slow down the rotation of the earth). The energy involved is far less than our energy demands, and only a small part is recoverable.

Card 19

BB *SEM* 72: 18

The sun pours out enormous amounts of energy, about 1.3 kilowatts per sq. meter at the top of the atmosphere, although most of this energy never reaches the earth's surface. Even so, enough reaches it so that 80 km square of surface on earth absorb the same amount of energy as we presently use in a year. Note that the desert of western Australia is about 1500 km square. But of course the sunlight is very *diffuse,* not concentrated like the heat of a stove.

Card 20

Abou-Hussein, M.S.M. "Ten-Year's Experience with Solar Water Heaters in the United Arab Republic." In the U.N. Conference on New Sources of Energy, *Solar 2.* Mayne Island: Cloudburst Press, 1978.

Part of a collection of specific applications of solar energy. This article was originally written in 1961.

Code: A-H SWC 78

Card 21

A-H SWC 78: 11

The costs and operating expenses of solar water heaters per year compared with kerosene, butane gas, and electric heaters in Cairo, Egypt (in 1961), were (U.S. dollars):

kerosene $14.00   butane gas $22.73   electricity $83.10   solar $9.00

Solar water heaters pay for themselves in 7 years. Still, the design and materials needed are not yet perfected.

Card 22

"An Atlas of Energy Resources." In *Energy, A Special Report*. Washington, D.C.: National Geographic Society, 1981.

Part of a well-illustrated and interesting series written as a special issue of the *National Geographic* in February, 1981. This particular article does not list an author.

Code: AER *ESR* 81

Card 23

AER *ESR* 81: 68–69

Surprisingly, enough sun *does* fall on most U.S. cities to provide significant portions of energy needed for home use. (There were charts and graphs for different cities.) For example, in Washington, D.C., a solar collector of 10 sq. meters on a roof can produce ½ of the hot water needed in *winter*. However, weather conditions do vary from year to year by as much as 20%.

Card 24

AER *ESR* 81:

The U.S. official goal for solar energy is for it to meet 20% of all our energy needs by the year 2000.

WARMUP II: ARRANGING NOTE CARDS INTO AN OUTLINE

You have completed the first step in using your notes, reading them over and getting general ideas. You are now ready for the next steps.

INSTRUCTIONS:
Read again the four steps listed at the beginning of Warmup I. Using the cards in Warmup I, proceed with steps 2 and 3 (and 4, if you have time). Disregard for the moment the cards with the bibliographical references. There are many ways you can organize these cards, but to give you a clear sense of direction on this first attempt, a

suggested outline is given here. A sentence outline is also provided in the answers section, but do not look there until you have completely finished your own work.

1. Cards that have to do with stored energy (oil, gas, and nuclear) that is being used in ways that make a change necessary.
2. Cards that give information about other forms of energy (other than stored energy or direct use of the sun) and their disadvantages.
3. Cards that discuss the potential, the expected use, the theoretical possibilities, the problems, and the direct applications and examples of direct solar power.

Use the cards listed in Warmup I.

PLANNING AND WRITING

When you feel you have made a satisfactory organization of the cards listed in Warmup I (following the four suggested steps), you are nearly prepared to begin writing. For this unit, plan to complete the first draft of an introductory and general paper on solar energy of about 600 to 1000 words. Follow these final steps before beginning:

1. Eliminate from your set of cards those that you are not planning to use, those that repeat information given in a better way in another card, or those that are not directly relevant to your topic. You may, of course, decide to use them all, or portions of all of them.
2. Arrange the cards in the order in which you are planning to use them. That is, the more general and introductory cards should probably come before the explanations or specific examples.
3. Plan your space and your time carefully so that you do not run out of either.
4. Before you begin to write, it would be wise also to write out separately an overall outline of what you are going to say.
5. As you write, make notes, in parentheses or in the margins, of which card you were using when providing the information.
6. Remember to take the date of publication into consideration. You cannot, for example, claim that water heaters cost only $9.00 per month, since that information was true back in 1961. In other words, things change, and you have to reflect those changes in interpreting older information.

The answers to the warmups are listed in the answers section.

❧ Unit 54 ❧

Understanding the Term Paper: References and Bibliography

Writing form: Term paper
Writing skills: Knowing when to acknowledge a source; writing the bibliography; using references or footnotes

INTRODUCTION

When you write a term paper, you present your original synthesis of facts and ideas that you have obtained from others. The overall organization, the point of view, the conclusion, and the wording are thus uniquely yours. Most of the information, however, is not, and you must give proper credit to the authors from whom you learned it. You must also use the proper format for crediting the sources.

TIP

You will produce a more positive impression if you turn in work that is neatly typed and follows the exact format requested or expected. Aids to help you (in addition to your typewriter and a clean ribbon) are a good supply of the right quality paper, a dictionary, and a bottle of white correcting fluid. Find out how to use them.

WARMUP I: KNOWING WHEN TO ACKNOWLEDGE A SOURCE

You need to acknowledge the author that you have read in the following situations:

1. The information that you found is not general or public knowledge, and you would not have known it without reading this source.
2. You want to use words, phrases, or sentences directly from the source. Normally not more than a total of five per cent of your paper should consist of quotations.

3. You want to use the same organization, system of classification, or point of view as the source and you recognize that these represent an original contribution by the author.
4. You want to use information that your reader might not believe unless you also mention where you got the information. The opinion of a recognized expert, even if it is about matters of common knowledge, can be very convincing.

INSTRUCTIONS:

1. Imagine that the following items are sentences that you intend to include in your term paper. Decide for each whether or not, on the basis of the four preceding guidelines, you need to acknowledge the source. You will need to go back to the sample reading selection in Unit 52 and to Warmup I in Unit 53 to find the original sources of information.
2. After you have marked *Yes* or *No*, find the exact source for items you marked *Yes*. If the sentence is a direct quotation, mark the sentence with quotation marks.

Yes _____ No _____ 1. The fossil fuels we are using today were laid down millions of years ago, and they are being used up very rapidly.

Yes _____ No _____ 2. The oil in the North Sea will begin to run out by 1984.

Yes _____ No _____ 3. The world will use about as much stored energy in a span of 25 years as it did in all previous history.

Yes _____ No _____ 4. Trees, grass, and seaweed use sunlight to grow, and they can be sources of energy.

Yes _____ No _____ 5. If all the available farmland were used to grow trees, the energy from that wood would still represent only about 10 percent of our needs.

Yes _____ No _____ 6. Huge satellites thousands of miles above the earth, like "giant butterflies," would collect and transmit solar energy.

Yes _____ No _____ 7. Despite the current frenzied search for new deposits, the dwindling of our proved reserves of oil and gas can only be slowed, not halted.

WARMUP II: WRITING THE BIBLIOGRAPHY

At the end of your term paper, you will need to list all the sources you have directly relied on in developing your paper. You will notice, as well, that there are bibliographies at the end of virtually all academic papers, articles, books, and even chapters of books.

If you are going to be writing many papers or articles, you will probably find it efficient to obtain a copy of a published guide such as Kate Turabian's *Students'*

Guide for Writing College Papers, 3rd ed. Chicago: The University of Chicago Press, 1977.

You may also find useful information in other places. Your academic field or department may customarily rely on a particular style sheet, and if so, you should be familiar with it. The editorial office of the printing press at your university may also have a preferred style or guide. Finally, if you are writing a thesis, your committee may have a preference about which guideline you should follow.

Probably the best format to use in writing a paper for an academic class is the one used in the articles the professor has written or the format used in the articles the teacher has assigned to the class. In general, these styles tend to be simpler than those recommended in the more conservative guides, and since your professor has indirectly approved of their use, they provide a ready and practical guide.

Here are some of the things you should include in your bibliography:

1. The authors and titles of articles and books to which you are directly referring.
2. The authors and titles of articles and books that you have read directly in connection with the writing of this paper that have shaped your ideas, even if you do not specifically refer to facts or information from them.
3. The authors and titles of unpublished works, such as reports or correspondence, from which you have drawn information or ideas.
4. The authors and titles of other types of materials, such as newspaper articles, films, or songs from which you have taken information or ideas.

Avoid the temptation to make your bibliography longer by listing material on the general subject that is not directly relevant. Especially avoid the temptation to list material that you have not read or are not directly familiar with.

INSTRUCTIONS:

1. Examine the following sample bibliography carefully. It provides the same references used in Unit 53.
2. Read the descriptions provided in the guidelines, and find examples for each of these explanations in the sample bibliography.

Bibliography

Abou-Hussein, M. S. M. "Ten-Year's Experience with Solar Water Heaters in the United Arab Republic." In the U.N. Conference on New Sources of Energy, *Solar 2.* Mayne Island: Cloudburst Press, 1978.

"An Atlas of Energy Resources." In *Energy, A Special Report.* Washington, D.C.: National Geographic Society, 1981.

Brinkworth, B. J. *Solar Energy for Man.* New York: John Wiley & Sons, 1972.

Wilhelm, John. "Solar Energy, the Ultimate Powerhouse." *National Geographic* 149 (March 1976): 380–97.

Guidelines

1. Be sure you are using the style expected for *your* paper. As mentioned, there are many different style sheets and many different possible correct formats.

2. List your sources alphabetically on a separate sheet headed by the word *Bibliography*. If the source has an author, use the first letter of the last name to determine the alphabetical order. If the source does not have an author, use the first letter of the first key word in the title.

3. List the last name of the author first, followed by a comma, then the author's first name, or the author's initials if no first name is given. In some fields *only* the initials are used. If there is more than one author, put the additional names in the normal sequence: first name first. Follow this entry with a period, not a comma.

4. List the date. In most cases it follows, after a comma, the publisher's name, or in the case of a journal, it follows the volume number. In many fields, however, the practice is to put the date immediately after the author's name.

5. Underline the titles of books, journals, magazines, newspapers, government documents, artistic productions, or anything published as a whole.

6. Follow the title of a book by a period. Then list the city where the publisher is located, followed by a colon, followed by the name of the publisher, a comma, the date and a period.

7. Use quotation marks before and after the title of an article or chapter. A period should follow the title and come before the second quotation mark.

8. In one common style, the name of the journal is followed without punctuation by the volume number, then a parenthesis, then the month and year of publication, then a closing parenthesis, colon, and page numbers. There is, however, great diversity from field to field. For example, some styles do not use quotation marks. In other styles the volume is followed directly by a colon and page numbers, and the month is not indicated.

9. Begin the first line of the bibliographical entry at the left margin of the page, and indent subsequent lines about five spaces.

10. Consult a guide for the accepted styles to use in listing documents, films, encyclopedias, and so on.

WARMUP III: USING REFERENCES AND FOOTNOTES

You bibliography provides a complete list of the sources you used, but you must in addition identify the specific part of your term paper in which you used the sources, as specified in the four guidelines in Warmup I. Fortunately, if you keep accurate notes, as suggested in the last unit, and if you follow the simple procedures outlined here, you will not find it difficult to provide correct references.

There are three possible methods of referring to your sources, and the terms *references* or *citations* will be used for all of them. The word *footnotes,* as will be explained, refers only to the last of the methods.

The easiest method, which happens also to be the preferred and most popular one, is to refer to the author and date right in the text of the paper. The page numbers are *not* listed unless there is a quotation. If your readers want to know more about the source, they can easily look in the bibliography. Here are three examples from a term paper on solar energy. Study them carefully.

1. Most people are not aware of the tremendous amount of energy that falls on the surface of the earth. According to Wilhelm (1976), the amount of energy from the sun falling on the Arabian Penninsula in one year is twice the energy contained in *all* the oil reserves in the whole world.
2. One way to collect the energy of the sun would be to install huge satellites like "giant butterflies" in orbit around the world (Wilhelm, 1976, p. 397).
3. It is possible to measure exactly the potential energy contained in the movement of the tides by measuring their effect in slowing down the rotation of the earth (Brinkworth, 1972).

The second style, which is not recommended or illustrated here, is to make a list at the end of your paper of all the references. The list is numbered. In your paper you also put numbers in the part of the text that refers to the corresponding note at the end. You normally would, in addition, also provide a bibliography.

The third method, which to most modern writers seems old-fashioned and cumbersome, is to place a note at the foot of the page (hence the term *footnote*). In the text you place a slightly raised number where you refer to a source. The same number is used in the footnote, which uses the format illustrated here. This method is presented because you *may* be asked to use it. If you are not, use the first method.

[1]John Wilhelm, "Solar Energy, the Ultimate Powerhouse," *National Geographic* 149 (March 1976): 385.

[2]Ibid., p. 397.

[3]B. J. Brinkworth, *Solar Energy for Man* (New York: John Wiley & Sons, 1972), p. 17.

[4]Wilhelm, p. 381.

1. The author's names appear in their normal sequence.
2. The first line is indented.
3. Commas, not periods, separate author and title.
4. Page numbers are always given.
5. If the same source is referred to in the following footnote, the word *Ibid.* is used.
6. If the same source is referred to, but after another footnote, only a shortened form needs to be listed. In this case, *Wilhelm* is the author of only one source, so only his name is required.
7. The city and publisher are given in parentheses.

Perhaps the most efficient way to use this method is to follow examples carefully, either those given here, those in a guide, or those in another paper. Unless you use this format frequently, you will probably not need to do it from memory.

PLANNING AND WRITING

You are now ready to write a short sample term paper of your own on the topic of solar energy. In the last unit you prepared a rough draft in which you made a record of which sources you used. Now it is time to rewrite the draft, use the first method suggested for providing citations, complete your bibliography, and complete the assignment. If this were a regular academic requirement, you would have to do the following:

1. Type your paper on standard-sized (8½ × 11 inch) paper, double spaced.
2. Begin with a title page on which you center the title, your name, the name of the course and professor, and the date.
3. Number all the pages after the title page, beginning with number 1. The number could be centered at the top, placed at the upper right corner, or centered at the bottom.
4. Provide the references as expected by the teacher.
5. List the sources used, alphabetically, on a separate page labeled *Bibliography*.
6. Provide an extra page for the teacher's comments.
7. Make a copy for your own records. (The teacher may not give you back your paper, or worse, it may get lost, so keep a copy.)

Your teacher will instruct you as to which of these requirements you must satisfy.

Unit 55

Writing the Term Paper: Picking the Topic

Writing form: Term paper
**Writing skills: Choosing an actual topic; planning the writing
  assignment**

INTRODUCTION

Units 55–56 are designed to give experience in actually writing a term paper. Even if your paper is short or covers a beginning topic, the exercise will take you through all the important steps in writing a formal paper and will give you valuable experience as a writer. In this unit the objective is for you to pick a topic and to plan the subsequent steps.

The editing exercise precedes and introduces the content of the other exercises.

EDITING

This section is a review of several types of mistakes, none of which is marked.

I am actually inrolled in industrial design career, the so-called Design 444.

The students are hard to get into the course, and the average of the pages to

read each weeks is about one-hundred and fifty. One of the requirements are a

paper on methods to design other equipments.

Since I have also been in computer science career, I decided to concentrate my mind to write on the both topics. What I mean to say is that I look for the

topic that would combine with the industrial design of computers by the same

computers. It is a topic that it appeals to me too much. A lot of informations

about it in the library, and the topic fit the course, because the professor said

me so. And he agree with the topic when I asked him if the topic was siutable

for the course.

I think the topic is at a right stage for this class because two reasons. At

first, it resemble topics covered in the chapters and biographies of our text.

Second it combine in a unique way several of major viewpoints of the course.

I also support that there is enought bibliographies for got the materials

that I need them. For examples, one of my proffesors papers list three

references . . . .

A suggested answer is in the answers section after Unit 60. Do not consult it
until you have completely finished your own work.

PLANNING AND WRITING: CHOOSING A TOPIC AND PLANNING THE ASSIGNMENT

In this unit your primary assignment is to choose a topic for a term paper. Since
you will not be ready to begin writing on the topic for several days, your writing
activity for this lesson will be to write about how you selected the topic, which
sources you intend to use, and why you feel the topic is appropriate for you.

The following questions are provided as a guide to you. Your writing may take either the form of a list of answers, or preferably, a coherent, well-organized composition.

1. What is the *general* field for which you are choosing a topic?
2. Are you writing the paper for a particular class? For publication? For a sponsor or agency? To fulfill the requirements of this class?
3. Identify the requirements as fully as possible. Use the following as a guide:
   a. The limitations placed on the selection of a topic.
   b. When it needs to be finished.
   c. How long it has to be and whether it needs to be typed.
   d. Whether it is an opinion paper, a book review, or library research.
   e. Which format (if any) must be used for footnotes and bibliography.
   f. Whether you are to turn parts in (such as an outline) before you turn in the finished paper.
   g. How much help the instructor is willing to give you.
4. Is this an introductory, moderately specialized, or highly technical paper?
5. List three topics that you have considered using.
6. Which factors influenced you in selecting the topic you finally selected? For example, did you talk with the professor about it? Did you find some useful and interesting articles on the topic? Is the topic highly relevant to your other academic work?
7. Did you find it necessary to broaden the topic (to make it more general) or to narrow it (make it more specific) after you started? Why?
8. How personally interesting is the topic for you?
9. Do you expect to be able to find enough information to complete the assignment satisfactorily?
10. Which means have you discovered for finding sources? For example, have you found recent bibliographies? Is some particular index of special use? Has the professor provided a reading list?
11. How well do you think, at this moment, that you will be able to do on completing this assignment satisfactorily and on time?

To complete the next unit you will need to bring to class a complete source that you intend to use. If you cannot bring the journal or book to class, make a photocopy of the article or chapter.

Unit 56

Writing the Term Paper: Finding and Using Sources

Writing form: Term paper
Writing skill: Listing sources correctly

INTRODUCTION

In this unit you will use at least one book, article, or document of your own choosing. Bring the material or a photocopy to class, or alternatively, take this unit to the library and do the work there. You will be reading the material, citing it in bibliographical and reference form, and examining it to see aspects of the format that you yourself might find relevant in writing your own paper.

The background information on taking notes, referring to sources, avoiding plagiarism, and so on, that you will need to complete this unit is in Units 52 through 54. Review these units if the information is not fresh in your mind.

WARMUP AND WRITING

Find an interesting , recent, relevant, and useful source of information for your topic. If your topic is one of general or popular interest, a good source might be an article from a popular magazine. If your topic is specialized, a good source would come from a professional or technical journal.

To help you gain practice in using sources, we suggest you respond to the following nine steps. The editing exercise provides some sample responses, so you may wish to complete it first.

To complete the writing assignment for this unit, provide the responses to the nine instructions. You may either give a list of responses, or preferably, you will develop a coherent, well-developed composition. In addition to doing this short assignment, of course, you will be doing the much more extensive task of finding sources and taking careful notes, as explained in Unit 52.

1. List the article as you plan to list it in your bibliography (as indicated in Unit 54).
2. Explain how you are going to cite your references in the text of your paper. The most reasonable method seems to be the one recommended in Unit 54 (putting the author and date of the source right in your text).

3. Consider all the other sources you are using and explain how valuable you consider this specific source to be. Tell why.
4. Write a short (less than 50-word) *summary* of the article, giving only the main ideas or point of view.
5. Discuss aspects of the article that made it easy or difficult to read, such as use of explanations, graphs, or examples; difficulty of the topic; clarity of the organization; and effectiveness of the written language.
6. Examine the introduction and discuss its length, interest, appropriateness, clarity, and usefulness in leading you into the article.
7. Examine the conclusion and/or summary and discuss its effectiveness.
8. Consider which changes you would make if you had written this article and were revising it.
9. Take notes (as directed in Unit 52) on the information, using separate note cards and writing only one key idea on each card. Be sure your first card gives the complete bibliographic reference and that each subsequent card refers to that reference (by using some type of code). Write down the number of the page on which you found the information. For the most part, use *only* your own words and phrases, and if you write down the author's words, be sure to use quotation marks in your notes.

When you use other sources, you will of course not need to follow all these steps. The purpose of this exercise is to help you become aware of many of the features of a good paper, features that you will deal with in your writing.

EDITING

Imagine that the following entries represent the responses to the nine statements just given. There are numerous errors in language, format, and mechanics. The technical information, however, is accurate. Correct the mistakes.

1. Todd M. Doscher, Enhanced Recovery of Crude Oil, *American* Scientist,

   Pages 193 to 199, March–April 1981, Volume 69: No. 2.

2. T.M. Doscher, "Enhanced Recovery," in *American Scientist,* 69:196.

3. The article offers a readable, introduction, yet interesting and informational data on the matter of getting the oil from the oil wells. Since this is

   at the suitable level and amount of difficulty for my class, so it is

   convenient for me.

4. The article make a summary of basic principals of the oil recovery, and explain Darcy's equation. Over half of that article discuss two basic methods to recover the oil after the originally pressure dies down: steam (both steam soak as well as also steam drive) and flooding (waterflooding and also the chemical flooding).

5. There were some technical vocabularies, but the chapter is well organizated, clearly, and good illustrations.

6. The introduction is longer. As the matter of fact, if you will include the informations about how the oil had been formed and normally productions proceedures, it is about one-forth of whole.

7. Its conclusion is only long one paragraph, and he didn't label it as the "Conclusion."

8. Example of a note card:

   TMD ERCO *AS,* p. 196

   At least the 25% of energy in effect recovered has been used just in recovery process itself in the steam-drive system.

The answers are in the answers section. Do not consult them until you have completed your own work.

❦ Unit 57 ❦

Writing the Term Paper: Developing an Outline

Writing form: Term paper
Writing skill: Using note cards to develop an outline

INTRODUCTION

You will use the note cards you have written on the articles and books you have read in order to form an outline for your term paper. The activities of this unit are based on the concepts developed in Unit 53.

TIP

Objectively speaking, we cannot claim that any writing is perfect. Writing is a creative art, not a science, and there are as many ways to say things as there are people to say them or hear them. Don't, therefore, set perfection as your goal. Attempt, rather, to say what you want to say as well and as interestingly as *you* can.

WARMUP I: READING YOUR NOTE CARDS

INSTRUCTIONS:
Read all your note cards through quickly to review the material you have collected. While doing so, you should be trying to review what you have read and also tentatively to note the natural ways in which the information falls into groups.

WARMUP II: SORTING YOUR NOTE CARDS

INSTRUCTIONS:
Read through your note cards again. This time put them into piles according to the content of each card. In other words, see how many cards you have on the various ideas, parts, or subdivisions of the topic.

After you have your cards in separate piles, read through each pile. Reconsider your original decision to put each card into that pile, and if you feel a card does not belong, either put it into another pile or set it to one side. Arrange the cards in each pile roughly from easy (introductory) to difficult (more complex).

Each of your piles should be of about the same size and importance. If some of the piles are very small, you should incorporate the cards with other cards, find more information on that aspect of your topic, or set them to one side.

WARMUP III: DECIDING ON THE FINAL ARRANGEMENT

INSTRUCTIONS:
Take a break from your notes for at least an hour. Leave them for a day or more if possible. After this break, your mind will be fresher and you will be readier to make a final decision.

After your break, without forgetting the organization that you developed in Warmup II, resort all the cards one more time. If you find yourself developing a completely new set of piles, take the trouble of once more reading through each pile and resorting and rechecking. Eventually you will arrive at a way of grouping your cards that makes sense to you and that you believe is the most logical and effective way of convincing your reader of the importance of your ideas.

WRITING I: DEVELOPING AN OUTLINE

Some good writers at this stage develop an outline of what they are going to say. In fact, some even write a short general summary or rough abstract.

INSTRUCTIONS:
If your teacher directs you to do so, develop an outline for your paper. Include these features:

1. Provide a general summarizing statement at the beginning, giving your thesis (your central idea).
2. Indicate how you intend to introduce your paper. Will you use an example, a story, or some important information?
3. List the three or four main ideas you intend to develop. If you have more than three or four, you should consider reducing them or regrouping them. If your overall structure is too complex, your reader might get lost or confused.
4. For each of the main ideas, list two or three (or more) ideas, facts, sets of data, or the like that you intend to use to support your main ideas.
5. Indicate how you will end your paper, either through a summary or conclusion or by other means.

WRITING II: ARRANGING YOUR CARDS TO SERVE AS A GUIDE

Whether or not you have an outline, you will want to have your cards arranged in such a way so that as you write, you can refer to them one by one. In other words, the cards will represent a type of outline.

INSTRUCTIONS:

Go through your cards once more, this time imagining yourself writing about what is on the cards, one by one. If you find your order does not lend itself to this type of mental writing, arrange the cards until it does. If you do not have a clear idea at this point what you will say in the introduction, do not become preoccupied. Often an idea for a good introduction comes *after* you have written the main body of the paper.

WRITING III: WRITING THE FIRST DRAFT

INSTRUCTIONS:

Sit down in a comfortable, quiet spot with an adequate supply of paper and begin to put your plans into words. Begin with the introduction, but if you cannot develop a good idea, go on to the next part. Follow your outline (if you have one) and your note cards, allowing yourself the luxury of changing your plan if, as you write, you think of a better one. If you decide that the information you are using is not general information and that you need to give an author credit (as explained in Unit 54, Warmup I), make a clear note, either in the text itself or in the margin, of the exact source or the exact card from which you obtained the information.

Remember one final important requirement. You must never use the words or ideas of another writer as if they were your own. Avoid plagiarism by clearly marking quotations and by correctly crediting the sources of your ideas.

After you have written the rough draft, read it over quickly and make general and obvious changes. But then stop. Unless you are in a terrible hurry, you need a rest in order to regain your objective perspective. Take a break, and then, when your mind feels fresh, come back to your work, ready (as you will be in the next unit) to make necessary revisions and corrections.

❦ Unit 58 ❦

Writing the Term Paper: Finishing the Paper

Writing form: Term paper
Writing skills: Revising the first draft; preparing the final paper; using the final checklist

INTRODUCTION

Having completed the steps in the preceding three units, you are now ready to start finishing your paper. You may need to go back to the library to check a source, buy some more typing paper, prepare some coffee to help keep you alert, or clean your typewriter keys, but basically you are ready for the concluding steps.

TIP

Look for criticism if you want to have a good product. Asking your spouse, a personal friend, or even a classmate will not help you unless they are free to be honest and to point out your weaknesses. Ask well-informed critics to read your writing. Then take their advice.

PLANNING AND WRITING I: EVALUATING YOUR FIRST DRAFT

INSTRUCTIONS:
Read through the draft you wrote in Unit 57 and answer the following questions. If your answer is negative in any case, make the necessary changes.

1. Do you believe the overall organization is the best one to use, the one that will be convincing, clear, and attractive to your readers?

2. Is the first draft the right length? If it is too short, do you know where to add to it? If it is too long, do you know where to cut it?

3. Have you included the proper, relevant information adequately to support the major ideas in your paper? If you have not, do you have the time to do more reading, and are the right sources available to you?

4. Do you have the correct references for all the information you have used?

5. Have you decided how to introduce your topic in an interesting way?

PLANNING AND WRITING II: REVIEWING THE REQUIREMENTS FOR THE FORMAT

In the planning and writing section of Unit 54 and other places, requirements have been listed for completing the final draft of the paper. Here is a comprehensive summary of what you should do:

1. Type your paper on standard-sized (8½ × 11 inch) paper. Except for the bibliography and the abstract (if you have one), use double spacing.
2. The outside (first) page should be your title page. The following information should appear on it, neatly centered on the page:
   a. The title, with the key words capitalized.
   b. Your name.
   c. The name of the professor or sponsor (if any).
   d. The course or project for which the paper is being written.
   e. The date on which it was completed or submitted.
   Check the title page of this or any other book for ideas on how to design a title page. There should be no number on this page.
3. Number all the pages after the title page. If you include pages before the text of your paper, such as a table of contents, number these with small Roman numerals (i, ii, iii, and so on). The first page of the text should be number 1. The number may be at the upper right, upper center, or bottom center. Be sure your pages are in the correct order before you number them.
4. If your paper is long or complex, or if you use many tables or graphs, provide your reader with a table of contents. Center the words *Table of Contents* at the top. List the parts of your paper along the left margin and the pagination along the right margin. See the table of contents in this or other books for examples.
5. If required to do so, provide a concise statement of the purpose, content, and major conclusions of your paper. Single-space this abstract and place it before the introduction with the title *Abstract*.
6. Unless your paper is very short or simple, provide headings for the major divisions. See the headings in this book for examples. If you have headings *within* headings, you can use a system such as this:

   MAJOR HEADING

   Intermediate Heading

   Minor Heading

7. Begin with an interesting but brief introduction (which should be marked by a heading using one of the three styles mentioned in number 6). Likewise, include a summary or conclusion (marked with a heading).
8. Throughout your paper, provide the type of references expected by the teacher, sponsor, or publisher. For details see Unit 54.

9. Include a list of all the sources you used, directly or indirectly, in developing your paper. Unless you are sending this to a journal for publication or unless there are only a few references, use a separate, numbered page. Head the list with the word *Bibliography,* centered. Single-space each entry, leaving a double space between entries.
10. Leave a blank page at the end of the paper for the teacher's comments.
11. Make a copy for yourself. The teacher may not return the original, or worse, it may get lost.
12. Staple or otherwise bind your pages together so that it is easy to open and read them. Enclose the paper in some type of protective folder, and put your name and the course number on the outside of the folder.

PLANNING AND WRITING III: FINAL CHECKLIST

After you have finished all the requirements but before you are ready to turn in your paper, make a final check of your work. If you can say "yes" to all of the following questions, you should feel confident that you have done a good job. This checklist is a modified version of the checklist you have used throughout this textbook.

1. Meaning: Do you have a central idea that is made clear through the introduction, the conclusion, and the body of your paper? Is this idea your unique contribution (and not merely a regrouping of miscellaneous ideas and facts)?
2. Organization: Have you developed a plan for presenting the information that is clear and attractive and that fits within the expected format? Have you used headings to label the major divisions clearly? Does your introduction lead the reader interestingly and specifically into the topic and avoid generalities, irrelevant information, or misleading promises? Does your conclusion neatly draw together the principal facts in a convincing way without overgeneralizing?
3. Content: Have you done a thorough enough job of reading the important sources so that your paper is authoritative, well supported, and accurate?
4. Vocabulary, sentence structure, and grammar: Have you used the appropriate vocabulary without merely copying whole sentences and phrases from the original (that is, without plagiarizing)? Have you, or has someone who is qualified to do so, checked the grammatical accuracy and the variety and effectiveness of the sentence structure?
5. Mechanics: Is your paper neatly typed (or very neatly written) on the right type of paper, double spaced with proper margins, and correctly numbered? Does it have a title page and a bibliography? Do the headings and paragraph divisions look neat? Have you carefully checked the alphabetizing of the bibliography, and are you sure the form in each entry is exactly right? Are your spelling and punctuation as accurate as you can make them?

In other words, if you were the teacher and had to give your paper a grade, would *you* give it a good grade?

❧ Unit 59 ❧

My Plans for the Future

Writing forms: Chronology; explanation
Writing skills: Review of skills used in other units

INTRODUCTION

Soon you will be leaving this stage in your learning of English and moving on to new activities and new opportunities. What are your plans? What do you hope to achieve, and where do you expect to go?

This unit offers you a chance to share what you are planning to do, as a way of saying goodbye. Your teacher will probably keep this last composition as a memento of your participation in this class and read it later on as a way of remembering you.

WARMUP AND PLANNING EXERCISE

By yourself, in small groups, or as a class, discuss the following questions and issues. Be thinking of how to combine them into a "farewell report."

1. What are your plans immediately after this course? Are you going to have a vacation? What type, and where will you go?
2. What are your plans following the immediate transition? Will you go on in school? Are you going to another school? Will you go back to your country or back to work?
3. What are your plans in the next phase of your life? Do you plan to finish a bachelor's or master's degree? Do a project of some type? Take on new responsibility in your work? Get married? Travel?
4. What are your long-range hopes and plans? What do you think you might be doing in five or ten years? What personal changes do you see taking place, such as raising a family, moving to a new job, making a major contribution in your profession, or achieving a long-held ambition?

EDITING

For a suggested answer, see the answers section after Unit 60.

I make many friends between the people I had met in this class, and really I am going to miss them too much. But I have to move toward, and maybe never see any of them again in my future life. My first walk will be taking a small vacation by my car around about United States. Are many places which I like to see before I come home. I wish to take one classmate along with myself, and we already are doing extensives plans about what will we take and where will we go.

Afterward the trip I will return back to my country where my relations are waiting me to over take the family's business. I am not convenient to do since I do not interest in that business, and while profitable not personally rewarding with me. In quite frankness, my really hope is how to developing a strong leadership within the company herself, hopefully by the involving of my younger aged brother, who say he really want to play a severe role. I think is realistic expect the company to prospect by this way, left me free to pursue to my own interest.

In ten years in the future of my life I hope to have involved in the politics

and economics affairs of my country and that I will be in position to effect the

growth and prosperousness of whole nation. . . .

WRITING

Write a "farewell" composition outlining what you will be doing in the future, what your hopes are, and where you will be.

❧ Unit 60 ❧

Evaluation IV

Writing forms: Any of those from previous units
Writing skill: Writing under pressure for a grade

INTRODUCTION

In this unit you will write on one of three topics the teacher selects. You will not have time to prepare for the topic in advance, and you will not be able to use a dictionary or other aids.

The purpose of this exercise, as of the previous evaluation units, is to help you write under the kind of pressure you may experience in your academic course-work. It will also give your teacher an opportunity, under conditions that are equal for all the students, to evaluate how well you can communicate in English; organize a new topic; and select and present facts, events, and ideas.

The teacher will use Appendix II in evaluating your work. If you have time, before you begin to write look again at the appendix, particularly at the description and sample of the level you hope to reach on this evaluation.

WRITING UNDER PRESSURE FOR A GRADE

INSTRUCTIONS:
The teacher will choose three topics from the teacher's manual that fit the writing forms that you have studied. Be sure to plan before writing and to check your work after writing. Write as much as you can as well as you can in 30 minutes on *one* of the three topics. Do not use a dictionary.

ANSWERS TO EXERCISES IN PART III*

Unit 41

Warmup: Using Formal English

Abbreviations and short forms: thank you, and, telephoning, department manager.

Incomplete sentences:
This is just a note to say thank you.
His name is Graves; do you know him?
Do you think I'll be given the position?
I hope so.

Subordination:
I sent a routine letter of application in which I mentioned your name.
In addition to giving quite a bit of background on my education and experience, I made a few inquiries about the position.
I hope to be considered for the position, because your comments on the subject have interested me greatly.

Editing Exercise

There are so many ways of "formalizing" the letter that you should have your teacher check your answers.

Unit 42

Editing Exercise

Naturally, there are many ways of formalizing this letter. Here is one:

Dear Dr. Cornell:

Thank you for your prompt reply to my request for information concerning admission into your master's program. After reading the materials you sent, I have some further questions that I hope you will answer.

*Answers not included in this section are located in the Teacher's Manual.

First, the brochure I received does not mention a TOEFL requirement. Does Southeast Texas State University not require the TOEFL, or was I perhaps sent the wrong brochure by mistake? I am, as I mentioned in my first letter, not a citizen of the United States.

Second, the three professors who will be writing my letters of recommendation do not speak English. Should I have the letters translated here, or do you prefer to have that done yourself?

Finally, you mentioned needing a 250-word statement of purpose. What kind of information would you like? Do you want to know my purpose in wanting a master's degree in civil engineering, or why I want to pursue it at Southeast Texas State, or what I intend to do after receiving it? This is not clear to me.

Thank you for your attention and time. I look forward to hearing from you.

Sincerely yours,

In what ways is this letter different from the first one? How is it different from yours? Your teacher will tell you whether the language you have used is appropriately formal.

Unit 43

Warmup I: *Reading Abbreviated English (suggested answers)*

1. The Gandhis' two sons, Rajiv and Sanjay, were born in 1944 and 1946 respectively.

2. In March 1977 Morarji Desai succeeded Gandhi as Prime Minister.

3. In June of 1975 Narain won his suit, and Gandhi's 1971 election was declared invalid; as a result of this decision against her, she was in danger of losing her seat in Parliament.

4. In August 1975 the election laws were revised by constitutional amendment, and Gandhi's June conviction was reversed.

5. She was reelected to Parliament in November 1978.

6. In 1979 she was charged with harassing four government officials.

Warmup II: *Expressing Relationships Between Items of Information (suggested answers)*

1. When Prime Minister Nehru died in 1964, he was succeeded by Lal Bahadur Shastri, who immediately appointed Indira Gandhi Minister of Information and Broadcasting.

2. Because Gandhi was in danger of losing her seat in Parliament, she declared a state of emergency.

3. She imprisoned her political opponents, censored the press, passed laws limiting personal freedoms, and postponed the March 1976 parliamentary elections for a year.

4. The repressive measures of the state of emergency and the growing influence of her ruthless son Sanjay led to Gandhi's increasing unpopularity during 1975 and 1976.

5. By 1977 she had become so unpopular that she was overwhelmingly defeated in the national elections.

6. In spite of her overwhelming defeat in the 1977 national elections, twenty months later Gandhi was reelected to Parliament.

7. In 1978 she was reelected to Parliament, and two years later she was once more in the Prime Minister's seat.

Sample Composition for Unit 43
Indira Gandhi

One of the most remarkable figures of our century is Indira Gandhi, whose shrewdness and political savoir faire have brought her repeatedly to power in the face of great odds. She was born into the world of politics in 1917 as the daughter of Jawaharlal Nehru, who later became India's first Prime Minister. She was educated in India and England, and in 1942 she married Feroze Gandhi; their two sons, Rajiv and Sanjay, were later to become political figures in their own right. At the time of their marriage, the Gandhis were already engaging in political activities that were to lead to their imprisonment in 1942–43. Then in 1959, the year before her husband's death, Mrs. Gandhi was elected president of the Congress Party. When her father, the Prime Minister, died in 1964, he was succeeded by Lal Bahadur Shastri, who appointed Gandhi Minister of Information and Broadcasting. Upon Shastri's death in 1966, she became the first woman Prime Minister of India.

The next ten years gave Gandhi the opportunity to prove to the world her abilities and her political astuteness. Unfortunately, they were to end in a bitter lesson to her about the ultimate power of the electorate. She began her period in office with some success in increasing food and industrial production, expanding rail transport, and nationalizing banks. But even while she was recognized for her effectiveness in these endeavors, she was exercising her powers in ways that were to make her increasingly unpopular. In 1972 a defeated opponent charged her with violating election laws. He finally won his case in 1975, and Gandhi's 1971 election was declared invalid, endangering her seat in Parliament. The Prime Minister moved quickly to protect herself. Within two weeks she had declared a state of emergency, imprisoning her political opponents, censoring the press, passing laws limiting personal freedoms, and postponing Parliamentary elections for a year. By the time two months had passed, the election laws had been revised by constitutional amendment and her conviction had been reversed, so it seemed that her position was safe. But the harshness of the emergency measures made her more and more unpopular in the eighteen months leading up to the next elections. In addition, there was growing public resentment of her son Sanjay, who was seen by many as a strong but negative influence on his mother. Her enemies must have been elated when she was overwhelmingly defeated in the March 1977 national elections.

During the next twenty months Gandhi continued to wield great political influence even out of office. In spite of her 1977 defeat, in November of the next year she was reelected to Parliament, and although she continued to arouse criticism for possible misuse of power, she became Prime Minister again in 1980. This year was also marked by Sanjay's unexpected death, a crushing blow for Gandhi. But by 1981 her other son Rajiv had already won a seat in Parliament for his mother's Congress Party. During this second period as Prime Minister, Gandhi has given her attention to such issues as strengthening the power of the central government, lowering inflation, and building India's space and nuclear power programs, but she has been less successful in dealing with regional unrest, the sporadic breakdown of law and order, and un- and underemployment. At this point it seems that her political future will depend on whether experience has taught her to temper her desire for absolute power. If it has, it seems likely that the population of India will continue to enjoy the benefits brought to them by this tireless and capable leader.

Unit 44

Warmup I: Selecting Information to Use

Material that students have chosen to omit may vary considerably. The teacher may choose to give time for class discussion.

Warmup II: Summarizing Information (suggested answers)

1. After a first marriage that ended in divorce, in 1952 he married Nancy Davis, the present Mrs. Reagan.

2. In the course of his acting career, Reagan held important positions in motion picture industry organizations.

3. After two unsuccessful bids for the Republican Presidential nomination, in 1980 he overwhelmingly defeated incumbent Jimmy Carter to become the fortieth President of the United States.

4. Reagan takes a traditional conservative stand on such issues as military power, moral values, communism, and big government.

5. Reagan blamed Carter for the industrial slump during the first part of the 1980s, but when the economic picture brightened in the fall of 1982, he claimed a victory for his "supply-side" economic plan.

6. Reagan's foreign policy has been influenced both by his belief in military might and by his desire not to alienate the oil-rich Arab nations.

7. In accordance with his belief that the United States is "the only island of freedom that is left in the whole world," Reagan supports United States military preeminence as a defense against the U.S.S.R. and communism.

8. Reagan supports a reduction in the size and influence of the federal government and is strongly against government waste and excessive government spending, as is appropriate for one who believes that "government is not the solution to our problem; government is the problem."

Warmup III: Presenting Information (suggested answers)

1. Favoring both tax cuts and a balanced federal budget, Reagan is opposed to government waste and excessive government spending.

2. Reagan feels that a reduction in the size and influence of the federal government would curtail government waste and excessive spending.

3. A crisis of confidence resulted when Reagan's own budget director expressed lack of faith in the President's economic plan.

4. Reagan's desire to reduce government spending has led to cuts in federal assistance to programs such as welfare, arts funding, and federally guaranteed student loans.

5. Reagan's aid to the El Salvador government against guerillas, whom he believes are supported by the U.S.S.R., has been prompted by his belief in using military intervention against the U.S.S.R. and communism.

Unit 47

Warmup: Finding or Inferring Main Ideas

A. "Obviously, if handguns were not legally available to private citizens, American murder statistics would be drastically reduced." (The first sentence of the paragraph is not the main idea. Further reading reveals that the purpose of the passage is not to be impartial but to give the author's support to handgun control.)

B. 3. Man has not made any real progress because his basic nature has not changed.

C. The United States should decrease its dependence on petroleum as an energy source.

Reading and Writing: Summarizing a Longer Passage (suggested answer)

Feeble Political Response to the Energy Crisis

I. Reasons
    A. Legislators' lack of appreciation to the problem
        1. Its seriousness
        2. Its inevitability
        3. Its complexity
        4. Legislators spend their time on simpler problems with quicker solutions
    B. Conflicting pressures on legislators from special interest groups
        1. Gas company lobbies (want price deregulation)
        2. Utility company lobbies (want nuclear power plants)
        3. Environmental group lobbies (oppose nuclear power plants)
        4. Oil company lobbies
        5. High technology company lobbies
    C. More immediate demands on legislators' time
        1. Constant campaigning for reelection
        2. Quick, easy problems given priority
        3. Energy crisis a long, hard problem
II. Solutions
    A. Impossible to change political system for sake of energy crisis
    B. Possible to move public to press for energy crisis solutions that are
        1. Political
        2. Economic
        3. Societal
        4. Technical

Unit 48

Warmups and Writing

There are so many ways of expressing these answers that you should ask your teacher to tell you whether yours are correct.

Unit 49

Writing: Synthesizing Information from a Variety of Sources

There are so many ways of expressing these answers that you should ask your teacher to tell you whether yours are correct.

Unit 51

Warmup I: Appropriateness of Topics

The most likely answer is given first. If another answer seems possible, it is given second.

1. A   **2.** C   **3.** B   **4.** A   **5.** B, C   **6.** C   **7.** C   **8.** A   **9.** C
10. A, B   **11.** A, B   **12.** C   **13.** B   **14.** A, B   **15.** A   **16.** C
17. A, B   **18.** B   **19.** A   **20.** C

Warmup II: Selecting a Topic

The answers and explanations given here seem the most likely ones, although there may be different choices in different situations.

1. A   **2.** C   **3.** C   **4.** A   **5.** C   **6.** C, B   **7.** A   **8.** B, C   **9.** C
10. C   **11.** B (You probably should not judge the value of a graduate assignment by how personally rewarding it is.)   **12.** C   **13.** B (If many people are using the same books and articles, these materials will be hard for you to get and use.)

Warmup III: Evaluating Information Sources

The most likely answer is given first.
1. C   **2.** C (Librarians may be experts on where to find materials, but they should not normally be considered experts on the content or meaning of that material.)   **3.** C (Such an index would lead you to articles at much too superficial a level for a specialized paper.)   **4.** A   **5.** B (Such abstracts would likely be too specialized and require too much time to pursue unless you were writing a very important or lengthy paper.)   **6.** C (You would probably weaken the credibility of your paper by admitting that the information had come from such a source.)   **7.** A (If the article and bibliography were good, the list of sources would be recent and relevant.) **8.** C   **9.** C   **10.** A   **11.** A (The professor is indirectly grading his or her own work if you use such material, and you are not likely to get a bad grade.)   **12.** A   **13.** B (The catalogue lists only books, is not always complete, and may not list your specific topic adequately.)   **14.** C, B   **15.** A   **16.** C, B   **17.** C (You might be able to turn in an attractive and even a superior paper, but if it is not your own work, you are cheating, and if you are caught, you could be in very serious trouble.)   **18.** C, B (Your writing teacher is not an expert in the content of your field and in fact may not be able to answer all your questions about the form of a paper in your field.)

Editing Exercise

There are four main libraries on campus: the main library at the center of the campus, the science library near the auditorium, and the art and business libraries. The main catalogue, however, is in the main library. It lists books by subject or title. For example, if you know the title or the author of the book, you can look in the title catalogue, whereas if you want to find books on a certain subject, you can look in the subject catalogue. Each of the many cards contains important information about the location of the book and other information to help you decide if you want to look at it.

The computer searches of a large literature base are another feature of the library, as is the use of computers in locating a book within the library and helping to tell you if the book is checked out and when it will be back. To use a computer search to locate books and articles within a large literature base, you must do several things, such as fill out a form, select key words related to the main concepts of your topic, and pay a small fee, depending on the field and the size of the list.

Unit 52

Warmup I: Summarizing

This is a suggested summary. Yours may be different and still be correct.

According to K. Weaver, the twentieth century will have used up most of the world's hydrocarbon fuels, which took millions of years to develop. Many analysts think that we are finding only about half as much gas as we are using and that the reserves we now know about will probably be used up in ten years.

Warmup II: Taking Notes

These are suggested notes. Yours may be different and still be correct.

Card 2:
Twentieth-century civilization is using up most of the hydrocarbon fuels that were ever available on earth. There probably will be little left in ten or twenty years.

Card 3:
Present gas reserves will be used up in ten years. We are finding new gas each year, but only about half of what we use, so it won't last much longer.

Card 4:
Oil reserves in the U.S.A. will be almost gone by the year 2000, the Soviet Union's will be going downhill after the early 1980s, the North Sea fields will decline after 1984, and Arabic reserves probably will disappear within 10 or 20 years.

Card 5:
Coal is plentiful, but transporting it will be a problem, and so will the pollution it causes.

Editing (The first part of the editing exercise is listed under Warmup I)

Likewise, oil reserves will be very low in the U.S.A. by the year 2000, and North Sea and Russian sources will begin to decline in the 1980s. Coal reserves are very large, but methods of transporting coal will have to be expanded, and the pollution from coal could become a serious problem in just a few years.

Unit 53

Warmup I: Reviewing Note Cards

The best choice of the four possible topics is number 2. There is only a little information for the other three topics, not nearly enough for even a short paper.

Warmup II: Arranging Note Cards into an Outline

One way to arrange these cards is as follows:

We are using enormous amounts of stored fuels (10) in a way that is dangerous to our environment (12, 11), and at the rates of present use, we will soon use them up (3).

Most of our alternatives are based on the energy derived from the sun (2, 7, 13). Unfortunately, none of these individually or collectively can solve our problem (hydro, 17; photosynthesis, 16; tidal, 18).

There is evidence that the sun produces vast amounts of energy (4, 19), which is the alternative that we must begin to develop now (14).

Government (24) and business (5) are anticipating a large increase in use of solar power. There are several ways in which it might be collected. One is by using large collectors in orbit (8), but other applications are also promising (23, 6, 21).

Unit 54

Warmup I: Knowing When to Acknowledge a Source
1. No. This is general knowledge that any university student should already know.

2. Yes. This is not common knowledge. The voice of an authority will make the fact more believable, and if your readers disagree with the information, they will be able to blame your source instead of you.

3. Yes. This seems like fairly common knowledge, but since the exact figure of 25 years is used, it is best to cite the source.

4. No. Most people already know this.

5. Yes. This information and the particular interpretation given to it are not common knowledge. In fact, they may be disputed. You had better cite the source.

6. Yes. The phrase that is used here is not general usage, nor does it represent your own words. You need to give the author credit.

7. Yes. This whole sentence is a direct quotation. You must give the author credit and give the exact page number.

Unit 55

Editing Exercise (suggested answers)
I am currently enrolled in an industrial design course, Design 444. The course is hard for students to get into, and an average of about one hundred and fifty pages of outside reading are required each week. One of the requirements is a paper on methods of designing other equipment.

Since I am also taking computer science courses, I decided to write a paper that included [emphasized] both design and computer science by showing how a computer could be used to design another computer. The topic appeals to me, and the professor agreed that the topic fits the requirements of the course and that there is a lot of information available on it in the library.

I think the topic is at the right level for this class for two reasons. First, it resembles topics covered in the chapters and bibliographies of our text, and second, it combines in a unique way several of the major perspectives of the course.

I also believe that there are enough references to the sources [materials] that I need. For example, one of my professor's papers lists three articles. . . .

Unit 56

Editing Exercise
1. Doscher, Todd M. "Enhanced Recovery of Crude Oil." *American Scientist* 69 (March–April 1981): 193–99.
(Note: Another acceptable form, used in science fields, would be as follows:
Doscher, T. M. 1981. Enhanced Recovery of Crude Oil. *American Scientist* 69:193–99.

2. (Doscher, 1981) (Note: In some fields the comma is omitted and the form looks like this: (Doscher 1981).)
Another possible citation form, which is *not* recommended, would be as follows:
[1]Todd M. Doscher, "Enhanced Recovery of Crude Oil," *American Scientist* 69 (March–April 1981): 196.

3. The article offers readable, introductory, yet interesting and informative data on the subject of getting oil from oil wells. Since this material is at the appropriate level for the class and is neither too easy nor too difficult, it seems suitable.

4. The article summarizes the basic principles of oil recovery and explains Darcy's equation. Over half of the article discusses two major methods of recovering oil after the original pressure is lost: steam (both steam soak and steam drive) and flooding (water and chemical).

5. There is some technical vocabulary, but the article is well organized, clear, and well illustrated.

6. The introduction is relatively long. As a matter of fact [In fact], if you include the information about how oil was formed and normal production procedures, the introduction represents about one fourth of the total [of the whole].

7. The conclusion is only one paragraph long and is not labeled.

8. TMD ERCO *AS,* p. 196 (or, TMD, *AS* 81:196)
At least 25% of the energy actually recovered is used just in the recovery process itself in the steam drive system.

Unit 59

Editing Exercise (suggested answers)
I have made many friends among the people I have met in this class, and I am really going to miss them very much. But I have to move on [along], and I may never see some [any] of them ever again. My first step will be to take a short vacation by car around the United States. There are many places that I want to see before I go home. I intend to take a classmate along too, and we are already making extensive plans about what to take and where to go.

After the trip I will return to my country, where my family is expecting me to take over the family business. I am not anxious to do so since I am not interested in that business, and while it is profitable, it is not personally rewarding to me. Quite frankly, my real hope is to develop a strong leadership within the company itself, hopefully with the involvement of my younger brother, who says he really wants to play a vital [active] role. I think it is realistic to expect the company to prosper in this way, leaving me free to pursue my own interests.

In ten years I hope to have become involved in the political and economic affairs of my country and to be in a position to affect the growth and prosperity of the whole nation. . . .

APPENDICES

❧ Appendix I ❧

Checklist

Ask yourself the following questions after you write your paper. If your answer to each is *definitely,* you can be satisfied with your effort.

1. Meaning: Do you have a clear idea of exactly what you are trying to say, and do you believe this idea will be obvious to the reader?
2. Organization: Have you chosen the most effective plan to convey your central idea, and have you divided your material into paragraphs that will lead the reader quickly and convincingly toward your purpose?
3. Content: Do you support your general statements with clear, interesting, and specific examples, facts, reasons, or explanations?
4. Vocabulary: Do you correctly use words that are precise and suited to the topic? Do you avoid unnecessary repetition of words?
5. Sentences: Have you used well-connected sentences of various structural types that are not repetitious, choppy, unparallel, or run-on?
6. Grammar: Have you used articles, comparatives, counters, prepositions, singular and plural forms, tenses, uncountable nouns, word order, and word and verb forms correctly?
7. Mechanics: Have you spelled words correctly; punctuated transitional words, phrases, clauses, and sentences properly; and made your paper as neat as possible?

❧ Appendix II ☙

Evaluation

This appendix provides an objective measurement with which the skill and progress of the advanced writer can be determined. The student needs to provide a writing sample that has been written in a thirty- to forty-minute period, on one of three alternative topics given at the beginning of that period, without the use of a dictionary or other aid. The teacher uses the scale and samples given here in determining a score. The scales and descriptions are not a fixed, inflexible standard, but rather a guide with useful explanations and examples that both teachers and students can use in seeing whether their efforts are bearing fruit.

The lowest grade on the scale represents approximately the level of proficiency a student should have reached before attempting to use this text-book. A score of 80 represents a level of proficiency that extensive experience suggests is acceptable for foreign students entering most United States universities. Properly prepared native speakers would normally score in the range above 90, based on language proficiency if not on organizational skill.

Progress along this scale depends on the students' capabilities and effort. *Average* improvement would vary between *about* one point for each week (at the lower end of the scale) to *about* half a point per week (at the upper end). Improvement in writing, however, can be neither predicted nor forced, and a host of variables, including personal ones, can allow one student to progress very rapidly while another progresses hardly at all.

GRADING SCALE AND EXPLANATION (BASED ON A 30-MINUTE EXTEMPORANEOUS COMPOSITION)

65

Meaning: The main ideas are clear, but some parts may be hard to interpret.

Organization: Varies from well to poorly organized.

Content: Tends to have some good support along with generalities and irrelevant details.

Vocabulary: Very basic (2000-word level). Less common words are often incorrectly used or misspelled.

Sentences: Choppy, rambling, or overly simple for the most part.
Grammar: Frequent mistakes even on basic forms.
Mechanics: Spelling, punctuation, and appearance may be poor.

70

Meaning: Most of the ideas are clear, with a few confusing parts.
Organization: Varies from well to ineffectively organized.
Content: Most of the composition consists of useful support, though there may be several irrelevant details and meaningless generalities.
Vocabulary: Basic level with some correct usage of more unusual words.
Sentences: A combination of well-designed sentences with choppy, rambling, or very simple structures. Some use of appropriate sentence transitions.
Grammar: A wide range of patterns, the simple ones used relatively accurately, the more complex ones usually with errors.
Mechanics: A range from error-free to "careless," though normally with minor mistakes in spelling and punctuation; handwriting legible.

75

Meaning: Generally clear throughout. One or two confusing sentences.
Organization: Generally a clear organizational plan, especially in compositions on personal or concrete topics.
Content: Most of the ideas are adequately supported, even if somewhat generally. May contain several clear examples, explanations, descriptions.
Vocabulary: A wide range, including words specifically related to the narrow topic. Numerous errors with advanced vocabulary are still present.
Sentences: Generally accurate use of a wide variety of structures, though some structures are obviously avoided or incorrectly used. Few mistakes with the basic types. Frequent and normally accurate use of transition markers of a more sophisticated type.
Grammar: Frequent complex sentences with few errors. Advanced patterns (such as conditionals, perfect tenses) still show errors.
Mechanics: Spelling, punctuation, and appearance show few errors.

80

Meaning: A directed and clear presentation of a point of view.
Organization: The steps in the development of the theme are normally clear and appropriately labeled.
Content: Few sweeping generalizations are made, with an obvious attempt, usually successful, to give reasons, facts, or examples as support.
Vocabulary: A range normally appropriate for the topic, with an occasional word that is a false cognate or that has the wrong connotation, and some circumlocutions.
Sentences: A limited number of obvious mistakes along with a good variety of the most appropriate patterns for the topic. Sentences are normally in the correct order, have a good variety of length with a minimum of unnecessary

repetition, and are logically joined with transition markers, which are usually correct.

Grammar: Control of all but the most difficult patterns, with occasional or careless mistakes.

Mechanics: Normally highly accurate use, though some writers may have consistent problems and still be very effective.

85

Meaning: Almost always very clear.

Organization: Obvious and appropriate paragraphing and development.

Content: Carefully chosen reasons, facts, and examples, with an occasional weakness in support.

Vocabulary: A wide range, including specialized and technical words, though there may still be several obvious errors in meaning or form.

Sentences: An appropriate variety of types and lengths, with clear transitions and only a few errors, if any.

Grammar: A limited number of obvious errors, with perhaps a few seemingly careless mistakes.

Mechanics: Few serious errors.

90

Only minor weaknesses in meaning, organization, or vocabulary. The grammar is still not fully idiomatic, but it contains few mistakes.

95

Appropriate use of most features, with very few mistakes of any kind.

100

A level of writing that would be considered entirely satisfactory by a professional teacher. There are no obvious mistakes.

Note: An educated native speaker of English might or might not fit into the advanced portion of the preceding scale. Some native speakers, for example, are fluent and accurate grammatically but lack skills in organization and selection of content. As with non-native speakers, the scales need to be interpreted or interpolated in special cases.

SAMPLES OF VARIOUS LEVELS (BASED ON A 30-MINUTE EXTEMPORANEOUS COMPOSITION)

About 65 or Below

"The Knowledge outside the classroom"

I'm a University Professor in my country for long time and I always had been seeing that this phrase is true in the most cases. I don't know where is this statement but I think that this is oldest. There are a variaty of the reason that can explain that people get most of their knowledge outside the classroom, because many things and activities of life is imposible that a teacher can teach in a classroom in everywhere in the world

For example, in the ferst time of life a child needs for himself know a lot of things with his friends in the school or in the garder-schools, that don't is able get with his teacher. For the other hand, he can get a lot of the knowledges in his home. His parents can teach much activities such as the religion, culture etc, that nobody should do. After this, when the child became the age of the man also he will need the life's school, especially he will go to University where there is a lot of the knowledge that he will be able to get outside the classroom.

Later, when he get a career in his university studies he will think that his profesional activities can give much experience that is a knowledge imposible to get in a classroom and he had needed to do everything in his life.

By the way, there are a lot of things that anybody can get in the classroom, and I think that also it is necessary for the life.

In conclusion, it is difficult for me say what is the truth because anyone needs to go to both ways of teaching.

About 70

Everyone has his own opinion about many things such as smoking, politics and what have you. I have my own opinion about knowledge, and how can we get the knowledge.

In this report I intend to tell the reader if the knowledge we get it from the classroom is more than what we get from out of classroom.

I entirely agree with this statement. I think the classroom deson't give us all what we need it maybe give us definite kind of knowledge not all the kind of knowledge.

In the beginning of life there was no classroom, but we read about many people have a big deal of knowledge. There was no classroom told the first man in the world how to plan, how to build his huts. I read about many potteries that have a good poems in the first and second centuries, they knew how say those poems without any classroom. In enicient the women knew how to sewing there dresses without any teacher.

I would like to give you an example to support my opinion. If we take two children. The first one we tell him to get his knowledge just from classroom, the other one we leave him get his knowledge from any where he wants. What do you think about which one of them will get more knowledge? I think the second one will get much more than the first one, because he will get his knowledge from his environement, from his parents, from the books he will read, from the T.V, and from his trails.

From what has been said, it may be concluded that, I have described why I agree with that statement which says "A person gets most of his knowledge outside the classroom" and I have said the classroom just give us a definite kind of knowledge but we can get all kinds of knowledge outside the classroom.

About 75

I'm absolutely agree with this statement. Most of people get most of their knowledge outside the classroom. The persons who didn't attend the classroom have a lot of knowledge. Because they can get knowledge from newspapers, TV, radio, and many kinds of books, they usually have a lot of knowledge.

In old days, it was difficult to get knowledge outside the classroom. But the development of masscommunication, like newspapers, TV, radio, make us possible to get knowledge at home.

The amount of knowledge that one can get in the classroom is not so much. According to the persons who disagree with this statement, the persons who didn't attend the classroom must be illiterate and have no knowledge.

But in fact, the person who didn't attend the classroom have a lot of knowledge. This fact can verify my opinion pretty well. Of course, attending the classroom is helpful for all persons to improve their knowledge, but it's not so critical point.

Deligence in reading books make the people have more knowledge than the people who attend the classroom. The best example is the president of the U.S., Lincoln.

He never attended the classroom but he had a lot of knowledge.

He could pass the qualifying examination of lawyer because he was deligent in reading books. Moreover he could be the president of the U.S.

It is the story of old days.

Nowadays it's easier to get knowledge than in old days because the masscommunication is well developed.

If someone had different opinion from that of mine, I would like to discuss with him about this problem. I can give him a lot of examples. I'm sure I can get victory over them in discussion.

In conclusion, the statement "A person gets most of his knowledge outside the classroom" is true.

About 77

A person gets most of his knowledge outside of the classroom

A classroom is a proper place to study basic knowledge. But it is not enough to study everything there. No one can study everything what he needs in the classroom because the lectures were planned for many people but not for specific person. So a person will get a very limited knowledge in the classroom. If he needs more than what he got from the classroom he should study outside the classroom. I aggree with this idea.

Laboratory is one of an example where people can learn many things and prove their hypotheses. Library is an other example where people can read many books and absorb what they read. Also from laboratories people borrow books to read them in their houses so that they can read more comfortable.

The fact is we all are studying everything not only in the classroom but also outside. For example if we are studying English in a classroom we should practice them also outside the classroom. Without practicing them outside the classroom it is impossible to speak well English.

There are much other knowledge that we got from outside of classroom, not because it should be practiced in the laboratory or in the society but because it is impossible to be taught in the classroom for example the knowledge habits of a society.

So a classroom is a very important place to study a basic knowledge. In the classroom we can only study a little part of our knowledge. But with that knowledge we can expand other knowledge and as a matter of fact we get much more knowledge outside the classroom because we have much more time outside of classroom.

About 79

A person gets most of his knowledge outside the classroom

I think in part that is thrue, but in another part it isn't. Because I think everyone has to learn first in the classroom, and after certain knowledge, they are ready to go out and learn outside of the school. The knowledge that they obtain in the school, will be the base for them to learn outside. I think that really makes the difference between two persons, one with theoretic bases and another with superficial knowledge about the same statement. I traveled several times as a tour guide, with groups from my country, and I learned a lot and also I could see really clear this point, who has bases and who hasn't. It is very interesting to see how the people see the same thing and how they understand completely different. After they have very good bases, they can learn a lot outside of the classroom so fast and easy. Also I think the knowledge that they obtain in the classroom is completely different, than the knowledge that they obtain outside of the classroom.

I think both are really important and everybody needs both. Because one can't exist without another. Knowledge inside the classroom is so important as knowledge outside the classroom. The human being has to have both to feel complete and free, especial now when the life is getting more complex everyday.

About 82

A person gets most of his knowledge outside the classroom

The main aspect of learning is not what you get in your brain, but how much of that input remains there. You can pass all the courses in a four-year program, in a high school, college or university, and still, your knowledge would be a very small one.

In college or university, you learn a lot of theories, but only those which are supported by real-life experience, remain in your brain, and become, a part of your personality, and your culture. Other theories, which are not supported by real experience, or you do not practice in real life, you forget pretty soon as if you have never learned. Consequently, some knowledge goes into your brain, some remains there and some goes out. The knowledge that you get in the classroom, has a very theoretical and abstract nature, while the knowledge you get outside the classroom has, in contrast, a very practical nature. So, a relatively greater amount of the later knowledge infuses in your brain.

Another aspect of that subject, is, that one tends to learn from his own experience, much more than from somebody else experience. Classroom's knowledge, is a summary of man's experience, while the outside classroom's knowledge is your own experience.

About 95–100

People Learn More Outside the Classroom

I believe that we get more knowledge outside the classroom than we do inside. A classroom can give us only limited kinds of information. If we look at the beginning of civilization, for example, we will note that people back then did not have formal classrooms, yet many of them were well informed. There were no classrooms to teach the first men how to plant or how to build huts. The great early poets of the first and second centuries didn't learn their poems in a classroom, nor did the women find out how to sew their clothes there.

Let me use another approach to support my opinion. Suppose there were two children, the first limited to getting his knowledge entirely from the classroom, the second one able to get information from any source. Which would learn more? Most likely the second one because he would learn from his environment, from his parents, from the books he read, from TV, and from private study.

Both history and common sense suggest, therefore, that the greatest source of useful, practical knowledge comes from outside the school. What we get in a classroom is not only a small part of that total, but of a specialized and abstract nature.

❧ Appendix III ❧

Transitional Expressions

Part of writing well involves using expressions whose function is not to add information so much as to show the reader how the items of information are related to each other. We say that such expressions provide transition between the ideas presented. Although you would not want to include transitional expressions in every sentence, you should use enough of them to help your reader follow your ideas clearly. This appendix presents some of the most common transitional expressions for the writing forms of chronology/process, comparison/contrast, and cause and effect. Each expression is given in the context of a correctly-punctuated sentence to serve as a model, and in some cases explanations are included as well.

Expressions of Chronology/Process

Events in a Narrative/Steps in a Process

To begin with,
First* } cut a piece of copper sheeting to the size desired.
The first step is to

Second,
Next, } scrub the copper piece with some detergent and fine steel wool.
Then

After that, apply the powdered glass in whatever color and pattern you like.
After you apply the powdered glass, }
After applying the powdered glass, } fire the copper piece in a kiln.

Finally,
The final step is to } fire the copper piece in a kiln until the glass melts and
Last,† } fuses to the metal.

When you remove the piece from the kiln, you will have a beautiful and durable copper enamel.

**Do not confuse *first* with *at first,* which means that a situation or attitude changed in time. (Example: *At first* he was furious, but later he calmed down.)

†Do not confuse *last* with *at last,* which means after a long wait. (Example: When Bashir found a good job, *at last* we could afford to get married.)

Afterward ⎫ I learned that someone in my class had been a spy for
Later ⎭ the government.

We *eventually* came to love the town, the university, and even our tiny apartment.

Simultaneous Events

During the operation the patient's vital signs must be closely monitored.

While the surgeon is performing the operation, ⎫ he or she explains the
As the surgeon performs the operation, ⎭ procedure to the medical
students in the gallery.

The surgeon performs the operation and explains ⎫ *at the same time.*
the procedure ⎭ *simultaneously.*

Other Time Expressions

I won't be able to return to my country *until* I finish my degree.

By the time she was twenty, my mother was a married lady with three small children.

Once the robbers memorized the floor plan, they were able to find the right door even in the dark.

Whenever the dinner bell rang, the dog's mouth began to water.

As soon as I graduated, I returned home and married my childhood sweetheart.

My parents have lived in that house *as long as* I can remember.

⎧ I haven't seen my grandmother { *in* / *for* } three years. ⎫
⎨ It's been three years *since* I saw my grandmother. ⎬
⎩ I haven't seen my grandmother *since* I left home three years *ago*. ⎭

Before the war ended,
Before ⎫ the end of the war, ⎫ the political system broke down completely.
Prior to ⎭ ⎭

The economy began to recover { *after* / *following* } the signing of the peace treaty.

Additional Information

The patient had received a ⎧ *, and* ⎫ he had contracted pneumonia
terrible wound ⎪ *; additionally,* ⎪ because of his weakened
⎨ *; also,* ⎬ condition.
⎪ *; furthermore,* ⎪
⎪ *; moreover,* ⎪
⎩ *and* had contracted pneumonia *as well.* ⎭

Expressions of Comparison and Contrast

Comparison

Many *parallels* exist between the two countries.

Like every President before him, Reagan blamed many of his problems on the previous administration.

The federal government began cutting aid to welfare programs.
In like manner,
Similarly,   } the state governments started trimming their own
Likewise,   welfare budgets.

Contrast

Although
Though
Even though
While   } I don't agree with what you say, I will defend to the
In spite of the fact that   death your right to say it.
Despite the fact that
Regardless of the fact that

[You can also reverse the positions of the two clauses, but note the difference in
   punctuation:]

I will defend to the death your   { *although*
right to speak freely,   *though* } I may not agree with what you say.
                                    (etc.)

I don't agree with what you say,   { *but* } I will defend your right to say it.
                                     yet

I don't agree with what you say;   { *still,*
                                    however, } I will defend your right to say it.
                                    nevertheless,

Attendance was good   { *in spite of* } the heavy rain.
                        despite

I had to tell him the truth *regardless of* his feelings.

I signed up for volleyball *instead of* tennis.
I don't like tennis, so I signed up for volleyball *instead.*
I don't like tennis. *Instead,* I signed up for volleyball.

[Here are a few expressions of contrast that are often misused:]

I can't afford a ticket; *otherwise,* I'd go with you.
I'm tired of listening to you complain all the time. *Otherwise,* I like you.
[*Otherwise* describes what might happen under different conditions (Example 1), or
   gives a contrasting side of the same situation (Example 2).]

Everyone thought I was well suited for engineering. *On the contrary,* I hated it.
[*On the contrary* means that the preceding statement is not true or that you disagree
   with it.]

If I tell him the truth, he may never speak to me again. *On the other hand,* he may
   thank me later.
[*On the other hand* presents an alternative to the preceding statement or adds new and
   different information, but both statements describe the same general situation, just
   as two different hands belong to the same person.]

In contrast to my country, the United States has access to two oceans.
[When you use *in contrast,* you are describing two contrasting situations or statements that are both true.]

Expressions of Cause and Effect

Cause		*Effect*
In past centuries, little was known about birth control or disease prevention	{ ; *as a result,* ; *consequently,* ; *therefore,* ; *because of this,* , *so* }	families had lots of children, many of whom died in infancy.

	Cause	*Effect*
Because *As* *Since* }	little was known in past centuries about birth control or disease prevention,	families had lots of children, many of whom died in infancy.

[You can also reverse the positions of the two clauses, but note the difference in punctuation:]

Effect		*Cause*
In past centuries families had lots of children, but many of them died in infancy	{ *since* *because* *as* }	little was known about birth control or disease prevention.

	Cause	*Effect*
In past centuries, *because of*	ignorance about birth control and disease prevention,	families had lots of children, many of whom died in infancy.

Cause		*Effect*
In past centuries, ignorance about birth control and disease prevention	{ *was responsible for* *contributed to* *resulted in* *led to* }	large families and high infant mortality.

Effect		*Cause*
In past centuries, large families and high infant mortality	{ *resulted from* *were due to* *were a result of* *were a consequence of* }	ignorance about birth control and disease prevention.

In past centuries, people knew *so* little about birth control and disease prevention *that* families had lots of babies, many of whom died in infancy.

In past centuries, there was *such* ignorance about birth control and disease prevention *that* families had lots of babies, many of whom died in infancy.

Knowing little about birth control or disease prevention, people in past centuries had lots of babies, many of whom died in infancy.

❧ References ❧

The following books are recommended for further study.

GRAMMAR

Azar, Betty S. *Understanding and Using English Grammar*. Englewood Cliffs, N.J.: Prentice-Hall, 1981.

Frank, Marcella. *Modern English: A Practical Reference Guide*. Englewood Cliffs, N.J.: Prentice-Hall, 1972.

Leech, Geoffrey, and Jan Svartvik. *A Communicative Grammar of English*. London: Longman, 1975.

Maclin, Alice. *Reference Guide to English: A Handbook of English as a Second Language*. New York: Holt, Rinehart and Winston, 1981.

USAGE

Copperud, Roy H. *American Usage and Style: The Consensus*. New York: Van Nostrand Reinhold, 1980.

STUDY SKILLS

Martin, Anne V., et al. *Guide to Language and Study Skills for College Students of English as a Second Language*. Englewood Cliffs, N.J.: Prentice-Hall, 1977.

Yorkey, Richard C. *Study Skills for Students of English as a Second Language*. New York: McGraw-Hill, 1970.